Family history and local history in England

David Hey

Longman
London and New York

Longman Group UK Limited,
Longman House, Burnt Mill, Harlow,
Essex CM20 2JE, England
and Associated Companies throughout the world.

Published in the United States of America
by Longman Inc., New York

First published 1987

British Library Cataloguing in Publication Data
Hey, David
 Family history and local history in
 England.
 1. Family – England 2. England –
 Genealogy
 I. Title
929'.2'0942 CS414
ISBN 0-582-00522-1   CSD
ISBN 0-582-49458-3   PPR

Library of Congress Cataloging-in-Publication Data
Hey, David.
 Family history and local history in England.

 Bibliography: p.
 Includes index.
 1. England – Genealogy – Handbooks, manuals, etc.
2. England – History, Local – Handbooks, manuals, etc.
I. Title.
CS414.H49 1987   929'.1'072042   86–10329
ISBN 0-582-00522-1
ISBN 0-582-49458-3 (pbk.)

Set in Linotron 202 10/12pt Bembo

Produced by Longman Singapore Publishers (Pte) Ltd.
Printed in Singapore

FAMILY HISTORY AND
LOCAL HISTORY IN ENGLAND

Contents

List of plates

List of figures

List of tables

Preface

The spectacular growth of interest in family history in recent years is a remarkable phenomenon and one that is worth pondering. Some theorists will no doubt explain it as mere escapism, an unhealthy desire to withdraw from the realities of life in the late-twentieth century to a time when family bonds were firmer and the individual supposedly more secure in a web of human relationships. There is probably a little truth in this, for many will say that material progress has brought less rather than more contentment, but the vast majority of family historians whom I have come across are only too well aware that their ancestors had a harder life than most of us have today. Knowledge of overcrowded houses, insufficient food, long and tedious hours of work and inadequate defences against disease soon shatters the myth of 'the good old days'. The golden age is illusory; nostalgia's all right, they say, but it's not what it was.

I believe that while a little romanticism certainly plays a part (after all, what hobby or pastime does not take us away from our everyday preoccupations?), the groundswell of interest in family history is a much more positive phenomenon. The desire to know who one's ancestors were is a natural human concern that has interested people throughout time and in all parts of the world. What is different now is that ordinary people have the opportunity and the means to pursue their family trees. Today we are more mobile and have more leisure time, and most important of all we now have numerous record offices that are open to everyone and which have well-qualified staff to guide the researcher and microfilm readers and other photocopying devices to make archives readily available. An interest in family history has always been there, but now everyone has the chance to pursue it. Thousands of people have discovered the pleasure of research which is peculiarly personal in its rewards. The proliferation of family history societies and conferences brings one into contact with fellow enthusiasts, and family history has become England's fastest-growing hobby.

Genealogy used to be a rather snobbish pursuit but nowadays all that has changed. Most of our ancestors were ordinary people but that does not make them uninteresting. In this book I have used the various branches of my own family as case-studies because their very ordinariness makes them typical. Nevertheless, when seen against the broader themes of English social and economic history their triumphs and disasters and their dogged persistence in a way of life takes on a wider relevance and gives human meaning to phases of human history such as the nineteenth century exodus from the countryside and the Great Agricultural Depression. In this book I try to interest family historians in wider concerns than the single-minded pursuit of their own family tree, for it is my belief that the great surge of interest in family history will help to deepen our understanding of local and national history once we get a series of good family histories in print. In researching my own family I have been able to discern interesting patterns amongst the welter of generations and I have become increasingly interested in the local history of the places where my ancestors lived. I hope that my own experience will encourage other family historians to raise their sights in this way.

As well as writing about my own research I have drawn upon the published work of other scholars who have studied local communities in depth or who have written about surnames, population mobility and other matters of interest to family historians. The chapter on the Middle Ages, in particular, relies heavily on this recent work and I am indebted to all the authors. Other sections draw upon material that I have assembled for classes in the Division of Continuing Education at the University of Sheffield and for talks to various family history societies and I have benefited from the subsequent discussions.

I would particularly like to thank Mrs Pamela Broadhead for typing the manuscript.

Acknowledgements

Acknowledgement is due to the following for permission to reproduce plates in the text: National Monuments Record (2.6 & 3.15); Sheffield City Libraries (2.9, 3.4, 3.9, 3.10, 3.12 & 3.16); The British Library (1.3); Essex County Council (2.5); Yorkshire Archaeological Society (2.7); Society of Antiquaries of London (2.8); Aerofilms Limited (3.3); Luton Museum and Art Gallery (3.6); Powell and Young, Solicitors, Pocklington, and Humberside County Council (3.11); Walter Scott (Bradford) Ltd (copyright holders) (3.13); Somerset Record Office (4.1); W. F. E. Gibbs and P. J. Wood (4.4); and the Public Record Office (4.2 (Document RG II/4618. Crown-copyright material in the P.R.O. is reproduced by permission of the Controllor of Her Majesty's Stationery office)).

The author is also grateful to the following for the use of documents: The Royal Institution of Cornwall (HA/9/20 (manor of Binnerton court paper)); North Yorkshire County Record Office (ZBQ (Husthwaite Manorial Court book)); Borthwick Institute of Historical Research, York (wills and inventories); Lichfield Joint Record Office (inventory of Thomas Eyre).

The author, would, finally, like to thank the staff of the following record offices for their assistance: Borthwick Institute of Historical Research, York; the Public Record Office; West Yorkshire Archive Service; Sheffield Central Library; Huddersfield Central Library; South Yorkshire Record Office; North Yorkshire Record Office; Somerset Record Ofice; Yorkshire Archaeological Society; and, particularly, all those anonymous people who over the years have explained how to use the microfilm readers at the Public Record Office Census Room.

I am the family face;
Flesh perishes, I live on,
Projecting trait and trace
Through time to times anon,
And leaping from place to place
Over oblivion

Thomas Hardy, *Heredity* (1917)

Let not Ambition mock their useful Toil,
Their homely Joys and Destiny obscure;
Nor Grandeur hear with a disdainful Smile,
The short and simple Annals of the Poor.

Thomas Gray (1716–71),
An Elegy written in a Country Church Yard

For Emma and Jonathan

Introduction

This is a book of encouragement and advice for those thousands of family historians who have already made some progress in tracing their family tree and have become interested in the places where their ancestors lived and worked and raised children. It is not primarily concerned with the mechanics of tracing ancestors for there are already enough good books to guide the enthusiastic researcher step by step. My aim, rather, is to encourage family historians to widen their interests so that they will be able to feel the excitement and pleasure of the study of local history. To know that one's ancestors shared and helped to shape the experiences of some remote village or quiet market town or perhaps a burgeoning industrial city is to enrich one's understanding of English social history. The past comes alive when it is intimate and personal. Some local historians, forever on the defensive about the academic credentials of their own subject and resenting the invasion of libraries and record offices by hordes of genealogists, have rather looked down on the pursuit of family history, but in my view they are quite mistaken. By pursuing his or her family tree the family historian becomes acquainted with the methods of local historical research and he or she quickly becomes interested in wider concerns. Family history is an excellent introduction to local history and the two subjects go naturally together. One day we shall have a number of substantial family histories on our shelves, not just the histories of aristocratic and gentry families but of the ordinary men and women who were far more numerous and whose stories are often just as interesting as anyone else's. When that day arrives we shall have a much better understanding of the social and economic history of England.

In this book I bring to the attention of family historians recent work on matters that were of vital concern to their ancestors; work on the family, mobility, population trends, housing, health and so on. I also try to show just how diverse and extraordinarily complex were the rural and urban communities of provincial England, even before the great changes associated with the Industrial Revolution. By becoming aware of this background and by acquiring a fuller sense of the past I hope that family historians will gain a better appreciation of the lives of their ancestors and the history of their everyday surroundings. They will come to realise that family history and local history are inextricably intertwined.

I spent my childhood in a fairly remote Pennine hamlet where the personal history of local people and their families was a matter of everyday conversation. This sort of history had an endless appeal for it was about the people we knew, their virtues, their dark secrets, their triumphs and their sufferings. To listen to this sort of talk was delightful and much more interesting than the history we learnt at school. In this way history was not something remote both in time or place, not something unreal because it was so distant and cut off from our daily lives, but an enrichment of the present, an explanation of why one's neighbours were what they were and of how the place that we lived in had come to be what it was. History was separate neither from the present nor the future, for the tales of the past showed that while material circumstances might alter human nature remained the same. Later I was to find that many other people in widely different parts of England, especially in rural areas but more surprisingly to me sometimes in our industrial towns, shared this sense of identity with a particular place within a wider neighbourhood and knew the detailed family histories of their neighbours. To them, as to me, family history was an integral part of the local history of their community.

It is often assumed that in earlier times an interest in family history was confined to the nobility and gentry. I think this assumption is quite wrong. It has arisen because only the rich and

---

Plate 1.1   George and Mary Hey *c.* 1906
My grandparents, George Hey (1854–1916) and his second wife, Mary Ann Garland (1866–1948), taken outside their home at Bullhouse Lodge. George was at that time working as a waggoner just down the lane at Bullhouse corn mill.

Like most family photographs it has neither names nor date written on it. I have a number of family photographs which I cannot identify and one that has the unhelpful comment on the back: 'This was taken 10 years ago'. Future generations will be helped if we all label our own photographs.

This photograph does not even have the name and address of the photographer. (As many studios were short-lived, commercial and trade directories sometimes provide an approximate date.) However, George and Mary lived at Bullhouse Lodge for most of their married life, that is from 1900 to 1910, and a photograph taken there of my father at the age of two was probably taken at the same time, for a visit by a photographer was a rare event. This enables me to date the photograph tentatively to about 1906, when Mary was forty and George was fifty-two, which seems about right. It was, of course, common for the man to be seated and the woman to stand in photographs of this period.

powerful families published accounts of their pedigrees, with all the usual accoutrements of heraldry and vanity. Ordinary men and women talked about these things but their memories were never written down. Their information was passed on orally if at all. But occasionally we get passing references in diaries or memoirs that reveal that the humbler ranks of society had an enormous curiosity about the histories of their own families and those of their neighbours. Thomas Bewick, England's finest wood-engraver, was well aware of this interest. When he wrote about his early life in the countryside on the south bank of the Tyne in the 1750s and 1760s he spoke warmly of the old inhabitants of the cottages scattered round the edge of the common:

> After I left the country, I always felt much pleasure in revisiting them, and over a tankard of ale to listen to their discourse. It was chiefly upon local biography, in which they sometimes traced the pedigree of their neighbours a long way back.

Family history has attracted scholars since at least the Middle Ages and has no doubt always been a natural human concern. Individual pedigrees such as that of the Northwoods of Northwood Chasteners, compiled in fourteenth-century Kent, were drawn up not just because of family pride but to protect descendants from legal claims on property. This safeguard remained a prime consideration in the Tudor and Stuart period. After successfully defending his rights against the claims of a new lord of the manor in the reign of Charles I, Richard Elmhirst, a Yorkshire yeoman, recorded his legal title to 456 acres in five separate pieces of property. In 1638 these holdings included 73 acres at his home at Houndhill and 70 acres only a stone's throw away at Elmhirst, the minor place name that had given rise to his surname. Having searched old records for details of his property he was able to pronounce that:

> Our Family as I conceive assumed their surname from a messuage in Worsbrough-dale in the County of Yorke, which now ys and for many Ages hath beene, our peculiar Inheritance, and doth not appear by any Evidence that I could ever yet see to have been the inheritance of any other Family.

Modern research into the family's history has confirmed this belief and has shown that in 1340 Robert of Elmhirst was a serf of the manor of Rockley; the family's rise to prosperity began in the sixteenth century with Richard's grandfather and was based upon sheep farming and the manufacture of cloth. The Elmhirsts are still resident at Houndhill, in the timber-framed house built by their ancestors.

The first collections of pedigrees, as distinct from individual family trees, were made in the second half of the fifteenth century. Amongst the first collectors were William Worcester (1415–82) of Bristol and Norfolk and John Rous (*c.* 1425–91), the chaplain of Guy's Cliff chantry at Warwick, two men who were also pioneers of English antiquarian and topographical studies. Rous made a collection of more than fifty genealogies and Worcester drew up the pedigrees of many ancient Norfolk families. Worcester's antiquarian studies inspired John Leland, whose *Itinerary* of his journeys throughout England between 1535 and 1545 was used in turn by Willian Camden. Camden's *Brittania* (1586) formed the basis of English antiquarian scholarship for the next two centuries.

The Elizabethan Society of Antiquaries did much to foster this growing interest in antiquarian and genealogical pursuits. Amongst its members were the heralds, the London historian John Stow and such county historians as Richard Carew of Cornwall, Sampson Erdeswicke of Staffordshire and William Lambarde, who published *The Perambulation of Kent* in 1576. These early antiquaries often had a legal training and were concerned with the rights of property: they brought a scholarly approach to the study of local and family history. They were concerned, however, only with the history of the leading families – the nobility and the squirearchy – and not at all with what William Harrison in his *Description of England* (1577) called the 'fourth and last sort of people . . . the day labourers, poor husbandmen . . . copy-holders, and all artificers as tailors, shoemakers, carpenters, brickmakers, masons, etc', in other words the great majority of the population. By the mid-seventeenth century several county histories had been published and numerous landed families had compiled their family trees – many of them spurious. Interest in genealogy and the descent of landed property was also manifested in architectural displays. In Northamptonshire the Elizabethan courtier, Sir Christopher Hatton, erected three pyramids at Holdenby, which were covered with the arms of the county gentry and those of the peers of the realm, and in the great chamber at Gilling Castle Sir William Fairfax arranged the coats of arms of the Yorkshire gentry on a plaster frieze that went all way round the room above the marquetry panelling. In Kent Sir Edward Dering started to collect the coats of arms of all the families of his county community, but abandoned the project after he had gathered 1,200 names beginning with A to F.

When Sir John Reresby, a Yorkshire squire, wrote his family history in 1679 he set forth the purpose of his work on the first page in the following terms:

> 1. To instruct posterity as well as the living how long it hath pleased Providence to continue us in the same name and place, and to incite them thereby soe to demeane themselves according to the rules of conscience and honour as to obteane a longer continuance of the same mercy.
> 2. To save such the labour of turning over a great many obscure papers as are curious to know what hath passed in their familie, and that please themselves (as I have done) with *olim memenisse* [recollecting past-things].
> 3. To preserve memorials of some things of use as well as of curiosity, which age as well as want of care to preserve hath near already consumed.
> 4. To restore such to their deserved places in the pedegree as have been omitted, either by neglect, or by cause yonger children, their memory it should seeme formerly seldome surviving their poor annuitys.
> 5. To show who have been the true patrons and foster-fathers of their families, that their memories may be honoured and examples followed.

By the Elizabethan and Stuart era genealogy had become a widespread and scholarly pursuit amongst the wealthiest classes. Some of the projects were indeed ambitious. If you have had trouble in compiling your own family tree, reflect upon this entry from Samuel Pepys's diary for 22 January 1661:

> I met with Dr Thos. Fuller. He tells me of his last and great book that is coming out: that is, the History of all the Families in England; and could tell me more of my own, than I knew myself.

It is some consolation to know that by this he meant only the important families; Harrison's 'fourth and last sort of people' were not included. A generation later, however, a Shropshire yeoman sat down to write the most remarkable local history that has ever been published and, incidentally, to show that the farmers, craftsmen and labourers of the parish of Myddle were just as interested in their own family history and the ancestors of their neighbours as were the rich and the mighty. At first Richard Gough contented himself with a conventional piece on the *Antiquities and Memoyres of the Parish of Myddle*, but when he had finished he embarked on a much longer work entitled *Observations concerning the Seates in Myddle and the familyes to which they belong,* a marvellously rich combination of local and family history. Gough set out the seating plan in the parish church and proceeded to write the history of each family in turn. Every man and woman got a mention and the descent of every family was traced as far as possible. Much of his information was obtained directly from his neighbours, as is evident from such comments as 'We have a tradition' and 'I have heard by antient persons'. These communal memories went back well over a century and their accuracy can sometimes be confirmed by documentary sources. Richard Gough did not rely entirely upon oral tradition, but like any good local and family historian he examined parish registers, manorial court rolls, deeds and leases and whatever other documents he could lay his hands upon; 'I have seene the antient deeds of most freeholders in this Lordship', he tells us. He was interested not just in the very human stories of his neighbours and their ancestors but was conscious of the historical and contemporary bonds of his community. He puzzled over the derivation of place-names, historical changes in the local landscape and the social structure of the parish. His legal training suggested the framework for his *Observations* for he was concerned to establish the ownership of pews and his deep religious beliefs led him to censor those whom he felt had fallen by the wayside. He wrote:

> If any man shall blame mee for that I have declared the viciouse lives or actions of theire Ancestors, let him take care to avoid such evil courses, that hee leave not a blemish on his name when he is dead, and let him know that I have written nothing out of malice. I doubt not but some persons will thinke that many things that I have written are alltogether uselesse; but I doe believe that there is nothing herein mentioned which may not by chance att one time or other happen to bee needfull to some person or other; and, therefore I conclude with that of Rev. Mr Herbert –
> 'A skillfull workeman hardly will refuse
> The smallest toole that hee may chance to use'.

Such sentiments will no doubt strike a sympathetic chord in the breast of many a family and local historian.

Gough's manuscript was not published until the nineteenth century and, alas, no one has seen fit to copy his approach. It has been said often and accurately enough that local histories were written by gentlemen for gentlemen; they were unconcerned with the ordinary families who comprised the mass of the population. The tradition of antiquarian scholarship continued to flourish in the eighteenth and early nineteenth centuries; then during the

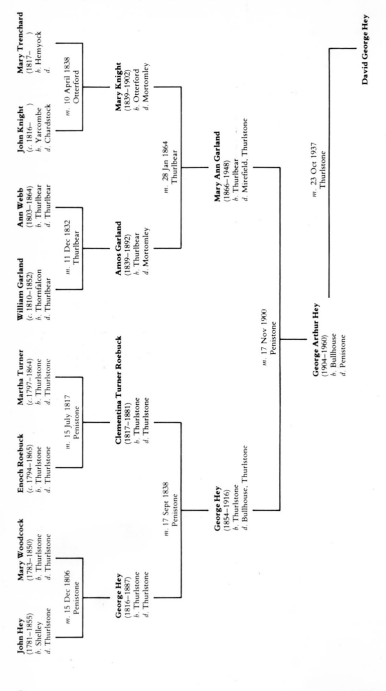

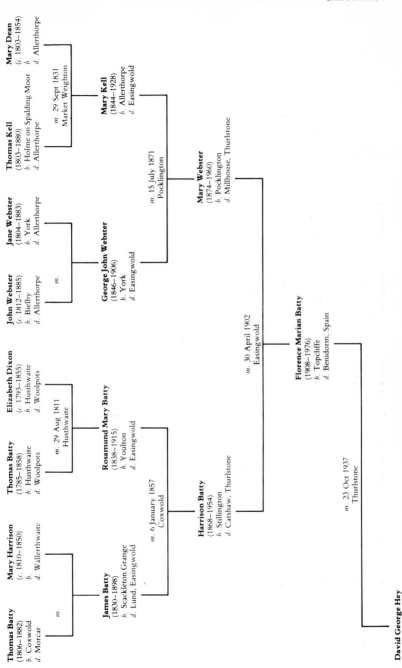

Table 1 Sixteen great-great-grandparents

reign of Victoria local and family histories appeared in print in all parts of the country. Towns and counties in every region of England had their historical societies which published annual journals or transactions, though it was not until 1911 that The Society of Genealogists was formed. It must be said that although a lot of excellent work was produced, many local and family histories were of a deplorable standard. One cannot help sympathising with the Revd Francis Kilvert who wrote in his diary on Shrove Tuesday 1870:

> Reading Edmund Jones' curious book which I brought from Hardwick Vicarage last night, an account of Aberystruth Parish, Monmouthshire. A ludicrous naïve simplicity about his reflections and conclusions. He thinks Providence took particular pains in making his parish which he thinks one of the most wonderful in the world.

Many a genealogist or antiquary was regarded as a figure of fun. William Swift, a nineteenth-century lawyer's clerk, was said to have seldom gone out; 'Spare, silent and austere with a face not unlike the parchments he handed out' was how one contemporary remembered him. For thirty-eight years he spent all his spare time researching into local and family history. He is commemorated as a genealogist by a memorial tablet in Sheffield cathedral. Such recognition did not normally come the way of the antiquary or family historian. As the anonymous writer of the preface to John Wood's *Remarkable Occurrences, Interesting Dates and Curious Information (Local and General)* put it in 1890:

> Literary distinction does not, as a rule, fall to the share of the local annalist; neither can he count upon his labours, save in very exceptional cases, being adequately rewarded, if looked at from the merely pecuniary stand-point. He does not work for either praise or pelf, but because he finds his self-imposed task to be a congenial one, and because he hopes that the results of his labours may prove to some extent beneficial to the present and succeeding generations.

The growth of interest in family and local history in recent years has been nothing less than phenomenal. Countless men and women from all parts of the land have discovered the pleasures of doing their own research, of following paths that no one has trod before. The rewards in terms of personal satisfaction are enormous. It does not matter who or what one's ancestors turn out to be. In these democratic and less snobbish times we are prepared to accept that most of our ancestors must have been amongst Harrison's 'fourth and last sort of people', simply because they formed the vast majority of the population. Every family has its share of saints and sinners, the well-off and the poor, the flamboyant and the diffident. Towards the end of Charlotte Brontë's story Jane Eyre surveyed the twenty scholars in her village school and reflected on her charges:

> They speak with the broadest accent of the district. At present, they and I have a difficulty in understanding each other's language. Some of them are unmannered, rough, intractable, as well as ignorant; but others are docile, have a wish to learn, and evince a disposition that pleases me. I must not forget that these coarsely-clad little peasants are of flesh and blood as good as the scions of gentlest genealogy; and that the germs of native excellence, refinement, intelligence, kind feeling, are as likely to exist in their hearts as in those of the best-born.

Every family's story is full of human interest, no matter what their social status.

But genealogy pure and simple soon becomes unsatisfying. It is not enough to construct a family tree of names and vital dates. Such a task is merely a first step towards a much fuller understanding of one's own family circumstances and of what older writers would have called the human condition. The next step is to construct biographies – as far as possible – of one's forebears, not just in the male line but in other branches as well, for how often has it been the mother rather than the father who has been the greater moulding force on an individual's character. A much rounder view of family life and influences is obtained by tracing all the grandparents of one's own grandparents, sixteen names in all, going back well into the nineteenth century. This task leads us to the third and most satisfying stage of all, the attempt to build up a picture in one's own mind of the kinds of communities in which one's ancestors lived. The sixteen great-great-grandparents will almost certainly have come from very different kinds of places and several of them will probably have moved quite a distance from their birthplace during their lifetime. Twelve of my great-great-grandparents came from the three Ridings of Yorkshire, but the other four belonged to Somerset families. They ranged from prosperous farmers to humble craftsmen and agricultural labourers. Through the study of family history one learns to see the great issues of English social history from all points of view, for most families will have straddled class barriers and will have had amongst their members both 'the shearers and the shorn'. The family historian is not one to talk in general abstractions. In his or her experience such things are largely meaningless. The life stories of one's own flesh and blood are too rich and varied to fit easily into such neat abstract patterns.

Nevertheless, the family historian is well advised to obtain as wide an historical background as possible, to understand that the lives of one's ancestors were shaped by the types of communities in which they lived, and that even before the Industrial Revolution these communities were very different in their social structure, their farming and other occupations, their houses and their whole way of life. Idealized images of the pre-industrial English village tell only a small part of the truth. Historical research over the past two or three decades has altered our perceptions of past provincial life in many significant ways, yet the results of this research are not widely known, and many a genealogist who wishes to become a family and local historian may be unaware of current opinion. This book attempts to remedy this situation and to encourage the amateur to widen his or her field of interest. Local history and family history are related subjects that are not the preserve of professionals. Amateurs can make either big or small contributions to our knowledge of the past and at the same time they can get deep personal satisfaction from their endeavours.

CHAPTER ONE
The Middle Ages

The family historian naturally works backwards from present generations into the remote past. All his early research is concentrated upon the twentieth and nineteenth centuries as he proceeds steadily back in time, proving one link after another in his chain of evidence. The Middle Ages are not his immediate concern and indeed he may never be able to trace his ancestors back that far. It was my original intention to write the book in the same way, but I soon found that the whole flow of the writing was in the opposite direction; the story of population change is one of growth, the account of industrial communities is one of increasing complexity, rural parishes and provincial towns altered in many subtle ways as the centuries passed. It became clear that the book had to proceed chronologically if it was to preserve its unity and not become hopelessly fragmented. So the chapter on the Middle Ages sets the scene and emphasises that even in the earliest periods for which we have evidence our ancestors were much more mobile than we once thought. Later chapters will become fuller as the evidence swells and as we approach the periods that are of greatest interest for most family historians, but a synopsis of the major studies of medieval communities will help our understanding of later eras and an account of recent work on surnames should appeal to all family historians who are interested in the ultimate quest for origins. This chapter forms an essential part of my argument that at its best the study of family history should be concerned with broad issues covering all periods of time for which we have evidence.

POPULATION AND THE ECONOMY

The family historian who tries to trace his ancestors back beyond the Elizabethan period is normally faced with grave problems of identification. For the period before parish registers were kept and before ordinary families began to adopt the practice of making a will, one has to turn principally to manorial court rolls and government taxation records. These sources do not give explicit genealogical data; it is unusual to get a good run of early court rolls and one can rarely proceed with confidence beyond the richer sections of society. But even if a direct line cannot be proved, the family historian can often point to probabilities and sometimes to the likely origin of a surname. The detailed local knowledge that comes not only from documents but from the study of places on the ground and from large-scale ordnance survey maps is as essential for a family historian dealing with the Middle Ages as it is for later periods. A background knowledge of medieval population trends and the structure of rural and urban societies is also necessary if one is to tread sure-footedly in an area beset with pitfalls for the unwary.

At the time of the great Domesday Survey of 1086 England's population stood somewhere between 1.5 and 2.25 millions. This figure is tiny in comparison with today's level, nevertheless a very high proportion of our present settlements were already in existence and had been so from time immemorial. During the two and half centuries after the Norman Conquest the national population grew quite rapidly, so that by the year 1300 it had at least doubled and may perhaps have trebled. At a minimum it had reached 3.25 millions and probably was much higher. Throughout the twelfth and thirteenth centuries existing settlements had expanded, new towns had been created and many new farmsteads and hamlets had been established on the edges of moors, woods and fens. These new, isolated settlements frequently gave rise to family names, a prolific group known as locative surnames.

By 1300 many families were living on the margin of subsistence. Medieval England was primarily an agricultural country; everywhere the growing of corn was a basic preoccupation. In later times those areas with a harsh climate and poor, thin soils turned increasingly to pastoral farming and to rural crafts which provided the wealth that enabled them to import their corn from more favoured areas. They were able to do this to a limited extent in the early Middle Ages, but agricultural yields were low and the growing pressure on available resources meant hardship and ultimately disaster. By 1300 smallholders with little to fall back upon in times of crisis amounted to at least 1.5 million people and perhaps as many as 2.5 millions; they formed an increasingly high percentage of rural society. Everywhere in England the basic pattern was one of small, family farms. Some families with sufficient land to survive remained rooted in one spot, but in general the Middle Ages was just as remarkable as later periods for the amount of movement from place to place. Mobility was usually restricted to a few miles within a well-defined neighbourhood, but the new towns that were founded during this period were often a magnet for migrants from much further afield. The family historian is well-advised not to place too much reliance on textbooks that stress that serfs were legally tied to the manor, but to study instead recent work on the origins and ramifications of surnames and detailed studies of particular manors. In practice, medieval people appear to have been just as mobile as were their sixteenth and seventeenth century descendants.

By 1300 most of the country's available agricultural land was being farmed, even on those soils that were of little value. Given the primitive technology of the time, the expanding population had no alternative but to spread on to the moors and into the woods and marshes. A crisis point was reached long before the Black Death of 1348–49. Historians are now well aware of the impact of the series of harvest failures and livestock disasters that befell many parts of the country between 1315 and 1322 and which checked, if it did not reverse, population growth. The Black Death was the major catastrophe, which reduced the population by between a third and a half, but the fourteenth century witnessed recurrent plagues and other epidemics. Some places suffered heavy mortalities in the major visitations of 1361–62 and 1375. Bubonic plague remained endemic throughout the Middle Ages and other diseases were also virulent. Throughout England population levels fell considerably and marginal land reverted to its former waste condition. Estimates of national population figures for the later Middle Ages vary considerably because we have few firm statistics to guide us, but by 1500 the country may have had only half the number of people that it had supported in 1300.

Those families which survived these recurrent disasters found themselves in a far stronger position than they had been in at the beginning of the fourteenth century. The poorer sections of society benefited because more land was available for all and because wage levels rose as demand outran supply. The richer families also fared well. During the later Middle Ages an energetic farmer with an eye to the main chance was able to enlarge his estate and rise to the status of yeoman or minor gentleman; many of the farming dynasties of England were founded during this period. The average size of holdings of all classes of rural society increased and for the great majority of those rural families which had come through the terrible experiences of the fourteenth century a better standard of living was the reward.

Cuxham and Wigston

The family historian who wants to gain some understanding of life on the rural manor during the Middle Ages should first of all consult two classic local studies: Professor P.D.A. Harvey's *A Medieval Oxfordshire Village : Cuxham 1240 to 1400* (1965) and Professor W.G. Hoskins's *The Midland Peasant: The Economic and Social History of a Leicestershire Village* (1957), the story of Wigston from its origins to the end of the nineteenth century. The small parish of Cuxham is situated between the Chilterns and the river Thame and is less than a square mile in extent. Its woodland had all been cleared by the time of the Domesday Survey, when the area under the plough was already as extensive as it was to be in the fourteenth century. Cuxham's three open-fields retained their simple medieval descriptions of North, South and West until their enclosure in 1846–47. During the Middle Ages the local farmers followed a simple, three-course rotation of spring corn, winter corn and fallow. According to the Oxfordshire Hundred Rolls of 1279 only two Cuxham families were freeholders; the other twenty-one were either unfree peasants or cottagers. The immediate effects of the Black Death, which struck the village in the winter and spring of 1349, were severe. None of the twelve villeins recorded in the manorial court rolls in January 1349 was still there at the end of the year, and only four of the eight cottagers remained in the village in 1352. Three years after the plague had gone many properties still lay vacant, but by May 1355 new tenants seem to have been found for all of them. The local population had been partly replenished from outside. Nevertheless, nearly three decades after the visitation the 1377 poll tax returns list only thirty-eight inhabitants over 14 years old, that is a third of Cuxham's estimated population in 1348.

At the conclusion of his study Professor Harvey warns that in his experience little information obtained from manorial records can be safely taken at face value and that one cannot argue from omissions. The family historian treads on dangerous ground when he ventures into this area. Nevertheless, there is much to be gleaned even from such unpromising territory. For example, Cuxham's manorial records shed some interesting light on surname development. In general, children of manorial tenants started in life bearing their father's usual surname, but in two cases a name taken from the mother's Christian name was used as an alternative, and more often an occupational name eventually replaced the original one. A greater problem for the family historian is posed by the arrangement whereby if a man entered a tenement through marrying a widow, he normally assumed the surname of her first husband. For instance, when Robert Wald-rugge married Agnes, the widow of Robert Oldman, in 1296 he became the second Robert Oldman to farm that property. If it had not been established that the first Robert Oldman had died in 1296 it could have been reasonably assumed that he was the Robert Oldman who became reeve in 1311, whereas in fact the reeve was the Robert Waldrugge who had changed his name. At this period surnames were still in a state of flux; fortunately for the family historian most of them soon became stable.

The Leicestershire village of Wigston was also farmed on an open-field system until the era of parliamentary enclosure, but it was always far more populous than Cuxham and it contained a large and persistent class of small freeholders who had considerable independence from the absentee lords of the manor. At the time of the Domesday Survey two out of every five Wigston peasants were free. Wigston was the largest village in Leicestershire in 1086, and though it declined considerably for a time after the Black Death it retained this position throughout most of the succeeding centuries. By the Tudor period most of the unfree peasants were copyholders of inheritance, in other words they had the right to pass on their landed property to their successor, subject only to a small payment or fine on entry and a small annual rent thereafter. Both the fines and the rents were certain and could not be altered at the will of the lord. In inflationary periods this arrangement benefited the tenants considerably. Early fourteenth century tax returns show that Wigston already had a class of larger and comparatively wealthy farmers, for nearly 70 per cent of the tax was contributed by only 10 of the 120 or more families in the village. Throughout the Middle Ages local farmers continually bought and sold land, mostly in very small parcels. The impression gained from the records is of a vigorous, thriving free peasantry and of economic inequality. In Wigston the inheritance system was primogeniture; although provision was often made for a widow, younger sons and unmarried daughters this was almost invariably in the form of a life interest only so that the ancestral tenement passed to the eldest son unimpaired in size. Younger sons became craftsmen and labourers.

During the fifteenth century some old Wigston families disappeared, but in Professor Hoskins's words, 'a solid core of middling peasant freeholders lasted right through this century of change and movement'. Such families had sufficient land to survive but insufficient resources to move out of the parish to larger farms. In general, it was the wealthiest and the poorest families which left the village. The Astills, Smiths, Herricks, Palmers, Simons, Moulds, Stantons and Clays, and possibly the Shepherds and Cooks remained in Wigston from the fourteenth to the sixteenth centuries, but they formed only a small proportion of the whole community. Hoskins has estimated that only about 10 per cent of the Leicestershire families recorded in the 1524–25 lay subsidies had persisted in the same place since the poll tax returns of 1377–81. The fifteenth century had seen a great reshuffle of the local population.

By the reign of Henry VIII a quite disproportionate share of property in scores of Leicestershire villages was held by one, two or three families who had managed to build up sizeable estates over the last 100–150 years. In this respect the differences between neighbouring communities was sometimes marked. Immediately south of Wigston the villages of Foston and Wistow shrank until only a hall and a church were left and sheep and cattle grazed the ridges and furrows of the former open-fields and the mounds and hollows that marked the sites of houses. In Wigston, however, life went on with a 'monumental stability'. There, the 1524 subsidy returns reveal:

> a solid community of middling-sized farmers, small yeomen and husbandmen, with no overshadowing yeoman family at the top, dominating the place as the Bents did at Cosby, the Bradgates at Peatling Parva, the Hartopps at Burton Lazars and the Chamberlains at Newton Harcourt and Kilby, to cite a few outstanding examples out of many from Leicestershire records.

Plate 1.2   Steetley Church, Derbyshire
This north-east view of the church was published in the Derbyshire volume of Daniel and Samuel Lysons, *Magna Brittania*, V (1817). It shows the church abandoned and forlorn, the entire roof of the nave having collapsed. Steetley was a deserted medieval village, a chapel of ease in the parish of Whitwell, and its church had become redundant.

However, sufficient remained to show that it had been a fine example of a small Norman church consisting of a nave, chancel and vaulted apse. Carved heads formed a corbel table all round the church and the apse retained its pilasters, decorated string course and splayed windows. On the other side of the church is a beautifully-carved Norman door, which leads into a memorable interior. It is not known who was responsible for erecting such a lavishly decorated building. Pevsner writes: 'There are few Norman churches in England so consistently made into show-pieces by those who designed them and those who paid for them.' The church was splendidly restored by the Victorian architect J. L. Pearson in 1876–80.

Even in the Middle Ages the local history of one parish could be very different from that of its neighbours.

Halesowen

The studies of Cuxham and Wigston were made before historians developed the techniques of family reconstitution in order to obtain fuller demographic information. These techniques were first used to extract data from parish registers but they have recently been applied to medieval manorial court rolls in Zvi Razi's study of *Life, Marriage and Death in a Medieval Parish: Economy, Society and Demography in Halesowen, 1270–1400* (1980). This book is not only of great interest to economic historians who are concerned with population trends and structural changes in the fourteenth century but is one that every family historian who wishes to extend his researches back into the Middle Ages should read. It triumphantly demonstrates that a great deal of reliable genealogical information can be obtained from a good run of manorial court rolls. Halesowen is unusually fortunate in having such a complete set, for in many places none survives at all, but Razi has shown that where manors are richly documented the local and family historian can proceed cautiously but accurately, providing of course that he has a working knowledge of medieval palaeography. Dr Razi concludes that the range of activities recorded in surviving rolls is so wide that a villager could hardly avoid appearing before his manor court from time to time. He believes that the adult male population of Halesowen is almost totally represented in the surviving documents.

Halesowen was a large manor with a small market centre and scattered settlements in twelve rural townships to the west of Birmingham. The manor was 8 miles long and up to 2½ miles broad and covered about 10,000 acres. For the period 1270–1400 there are 215 surviving rolls covering 1,667 sessions of the court; the rolls of only 16 years are missing. With such a good sequence of detailed records positive identification of individuals is possible. Some people appear only once or twice but 80 per cent of the recorded names appear more than 10 times and certain individuals are recorded over 200 times. Each of the 5,002 names noted in the Halesowen court rolls between 1270 and 1400 is mentioned on average 15 times.

Even so, the historian is faced with severe problems of correct identification. First of all, as peasant surnames were unstable before the mid fourteenth-century villagers appear in the rolls under more than one name and often under two. Dr Razi writes:

> They were named indiscriminately by the scribes according to occupation or function, township, locality, place of origin and family relationship. For example, Alexander, a villager from the township of Romsley, who appears in the records between 1274 and 1293, lived in the small hamlet of Kenelmestowe near the Church

of St Kenelm and was a clerk by profession. He therefore had three
surnames – 'de Kenelmestowe', 'de St Kenelm' and 'the Clerk'. His
son Clements was called 'Clements the son of Alexandra of St
Kenelm' and 'Clements Tandi'. But in 1293 Clements married
Emma de Folfen and entered with her the family holding.
Henceforward he appears in the court rolls as 'Clements de Folfen'.

After the Black Death surnames stabilized and few villagers had
aliases.

A second problem – one that the genealogist will be familiar
with in later periods – is that it is common to find two or more
people with the same name. This difficulty is partly the result of
the fashion to name eldest sons after their father or grandfather,
thus making it hard to distinguish between the generations.
Pedigrees are rarely recorded in manorial court rolls, so any
genealogical data has to be extracted laboriously. Some problems
will never be solved, but Dr Razi claims that by studying every
detail of the context of an individual's appearance in court, such
as his associates and his location, it is possible to make correct
identifications in a high proportion of cases. Discovering the
familial ties of medieval villagers is made easier by the fact that
many of the social and economic activities reflected in the records
of the manorial court were conducted within a family framework.
Razi provides examples of the ways in which he reconstituted 677
families by explicit genealogical information obtained from the
1270–1400 rolls and the inferences which enabled him to establish
links between the members of another 364 families. Altogether,
he was able to identify 2,057 men and 1,378 women who were
residents within the manor during those 131 years. Another 372
people (11 per cent) could not be identified and a further 178
apparently were outsiders.

By the late thirteenth century differences in the villagers' standard of living were already marked. In the absence of rentals or
customals it is difficult to establish the number of free and
customary tenants in the manor of Halesowen, but 504 of the 788
families (64 per cent) that were reconstituted by Dr Razi from the
court rolls of 1270–1349 were of unfree status. The holdings of
peasant families were often referred to as virgates or as fractions
of virgates. A virgate probably amounted to 25 to 30 acres of
arable land in the open fields, together with pasture rights on the
fallow and commons, a small plot of meadow and a few pasture
closes. Middling families held half virgates and poorer ones much
less. But even though land was in short supply and primogeniture

was the dominant inheritance system many families were able to provide for more than one son and one daughter to marry and settle in the parish. Parents tried to give their younger children a start in life while keeping the family holding intact. Young couples were prepared to begin their marriage with only a cottage or a smallholding of a few acres. They married young – probably between the ages of eighteen and twenty-two on average – and did not wait until they had inherited the family holding.

The mean family size in Halesowen was 5.8, roughly the same as in some contemporary East Anglian villages which have been studied and which practised partible inheritance. Claims that different inheritance customs produced different population densities appear to be unfounded. As in later times, wealthier families tended to have more children than the poor who were unable to support many offspring on their limited resources. Contrary to later practice, however, illegitimacy rates were high; women who bore children out of wedlock were not stigmatised nor were bastards treated as outcasts. A study of the court rolls also shows that people moved in and out of the manor frequently, though they probably did not go very far. The rolls for 1270–1348 note the departure, with or without licence, of sixty-seven men and women of unfree status; many others probably left without their move having been registered.

The population of Halesowen continued to rise until the devastating visitation of the Black Death in the summer months of 1349. Population growth was checked but not reversed by the famines and pestilences that occurred sporadically between 1293 and 1318. Many cottagers and smallholders died during these earlier crises but not in the same numbers as during the disaster of 1349. The Black Death may have killed 81 of the 203 male tenants whom Dr Razi has identified in the Halesowen court rolls. Whole families were wiped out. At least 40 per cent of the tenants died and in none of the twelve rural townships did the number of deaths fall below 33 per cent of the local population.

But life soon returned to normal and tenants were quickly found for all the holdings. Some of these farmers were outsiders who were prepared to move to increase their standard of living. During the forty years after 1353 an average of 5.5 immigrants per year settled in Halesowen. The detailed biographies painstakingly compiled by Dr Razi from the manorial court rolls of 1350–1400 show that many of these incomers were previously related to Halesowen families by blood or marriage. They were quickly integrated into the local community and some were soon elected to manorial office. The richer families enlarged their holdings but poor families also benefited from the sudden availability of land. Economic opportunities also allowed even earlier marriages, so that men now commonly married at twenty and women at an even younger age. Illegitimacy rates fell sharply and the expectation of life increased. The Black Death had profound economic and demographic consequences that were felt for the rest of the Middle Ages.

Later outbreaks of plague occurred at Halesowen in 1361–62, 1369 and 1375, as in many other parts of the country. This long period of malaise changed the face of England. Though these plagues rarely wiped out a whole community in a single visitation, many rural settlements withered and eventually disappeared except perhaps for the church and the manor house. Deserted medieval villages are a feature particularly of the Midland Plain, parts of East Anglia, Lincolnshire, the North and East Ridings of Yorkshire and other farming regions where sheep and cattle replaced men. In those parts of England that are characterised by dispersed settlements rather than nucleated villages the effects of population decline are less obvious but were no doubt still severe. The rural market centres which had been established while the population was still expanding in the thirteenth century ceased to trade and declined to mere villages, and some of the mightiest towns and cities in the land descended into a long spiral of depression which was not broken until the Elizabethan age.

Towns

Late-medieval towns were very small by modern standards. About 75 per cent of them were simple market centres like Lutterworth, which at the beginning of Henry VIII's reign had only 116 houses. Such places were hardly bigger than the more populous of the villages and had a different character only on market days. More obviously urban were the 200–300 small towns with populations of 1,500 or more. They often had a semi-autonomous governing body and the characteristic householder was a craftsman. Next in rank came the thirty-three towns with between 2,000 and 5,000 people, places of regional importance with sophisticated urban economies. But all these smaller towns were overshadowed by the nine leading provincial cities and by

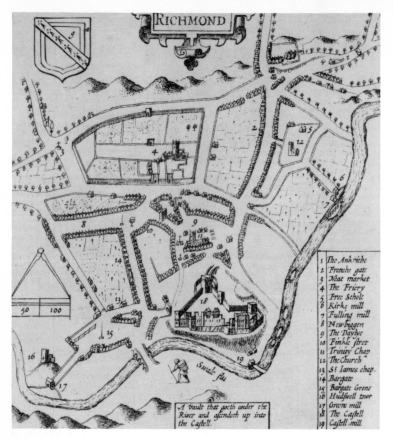

Reference key on map:

1. The Ankriche
2. Frenche gate
3. Neat market
4. The Friery
5. Free Schole
6. Kirke mill
7. Fulling mill
8. Newbiggen
9. The Daybe
10. Finkle stret
11. Trinity Chap
12. The Church
13. St Iames chap.
14. Bargatt
15. Bargatt Grene
16. Hudswell towr
17. Greene mill
18. The Castell
19. Castell mill

A vault that goeth under the River and ascendeth up into the Castell.

Plate 1.3 Richmond in 1610

This map was published as an inset in John Speed's map of the North and East Ridings of Yorkshire. It is now kept in the British Library as pressmark G.7884, plate 81. It gives a clear view of the topography of the town, which was still basically that of the medieval borough.

Richmond was a Norman word meaning 'strong hill'. In 1071, shortly after the 'harrying of the North', work began on a cliff-top castle high above the Swale. William I granted Alan Rufus one of the largest feudal holdings in the kingdom in order to defend this strategic position. At first, the outer bailey formed a large open space beyond the castle walls, but soon this was converted into a market place around Holy Trinity chapel. During the fourteenth century town walls were built above the bailey defences, whose curving lines are preserved by shop frontages. By the time that Speed drew his map a number of permanent buildings had been erected in the market place.

Extramural development took place along Frenchgate and Bargate and then along Newbiggen. The parish church and the friary stood beyond the town walls. By 1610 the congestion in the old market place was such that the livestock or 'neat' market had been removed to the edge of the town.

24

London, which had about 60,000 inhabitants in the year 1500. In the first half of the sixteenth century Norwich was next in size to the capital with a population of over 10,000, and Bristol, York, Salisbury, Exeter, Colchester, Canterbury, Newcastle and Coventry each had more than 6,000 inhabitants. This leading group included five county towns and diocesan sees, three major ports and three centres of inland navigation. Even these cities, however, were smaller and less buoyant than they used to be. They managed to recover from the fourteenth-century disasters but during the second half of the fifteenth century demographic trends and economic forces hit them hard. Many English towns decayed during Henry VIII's reign and for some the 1520s were a time of crisis.

Charles Phythian-Adams's masterly description of the decay of a leading provincial centre in *Desolation of a City: Coventry and the Urban Crisis of the Late Middle Ages* (1979) is essential reading for anyone wishing to understand this process and to form a view of the social and economic structure of a medieval town. The book explores all aspects of late-medieval urban life, including the pattern of the working day and the annual rhythms punctuated by holy days, when the ceremonies of the socio-religious guilds or fraternities provided colourful spectacles and unifying bonds. The inhabitants of Coventry saw themselves as belonging to an urban community that was very different from those of their lesser neighbours. Coventry was pre-eminent in the Midlands as a major distribution centre with important markets and fairs and for its ecclesiastical status as the joint head of a diocese. In 1450 Coventry was still flourishing with a population of about 10,000 or more; by 1523 such was the desolation that the inhabitants numbered only 5,699.

Late-medieval Coventry was a hierarchical society whose inhabitants had a great respect for wealth and age. Unlike the thirteenth and fourteenth century inhabitants of rural Halesowen, the citizens of early sixteenth-century Coventry did not marry young. The majority of men did not set up house, cottage or workshop until they were married; only 61 of the 1,302 heads of households enumerated in 1523 were 'single men' and at least half of these were widowers. Contemporaries drew a distinction between householders and the poorer cottagers. Even the simplest house had a hall and solar behind the workshop that fronted the street, whereas cottages consisted of little more than a chamber. The correlation between wealth and household size is marked, with an uninterrupted sequence of household densities ranging from 2.6 for the cottages to 9.2 for the wealthiest households with living-in servants. Significant variations in household size can be observed between the different wards of the city; in some parts poverty and homelessness were becoming major problems. Living-in servants formed about a quarter of the recorded population. Most of them were young and together with the children they comprised about half of Coventry's inhabitants. The youthful composition of medieval communities goes a long way towards explaining the hierarchical structure of local societies based on a veneration for age.

THE ORIGINS OF ENGLISH SURNAMES

As I have a fairly unusual name myself, one that is still uncommon beyond the former boundaries of the West Riding of Yorkshire, I have long been interested in the origins of surnames. Like many other family historians, I suspect, I have looked at dictionaries of surnames but have never been satisfied with the explanation on offer. Under my own name, spelt Hey, the dictionaries usually say 'see Hay'. But this advice ignores the fact that Hay is a Scottish name and that Hey is largely confined to the western and southern parts of Yorkshire, where it is still sometimes pronounced in the local manner and with a hard 'e'. Although it is common to find names spelt in a variety of ways during the centuries when spelling was phonetic, because of this pronunciation I have rarely seen my name spelt in any other way than the present one. Despite the fact that Hay and Hey are both derived from the same word meaning a hedged enclosure the two surnames have different origins. We can be even more specific than that in saying that although Hey is a common minor place-name, especially on the Pennine moors, the surname has been derived from one particular Hey in the ancient parish of Halifax.

Even today most English counties possess a substantial number of surnames that are common within their boundaries but which are rare or non-existent beyond. Many of these names were derived from hamlets and single farmsteads in the thirteenth and fourteenth centuries. Kent has its Hogbens, Hasteds, Blaxlands and Wickendens and Lancashire is the home of such distinctive surnames as Birtwhistle, Fasakerley, Postlethwaite and Rigby. Some of these names are found occasionally in other parts of England but not in the same numbers. If we trace them back through parish registers to the taxation records of the fourteenth century, especially to the poll tax returns of the late 1370s, they are often found to be confined to the locality from whence they originated. Today, Rigby is a common surname in Lancashire and Cheshire but is fairly unusual elsewhere; its restricted distribution in the Middle Ages shows that it was derived from a small place called Rigby in the parish of Kirkham. The Eleanor Rigby of the Beatles' song had a good local name. A much higher proportion of Lancashire surnames than of those in the country as a whole originated in this way.

It is common to find that by the sixteenth century such names had begun to spread beyond their original locality. If we look at the taxation records known as lay subsidies in the reign of Henry VIII and turn also to the earliest surviving parish registers we discover that by then many of these distinctive surnames had ramified within a much wider neighbourhood than the original parish. Our medieval ancestors were more mobile than we once thought. Locative surnames that can be identified with a single place of origin sometimes turn up in far away places even in the Middle Ages, for men and women occasionally travelled very long distances to find new homes and work. Medieval Norfolk, for instance, contained people who had come from as far afield as Yorkshire and Cumbria. Some locative names were formed when people moved to a new place; men were named after their native town or village in the form of John of Doncaster, William of Buxton, and so on. But many other families took the name of their residence as their surname while they were actually living there. In areas of scattered settlements, where such names can be identified with individual farmsteads, the genealogist has the exciting possibility of tracing a name back to its precise origins.

The first person to make a serious attempt to analyse the geographical distribution of British surnames was Dr H. P. Guppy, whose *Homes of Family Names in Great Britain* was published as long ago as 1890. Guppy's method was to extract farmers' names from Kelly's Post Office directories on a county by county basis. He chose to limit his study to farming families because they were the most stable group in provincial society, though of course they formed only a small minority of the entire population. Guppy was at pains to point out that his work was merely a preliminary examination of a fascinating topic. He observed that even some common surnames were distributed unevenly; the Browns were particularly numerous in the North, Chapman was essentially an eastern England name, and the Kings were mostly confined to the area south of a line extending from south Shropshire to the Wash. As for the widespread name Smith, 'Its great home is in Worcestershire and in the adjacent counties of Gloucestershire, Warwick and Stafford', though it was numerous in Essex also. Guppy's main finding was that counties varied greatly in their possession of names that were peculiar to their area. Cornwall and Devon were pre-eminent in this way, with localized names forming at least 40 per cent of the total. Next on Guppy's list came Lincolnshire and the North and East Ridings of Yorkshire with over 30 per cent of names having a restricted origin, then came the West Riding, Lancashire, Kent, Dorset and Somerset with over 25 per cent. These are very crude figures – those for the West Riding and Lancashire certainly need to be higher if the names of all occupational groups are considered – but they do point to the general truth that old-enclosed pastoral areas characterised by dispersed settlements produced far more localised names than the nucleated villages of the open-field arable areas such as the Midland Plain.

Guppy's pioneering work was not taken up until recent times. Instead, the study of the origins of surnames became the preserve of linguists who were concerned with the meaning of a name rather than with identifying its geographical origins and subsequent ramification. The classic works of this approach are Professor P. H. Reaney's *The Origin of English Surnames* (1967) and his *Dictionary of British Surnames* (1958). In the last few years, however, the study of English surnames has been revolutionized by Richard McKinley, the Marc Fitch Research Fellow in the Department of English Local History at the University of Leicester, and by Dr George Redmonds's work on the West Riding. McKinley has taken one county at a time and has painstakingly assembled surnames from medieval tax returns, manorial court rolls, etc., progressing chronologically to parish registers. He has thus been able to establish the incidence of each type of name at various periods from the twelfth century onwards. In the process he has shed a great deal of light on English social and economic history, particularly on the topics of social and geographical mobility.

Surnames can be placed in six categories:

1. those derived from personal names;
2. those derived from occupations;
3. topographical names, derived from features of the landscape;
4. locative names, derived from specific place-names or localities;
5. nicknames;
6. terms of relationship.

The locative names are particularly rewarding to study, for they are relatively easy to use when assessing mobility. They, more than any other type, often have a single origin. Perhaps the most interesting finding of all this recent work is the conclusion that a great number of our English surnames originate with single families.

In *The Surnames of Oxfordshire* (1977) McKinley states that no evidence has been found of true hereditary surnames in the county before 1066; the beginnings of family names are to be sought instead in the period immediately after the Norman Conquest. This appears to be generally true of the whole country. Sir Anthony Wagner tells us in his book, *English Genealogy* (1960), that the ancestry of two extant English families only – the Ardens and the Berkeleys – can be carried back to pre-Conquest Englishmen, though some other surnames are Old English in origin. Numerous descents can be proved from Norman families and some of these can be traced back in Normandy to the tenth century. In most cases, however, we have to look to the thirteenth or fourteenth centuries, and sometimes much later, for the origins of hereditary surnames. In Oxfordshire most of the rural population, including some landed families, did not acquire family names until the late-thirteenth or early-fourteenth centuries. About half the surnames that occur in the Oxfordshire Hundred Rolls for 1279 survived as hereditary surnames into the following century. Country folk in this county seem to have adopted this practice a little earlier than the poorer sections of the town of Oxford.

Locative surnames can be used for the study of population movements in a more systematic manner than any other category of name. Of course, places of origin cannot always be identified with certainty, for some place-names are common or at least are found repeated elsewhere, and both place-names and surnames have changed their form over a period of time. In the country at large over half the surnames derived from place-names can have

Plate 1.4 Fanshaw Gate Old Hall, Derbyshire
The medieval hall that occupied this site was demolished in 1636, but a pair of fanciful gateposts, a dovecote and a building with mullioned windows survive from the seventeenth century. This was the home of the Fanshawe family who moved to London in the sixteenth century. Between 1530 and 1674 a succession of Fanshawes held the post of Remembrancer of the Court of Exchequer. One of these men – Henry Fanshawe – founded a grammar school at Dronfield, the parish centre 3 miles from the family's original home.

The first element of the place-name is obscure, but shaw signified a small wood and gate was a Viking word in origin for a road, presumably the winding lane that passes in front of the hall. The Fanshawe family were recorded here in the first half of the fifteenth century and they continued to own the property until recent times. Other Fanshaws or Fanshawes still live within a few miles of the place which has given rise to their surname.

alternative identifications. Tracing the origin of a name can be a complicated business, especially if a bearer of the name has travelled a long way. Another problem with using locative surnames to assess the incidence of geographical mobility is the extent to which such names are representative of the nation as a whole. If we turn to topographical names such as Hill and Wood we find that they were borne predominantly by unfree sections of the

30

population, particularly those surnames which were both numerous and widespread. The groups of people who bore locative surnames appear to have had more varied social origins, but was that true of those families and individuals who moved from their original locality? Many such questions remain unresolved, for this new approach to the study of surnames has so far been applied only to a limited number of counties.

The 1279 Hundred Rolls demonstrate a certain amount of movement among the unfree population of Oxfordshire, though this took place over quite short distances. This mobility cannot be explained as merely the movement of serfs from one manor to another, and it was more common in some parts of the county than the rest. One might reasonably expect a considerable amount of migration in and out of Oxfordshire because of the county's central position, its lack of well-defined geographical boundaries and its several different types of countryside. It is exceptional to find an Oxfordshire family at any period of time that was continuously resident in the same village for over a century. Richard McKinley has shown, however, that if we take the county or even the smaller unit of the hundred as the relevant unit, rather than the parish, then we will find a great deal of continuity in Oxfordshire surnames. Families moved from parish to parish, but they moved within a limited area.

In an earlier study, *Norfolk and Suffolk Surnames in the Middle Ages* (1975), McKinley examined that part of the country which was the most populous and economically advanced at the time of the Domesday Survey. In some cases the richer East Anglian families had adopted hereditary surnames within a generation or two of the Battle of Hastings. The acquisition of surnames was, however, a gradual process over a period of four centuries. The most productive era in this respect stretched from the mid-twelfth century to the mid-fourteenth. This was the time when most English towns were founded. A high proportion of fourteenth-century East Anglian townsmen had names that had been derived from other places; in Norwich nearly half the freemen had locative surnames derived from places beyond the city, and in King's Lynn the proportion was nearly two-thirds. Towns also influenced surname development in another striking way, for many more of our occupational surnames were derived from urban than from rural crafts; the cloth industry was a particularly rich source.

A comparison can be made between the tax returns of the 1520s known as the lay subsidies and earlier taxation documents.

In Norfolk and Suffolk more than half the people recorded in thirteenth and early-fourteenth century sources with locative surnames were living within 10 miles of the places from which their names were derived, but by Henry VIII's reign their descendants had spread over much greater distances. Though families tended to move only short distances at a time, in the long run frequent moves resulted in a considerable migration of population. Social mobility, both upwards and downwards, is also apparent when the sixteenth-century population is compared with that of much earlier periods. All the regional studies that have been made so far suggest that such mobility was a national phenomenon, though its incidence varied from area to area. East Anglian people seem to have been amongst the most geographically mobile. Nevertheless, it is also true that many families did not move very far. Individual family names remained peculiar to particular localities. One intriguing puzzle that remains unsolved is why some families ramified at an early date and eventually spread to many different parts of the kingdom, whereas others have remained close to their origins. This is an exciting area of research which promises to yield many more unexpected results in the coming years.

With his *Surnames of Lancashire* (1982) Richard McKinley turned to a county that in the Middle Ages was remote from most of England, cut off as it was by the sea, the surrounding hills and the mosses that restricted movement from one area to another. Hereditary surnames were formed rather late in Lancashire. A considerable minority of the population were without family names in early-Tudor times and the process was not completed until the seventeenth century. Many surnames in common use in the Middle Ages did not become hereditary; those ending in the suffix '-daughter', for instance, were not normally passed on to descendants. Non-hereditary nicknames were widely used until the end of the eighteenth century, for in many localities a single surname was borne by a lot of the inhabitants. Nevertheless, most of the surnames which ramified beyond their original parishes were well established by the year 1400. Lancashire has a high proportion of locative surnames, far more than most other English counties. Many of these names were derived from minor place-names established in the thirteenth century when the expanding population created new farms in clearings on the hills and in the woods and marshes. The county's population was remarkably static before the Industrial Revolution. Localized names ramified within restricted areas and not many outsiders came in to settle. Few Lancashire surnames are derived from places beyond the county boundary, a fact that contrasts sharply with East Anglian experience.

A final point from the many observations in Richard McKinley's work that will interest family historians is that during the thirteenth and fourteenth centuries the categories of surname chosen by different social classes differed in several interesting ways. In Lancashire, for example, names with the suffix '-son' were rarely used by the better-off landowning classes. Such names appear in large numbers in Lancashire in the early fourteenth century, however, amongst townspeople and in the countryside amongst bondmen, small tenants and labourers. The category of family name can therefore often be a clue to the social and economic standing of one's ancestors in the Middle Ages. Occupational names and locative names are the most obvious types, but we still have much to discover about the origins of other categories.

A pioneering study of northern names was made by Dr George Redmonds in *Yorkshire: The West Riding* (1973). He showed that in this part of the country many landowning families were using hereditary surnames from the mid-twelfth century onwards and that these names were very often taken from the place where the family resided and held land. The vast majority of Yorkshire towns and villages had given rise to surnames before 1250 but most family names within the Riding were derived from minor settlements, especially in the period 1250–1350, but sometimes as late as the fifteenth century. A study of the court rolls of the huge manor of Wakefield emphasized the importance of the years 1275–1325 and 1350–70 as periods of stabilization of hereditary surnames. The 1379 poll tax returns show that a large number of West Riding families still did not possess a true surname, however. During the thirteenth and fourteenth centuries a person could still be referred to by a variety of different surnames. It does not appear to be true that population growth and the use of only a small number of Christian names led to the use of permanent surnames, for an elaborate system of diminutives and pet-forms enabled people to get around this problem. Rather, it was a more efficient administrative system that demanded firm identification.

Dr Redmonds has shown that the West Riding was the home of a large number of distinctive names, which in many cases had a single family origin. One has to remember how small England's population was at the time of surname formation. The enormous parish of Halifax, the largest in England with some 80,000 acres within its bounds, had only 831 names recorded in the poll tax returns of 1379. Well over a hundred of these became surnames which are still in use at the present day. An equal number became hereditary surnames but did not survive very long. These names were formed at a time when the reclamation of moorland and the clearing of woods was being actively pursued. The hills around Halifax have been wonderfully productive of locative surnames derived from isolated farmsteads. Most of these names have a single family origin; most of them had begun to spread by the sixteenth century; but even though they can now sometimes be found far afield most are still concentrated within 20 or 30 miles of their place of origin.

SOME CASE STUDIES

In the year 1593 Robert Furse of Dean Prior in the county of Devon wrote an account of his family for the benefit of his descendants and coupled this with instruction and advice on how to proceed in this troubled world. He set out his aims at the beginning:

> I do mynde bryfely to speke of all the everyche of them in the callynge that ys what there names were wythe whom theye marryed what issue theye hadde where the dwelled where theye dyed what londs they hadde and by whatt tytell and where the londs lyethe and the valye thereof of whom hyt ys holden and by what rente sute and serves and all other charges due for any parcell thereof and howe yt hathe dyssended and the perfytt names of the londs and howe and by whom hyt hathe bynne lesed and what yeres our anncestors leved what welthe or existimasion they were of what plesure for there recreasyon and pastym they moste delyted of what stature quallytes and personage they were of and whatt wylles and testements theye made.

Furse was therefore very much in the tradition of those sixteenth- and seventeenth-century family historians who were concerned to prove their legal title to property passed down to them by their ancestors. He was also in the tradition of the time in stressing that these blessings had come from God. His general introduction was followed by a prayer, then nine closely written pages of advice and exhortation. After that he was ready to start on his family history.

He tells us that he had collected his material from legal evidences, 'som by reporte off old awncyente men and som of my on knowlege and experyns'. Furse is the name of a farm in the parish of Cheriton Fitzpaine, which gave rise to the surname. Robert Furse assumed that the first six generations whom he knew to have owned the farm – starting with Roland de Cumba and proceeding with William de la Furse – were his ancestors, but we cannot be sure about that. He was on more certain ground by the sixteenth century when he reached Robert Furse, who began the family tradition of bequeathing a cow to his heir on the understanding that a yearly sum to the value of the cow should be given to some charitable cause.

> This Roberte was greatly to be commended for that he trayned uppe his son John Furse to be a lernede man for by that menes our credyt and levinge ys grettly incressed.

Up to this point the family had owned a tenement of 48 acres at Furse and another 39 acres at 'Westewaye' in Cruwys Morchard. In Robert's vivid phrase they were yet a 'little twig'. They became more substantial when John married an heiress, Annes Adler.

> He kepte a verye good house and was of grette welthe he meayntayned his son and here in lernynge at the yndes of the curte
> . . .
> Note here that John Furse and Annes his wyfe were too of the beste laborers that came ynto our harveste for we enjoyede moste of our londs from them. Any by there menes therefore we have good case to have them in memorye for in truthe theye were the Fyrst Fondasyon of all our credytt prayse God for hit.

Once he had completed the Furse family history Robert turned to the Moreseads, his mother's family. Their story is told in seven closely written pages. Here again the family name was taken from their place of residence – an estate in the parish of Dean Prior. Robert noted that:

> the custom and use was of olde tymes to call men after the names of ther mansyon howses but spessially those that were freholders for I have redde that wytheyn the parysche of Dene pryer there was Steven of Smallcombe, Sempeston of Sempeston, Rowdene of Rowdene, Nuston of Nuston and so of dyvers others.

Devon was a prolific source of locative surnames that have arisen in this manner, for the county's ancient settlement pattern was one of scattered farms on hills and in sheltered combes as much as one of towns and villages. In this it was very similar to the

Plate 1.5 Kirkburton and Shelley *c.* 1772

The first large-scale map of Yorkshire, surveyed between 1767 and 1772 for Thomas Jefferys, is an invaluable source for local historians in the North. Many other counties have maps of a similar standard from the mid or late eighteenth century.

The map marks three of the homes of the Hey family within the parish of Kirkburton. Birk House, near the southern border of Shelley township, was probably the home of the Thomas Hey who was recorded in 1505 and 1524, and it was certainly occupied by members of the family from 1568 to 1719. Joseph Hey (1629–75) seems to have been the first to move to Thorncliffe on the edge of the large common that lay to the east of Kirkburton village, and another branch had settled at Shelley Hill Top by 1688. The senior branches of the family continued to live in the parish after my great-great-grandfather moved a few miles south to Thurlstone about the year 1800, and George Hey (1811–93) became a successful businessman, benevolent employer and Chairman of the Local Board.

The Heys were a prolific family in Kirkburton and Shelley. The surname appears 300 times in the parish register between 1543 and 1800. My ancestor William Hey (1667–1710) had three sons who had eighteen children between them; six of these children were sons who eventually fathered branches of their own. Most of these Heys earned their living from weaving woollen cloth and farming a smallholding. Life went on much the same from generation to generation. They have left few records

36

West Riding, another region that was the home of numerous distinctive surnames.

In tracing my own family name in the West Riding I got back ten generations to John Hey of the township of Shelley within the parish of Kirkburton, who died in 1633. Gaps in the parish register prevent my proving an earlier line with certainty, but many Heys lived in the township of Shelley during the sixteenth century. The Thomas Hey of Shelley who was recorded in a manor court roll of 1505 and the lay subsidy returns of 1524 was probably my ancestor though I cannot be sure. Before that time I am on even more uncertain ground. Another court roll of 1476 mentions a John Hey of Shepley, the next village to Shelley, but I have not yet discovered any further information about the surname in this locality. A century earlier, however, the West Riding poll tax returns of 1379 name only one Hey, a certain Robertus del Heye, or Robert of the Hey, in Barkisland township a dozen miles or so away in the huge parish of Halifax. The site of the medieval hey or enclosure that appears to have been the ancestral home of everyone who bears my surname is now occupied by a seventeenth-century Pennine farmstead with mullioned windows known as Over Hey House, or 'ey 'us in the local dialect. The name of the farmhouse is pronounced in exactly the same way as Yorkshire people have pronounced my surname over the centuries.

Of course, only a portion of surnames can be traced back to their origins in this way, but most family historians will find that at least one of their branches leads in this direction and local historians who study those parts of England where the characteristic settlement pattern is one of dispersed farmsteads and hamlets rather than nucleated villages will be able to trace some of the distinctive surnames of their communities in this manner. One must be prepared for surprises because at first sight some

---

of their activities, but John Hey of Birk House, clothier, was named in a document of *c.* 1698 kept in the Public Record Office (E134 Wm3 East, 4) when he intervened on behalf of a friend and neighbour, Elizabeth Kaye, a widow who was being prosecuted for tithe payments by the vicar. John Hey 'lay downe A broad piece of gold & a guinea', which more than covered the vicar's claim, but this noble gesture did not placate the clergyman. He was accompanied on this mission by his relation, John Hey of Thorncliffe, clothier, and was commended by the justice, Sir John Kaye, for his action. Such personal glimpses of members of one's family in the seventeenth century are, however, rare.

surnames derived from place-names appear to have a very different origin. Curiously enough, in the place where I live all my near neighbours seem to have locative surnames, though one or two are not immediately obvious examples. Coming up the road we have the Midgleys, Broadheads, Heys, Blanksbys, Darwents and Appleyards and just over the brow of the hill is a farmer named Shufflebottom. Midgley is a straightforward West Riding name derived from a village in the parish of Halifax, not far from Over Hey House. Darwent may have come from Darwen in Lancashire but it is more likely to be a north Derbyshire name taken from the small settlement of Derwent that is now submerged beneath a reservoir. In turn the village took its name from the river. The pronunciation of Derby, the county capital on the southern stretch of the river, shows that Darwent is a feasible alternative to Derwent. The village name was indeed spelled Darwent in some sixteenth-century documents. Shufflebottom is a Lancashire name in origin, a gradual corruption over the years of the minor place-name Shipperbottom in the parish of Bury, a name first recorded in 1285. We are left with the Appleyards, Blanksbys and Broadheads.

One might reasonably expect the surname Appleyard to have had multiple origins. Surely, one may think, there must have been numerous yards where apples were grown or stored. But the present geographical distribution of the surname is intriguing. It suggests that only one Appleyard gave rise to a surname. The current Sheffield telephone directory has 64 entries for the name, whereas the Brighton directory has only 9 and the Bristol directory as few as 4. If we search the returns of those people who paid the poll tax in 1379 we find that a Thomas de Apilyerd was living in Thurlstone township, some 15 miles north of Sheffield. In a document dated 1297 Appleyard is referred to as a minor place-name in the same township. This place-name is now lost, but as no rival candidate has appeared it seems that this was the particular orchard which gave rise to the surname.

The Blanksbys have a similar origin. They too have not moved far over the centuries. Present-day ordnance survey maps mark Blingsby Gate on the northern edge of the park belonging to Hardwick Hall. A map of 1610 surveyed by William Senior has 'Blingsbie' written across a large field of 38 acres 1 rood 20 perches, and this site is still known to local farmers as the Blingsbys. It is covered by the typical platforms and depressions of a deserted medieval village. Domesday Book records it as

Blanghesbi, a Viking settlement incorporating the personal name Blaeingr. Over the centuries the place-name has changed to Blingsby, but the local surname Blanksby is nearer the original pronunciation. The surname is not often found more than 20 miles from the original village site. In a similar way the surname Bristow preserves the old pronunciation of Bristol and many other examples can no doubt be found all over England.

The final name amongst my group of neighbours is more difficult to trace back to its origins. Broadhead is a common name, not confined to one locality, and in some parts of the country it may have started as a nickname. It has multiple origins, and the Lancashire Broadheads probably came from a minor place-name in the parish of Scarisbrick – the del Brodheved of *c.* 1250. My neighbours, however, are descended from a different branch, for Broadhead is a very common name in Sheffield and other parts of south Yorkshire. They appear to have come originally from a little further north on the hills around Holmfirth in that part of the huge manor of Wakefield known as the Graveship of Holme. The 1545 lay subsidy roll for the wapentakes of Agbrigg, Morley and Skyrack records only three Broadheads, all of whom were resident in this graveship. The 1379 poll tax returns confirm this evidence, and the manor court rolls for 1348 refer to Juliana del Broydhed and also to Thomas del Bridheved, who surrendered 'his chief messuage and 25 acres of land and meadow and pasture in Upperthong, which are granted to Richard his son to hold to himself and the heirs issuing of his body'. The 6 inch ordnance survey map marks Broadhead Edge near Austonley and Upperthong within the Graveship of Holme. It is this topographical feature, the broad head or escarpment, which seems to have given rise to the local surname.

In his *Dictionary of British Surnames* Professor P. H. Reaney observed that his own surname, 'though not common, is a Sheffield name, always with this spelling. The correct pronunciation is Rainey, now being replaced by the spelling pronunciation Reeney. The above forms are all from the neighbourhood of Penistone and Sheffield. The name derives from Ranah Stones in the township of Thurlstone . . . . Rayner is a dialectical pronunciation'. Here then is another name with a precise geographical origin. Unfortunately, Professor Reaney did not apply this line of thought to the many other names in his dictionary which are derived in a similar manner. He relied instead on linguistic interpretations that do not satisfy the evidence of the past and present distributions of surnames. For example, under the entry for Bullas Reaney gives John de la Bulehouse (Hampshire, 1224), Henry de Bolus (Derbyshire, 1327), William Bolehouse (Somerset, 1327), Thomas Bulluse (Sheffield, 1478), etc. and explains the meaning of the surname as 'one employed at the bull-house'. This fails to take account of the present geographical distribution of the name in and around Sheffield and its frequent appearance in the early Sheffield parish registers. The surname seems to be derived from the hamlet of Bullhouse, which lies only three-quarters of a mile away from Ranah Stones. The place-name is still pronounced Bullas locally, like the surname, and it was written in the form Bullous in 1574. The meaning may be either bull-house or bole-house, i.e. a place where iron was smelted, but it is unlikely that the surname was attached to 'one employed at the bull-house'. Rather, it was probably attached to the family who resided here. The attribution of the surname is more specific than Reaney suggested. The same point can be made about his explanation of the surname Abdy, which he thought meant 'one employed at the abbey'. In 1379 Robert del Abdy paid the poll tax in Brampton township. Abdy farm lies close to the Brampton boundary and the English Place-Name Society's explanation of the place-name is 'property belonging to an abbey'. It is known that both Roche Abbey and Monk Bretton Priory had an estate in this area. The surname therefore did not have the general meaning of Reaney's suggestion but arose from the occupancy of a particular farm.

Dr G. Redmonds has shown that more than three-quarters of the West Riding's distinctive locative surnames that were recorded in 1379 came from Halifax parish, names such as Ackroyd, Bairstow, Boothroyd, Bottomley, Copley, Haley, Holroyd, Horsfall, Illingworth, Lumb, Murgatroyd, Priestley and Sutcliffe. The names of some famous Yorkshire cricketers can be recognised amongst them. Moreover, Halifax parish is the true home of some names which at first sight we might place elsewhere. The surname Sunderland brings to mind the town in County Durham, which may indeed have given rise to some branches of the surname, but the West Riding Sunderlands originate from a minor place-name near Northowram. Thomas de Sunderland was there in 1379 and the family resided at High Sunderland Hall until the middle years of the seventeenth century.

Dr Redmonds's method of using telephone directories to assess current distributions of names and then to work back through parish registers to the sixteenth century and then through manorial court rolls and tax returns to the period when surnames began is one that can be followed with profit by the amateur local and family historian. Some names will continue to defy interpretation, others will remain tantalisingly obscure, yet the amateur who knows his documentary sources, his chosen area on the ground and his local dialect will be able to make confident identifications that are well beyond the powers of the linguistic expert who does not have detailed local knowledge. In recent years it has become abundantly clear that many surnames have a single origin. The historian who is interested in an area of scattered settlement, where each farm has its distinctive name, can make a real contribution to our understanding of how surnames began.

Sheffield names

Let us take some of the surnames in the Sheffield telephone directory that can be shown to be local in origin. Names such as Crooks, Shirtcliff and Osgathorpe came from small settlements that now lie within the city boundaries and Creswick was the name of a farm on the northern outskirts near Ecclesfield. Hampshire does not come from the southern county of that name, as one might think, but in the north of England at least it is a shortening of Hallamshire, the name of the ancient territorial unit that comprised the parishes of Sheffield and Ecclesfield and the chapelry of Bradfield. The surname Housley is derived from a hamlet 6 miles north of Sheffield. In 1379 Lawrence and John of Housley were living in this township, quite possibly in the timber-framed building known as Housley Hall which survives behind an eighteenth-century exterior. The moorland chapelry of Bradfield, north-west of Sheffield, was the home of many other local names, such as Dungworth, Holdworth and Worrall. The 144 Broomheads in the current Sheffield telephone directory are descended from a family that lived on the edge of one of the wildest moors way back in the thirteenth century. Henry de Broomhead was there in 1290 and William Bromhead was recorded in 1379. In later times Broomhead Hall became a gentleman's residence but now only the grounds and the place-name survive. A mile or so further north at Windhill farm a roofless cruck-framed barn stands dramatically on the skyline of the wind-swept hill that was recorded as Wyndehill in 1289 and as Wyndill in 1523. The name was gradually shortened and softened

Plate 1.6 Housley Hall, Yorkshire (interior)
From the outside, Housley Hall appears to be an eighteenth-century, stone-built farmhouse of superior quality, the home of a prominent member of Ecclesfield parish, Mr Housley Freeman. But the stone shell masks a much earlier timber-framed structure. Housley Hall has a crown post roof, which is unusual in rural parts of Yorkshire, where such a design is fourteenth or fifteenth century in date. It is possible that this is the very building where Lawrence and John of Housley were living when they had to pay the poll tax in 1379.

Housley Hall is now surrounded by modern housing but it long remained a distinctive, isolated dwelling. The surname Housley, which is derived from this site, is still common locally, with ninety-seven entries in the Sheffield telephone directory.

over the years as the Windles moved from their ancestral home to more sheltered climes.

In pursuing this type of enquiry one has to work through every early record that one can lay one's hands on and to consult (where they are available) the relevant volumes of the English Place-Name Society's county surveys. In some cases the earliest surname evidence pre-dates the first record of the place-name, perhaps by a few centuries. Thus, the English Place-Name Society offer no explanation for the meaning of Rails farm on the southern edge of the chapelry of Bradfield; it is first mentioned in the 1770s. The surname evidence suggests that the earlier form was Ryles, now usually spelt Ryalls. Sixty-three people named

Ryalls appear in the Sheffield telephone directory and many of their ancestors appear in Sheffield's sixteenth-century parish registers. The local manorial court rolls of 1440–41 reveal how the farm was sited at the edge of uncultivated land for in that year Edward of Ryles, Agnes his wife and Richard their son were given permission 'to pluck up by the roots and clear away, in all lands that could be ploughed, thorns, brambles and thicket'. Two generations earlier in 1379 William Ryol and his wife, Isabella, together with Agnes Ryall, a widow, were assessed for the poll tax. The meaning of the place-name is still obscure but there is little doubt that this farm has given rise to the surname.

One of the most prolific Sheffield surnames is Staniforth. No less than 239 Staniforths are to be found in the local telephone directory; the baptism, marriage and burial registers show that the family had already many branches in the parish by the reign of Queen Elizabeth; and in 1379 John and Henry of Staynford were taxed amongst the inhabitants of the adjoining parish of Ecclesfield. The place-name has long since been lost but it was recorded in 1366 as Stanyford ('the stony ford') at a site close to the Sheffield–Ecclesfield boundary. Like the Appleyards, the Staniforths have preserved the memory of a minor place-name that is no longer in use. The surname Carr presents a different sort of problem. Several Carrs were taxed in 1379; Bradfield had a Richard and Roger del Kerre, Ecclesfield had a John and William de Kerre and Sheffield had a Thomas Carr, William att Karr and Peter in le Kare. The place-name is a common one signifying marshy land and the surname has arisen in other parts of the country as well as in South Yorkshire. As far as the local name is concerned Carr House in Bradfield is a possible source of origin, but Sheffield has a Carr Bank, Carr Field and Carr Wood. Some of these place-names may have been derived from an owner with the surname Carr. One may well ask which came first, the chicken or the egg? So far there seems to be no satisfactory answer to the problem of the origins of the local Carrs.

The same teasing puzzle is offered by the surname Bower. In 1379 Ecclesfield had a William del Boure and a Richard Bower and Bradfield's inhabitants included Agnes, Richard, Robert and John del Boure. Bower Hill in Ecclesfield attracts our attention as a possible source of origin until we read that in 1565 the land there was held in the tenure of John Bower. It is, of course, possible that the Bowers had resided here for centuries (though evidence for this is lacking) but we must be also prepared to accept the possibility that the place-name was formed during the time of John Bower's tenancy. Dr Redmonds has recently drawn attention to this problem in a study which includes two place-names from the Graveship of Holme, those of Choppards and Totties (*Old West Riding*, vol. 4 no. 2, 1984, 7–10). He was able to show that Robert Chobard or Chopard was frequently mentioned in the Wakefield manorial court rolls of 1297–1331 and that in 1313 he took possession of 14 acres with buildings in Littlewood in Wooldale, which was almost certainly the site of the hamlet known since that time as Choppards. The surname was probably French in origin but did not survive locally. In the same court rolls William Totti was recorded in 1314 when he took over a toft and 9 acres of land from William, the son of Hugh of Thurstonland, 'undertaking to keep the buildings in repair'. This land was 'left unoccupied by the heirs of Adam Cosyn'. The place-name Totties does not therefore commemorate the first tenant. Moreover, neither Totti nor Chopard remained long in this township so it cannot be said that place-names of this type stabilised after several generations of a family had held the same property. Caution is obviously needed when interpreting place-names and in identifying the homes of family names. In arriving at a decision about the most likely geographical site we must place most emphasis on the earliest records both of the place-name and the surname. It is not always possible to come to a firm conclusion, but the local expert who is both a family and local historian is the best person to suggest a derivation for this type of name.

A few surnames that became prolific in well-defined areas quite early on actually originated from further afield. Bagley had become a Sheffield surname by the mid sixteenth century and the stream known as Bagley Dike was no doubt named after one of this family. The best candidate for the source of this particular surname is Bagley farm, nearly 20 miles away near Tickhill. The place-name means 'badger-glade' and was recorded as far back as 1148. Sometimes a surname migrated considerable distances. Sheffield had many Scargills in the sixteenth century; two centuries earlier in 1379 Thomas Scargill was taxed at Sheffield and John of Skargill at Ecclesfield, but the surname is not derived from a local place-name. It has a Scandinavian ring to it and is probably derived from the place-name many miles to the north in the Yorkshire Dales. Norwegian settlers who came over the Pennines into north-west Yorkshire used the word gill to describe a ravine or a deep, narrow valley with a stream. The name Scargill is still known in Sheffield, though only one is found in the telephone directory. Other common Sheffield surnames which sound as if they have a place-name origin but which have not yet been identified include Hattersley, Hawley and Ashurst. John Ashurst was living in Sheffield by 1379, but these families may have migrated into the area early on. Their surnames are not necessarily derived from local place-names.

We may conclude by noting that some surnames which have not arisen from place-names may nevertheless have precise geographical origins. Some may have come from a single family. Thus, the nicknames Speight (meaning a woodpecker), Teal, Tempest and Verity are located firmly in the West Riding textile area. Diminutives from female personal names include Jowett, which is common in Bradford and Leeds, and Allott and Gillott which are found particularly in the Sheffield district. A Stephen Allott was recorded in Sheffield in 1379. Some of the surnames that have undoubted multiple origins may still turn out to be especially numerous in one or more of their original localities. Sheffield has more than its proper share of Machons, Drabbles, Rawsons, and Cutts. The last name in this group comes from a shortened form of the Christian name Cuthbert. A Ralph Cutte was amongst those who paid the poll tax in Ecclesfield in 1379 and numerous members of this family were recorded in the earliest Sheffield parish register.

Local history and family history can, therefore, be profitably combined to pursue telling lines of enquiry into the homes of family names. A family historian can trace his or her family tree back through the earliest records available to a particular locality and the local historian can use knowledge acquired through a painstaking study of the documents and a wide familiarity with the local landscape to suggest a possible or probable source for a surname. In this way the amateur enquirer can make a significant contribution to the wider study of English social history.

CHAPTER TWO
Early-modern England

BASIC RECORDS

Some records are worthy of special comment at the beginning of this chapter for they are sources that every family and local historian must learn to use straight away if he is to gain any understanding of the period before the Industrial Revolution.

Parish registers

Parish registers are the major source for anyone tracing his family tree in the centuries before the introduction of civil registration in July 1837. They are also of fundamental importance for the local historian as they provide demographic data essential to a proper understanding of his chosen community. In recent years the rigorous analysis of these data by the Cambridge Group for the Study of Population and Social Structure has indicated the general trends of population movement and has pinpointed the years when harvests failed, epidemics struck and the death toll soared. Anyone working seriously on the social and economic history of the sixteenth, seventeenth and eighteenth centuries must become acquainted with the major findings of this demographic research.

In 1538 Thomas Cromwell ordered each parish to keep a record of its baptisms, marriages and burials. Apparently, most parishes kept their records on loose sheets of paper, many of which were subsequently lost or destroyed. Very few registers go back as far as 1538. The system was improved in 1597, when ministers and churchwardens were instructed henceforth to keep their records in a bound register and to copy out surviving documents at least as far back as 1558, when Elizabeth came to the throne. At the same time it was ordered that in future an annual transcript of events should be sent to the bishop's office. Where they survive, bishop's transcripts are a valuable alternative source for the historian; they may cover gaps in the original registers and can sometimes be more readily consulted.

The first task of the researcher is to locate his records and to check whether or not they are more easily available in print or on microfilm. Since 1979 parish registers have been deposited in appropriate record offices if churches cannot meet strict requirements for their safety and preservation. It can take time to find exactly where the records one is searching for are kept. The newer dioceses which have been created since Victorian times normally use a local authority record office as their approved archive repository. This means that the original parish registers are usually housed in a different place from the bishop's transcripts which are kept at the record office of the appropriate ancient diocese. Thus, the original registers for the Sheffield district are to be found at Sheffield Central Library, whereas the bishop's transcripts for those parishes that were within Yorkshire are kept at the Borthwick Institute for Historical Research, York, and the transcripts for those places that formerly lay within Derbyshire are available at the Lichfield Joint Record Office.

At an early stage of his enquiries the local and family historian must become familiar with the shape and size of his parish and learn which places are located within its bounds. Parishes vary enormously in size, according to their geographical position and the special circumstances of their historical development. A moorland parish will obviously be larger than a parish in a fertile area that was densely settled in early times; a church that was an Anglo-Saxon missionary centre will usually have a larger parish than one that was founded later. Some parishes contained chapelries or chapels-of-ease, which may or may not have had independent rights to perform baptism, marriage and burial ceremonies. Such ceremonies were sometimes recorded in separate chapelry registers, but others were noted in the register of the parish church. The Institute of Heraldic and Genealogical Studies, Canterbury, has published a series of county maps showing the ancient parish boundaries and the starting dates of surviving registers, and various record offices have produced similar maps for their own area. These are essential tools for

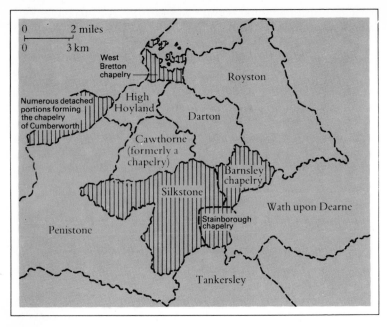

Fig. 2.1 The parish of Silkstone (Yorkshire)
The parish of Silkstone retained its medieval shape until well into the
nineteenth century. The inhabitants of Stainborough, together with those
from Cumberworth and West Bretton, had to attend the parish church
for baptism, marriage and burial services, but the inhabitants of Barnsley
were baptised, married and buried at their chapel of St Mary. Both Silkstone and Barnsley have registers that date from the sixteenth century.

family historians who are tracing their ancestors in unfamiliar
parts of the country. One must always bear in mind that the
settlement pattern of England's industrial regions was altered
beyond recognition during the course of the nineteenth century.
Some of today's populous places were insignificant before the
Industrial Revolution, but they have now far outgrown the village
that was clustered around the ancient parish church. Elsewhere, the
rate of growth has been such that ancient parishes have been
carved into much smaller units so that new churches could serve
the expanding population. A further complication arises when a
new settlement straddles the boundary between two parishes, so
that two sets of records have to be seen. One has to be aware of
such problems and refer to whatever maps and directories are at
hand.

   Having found the appropriate register, the researcher is soon faced with fresh difficulties, quite apart from the daunting task of reading sixteenth and seventeenth century scripts. In the first place he must be aware that until 1 January 1752 the old year began on Ladyday, 25 March. Thus entries for, say, the year 1680 will not end at 31 December but continue through January, February and most of March 1681; sometimes they will be written as 1680/1 for the period between 1 January and 25 March, and it is as well for the local and family historian to adopt that convention or else he will get in a hopeless muddle. In 1752 the old Julian calendar was replaced by the more accurate Gregorian calendar and in order to bring England in line with Europe the next day after 3 September was proclaimed to be 14 September. However, events such as annual fairs were often celebrated long afterwards on Old May Day, Old Michaelmas, etc., and the financial year still ends on 6 April, eleven days after Lady Day.

From 1754 onwards marriages were entered on printed forms, otherwise no standard procedure was laid down until 1813. In earlier times the quality of the information provided by a register varies from place to place and from incumbent to incumbent. Registers were often kept in a disorderly fashion with no attempt to separate baptisms from burials or marriages. It is common to find gaps when nothing is recorded, blank spaces where the minister has forgotten a name when he came to register it after the event, repetitions, erasures and insertions. A page from the register of the Leicestershire parish of Countesthorpe illustrates some of the difficulties one is likely to encounter.

> The Christenings Burials and Weddings in our towne from the 25th of March 1646 unto the 25th of March 1647.
> Robert the sonne of Thomas Wyers husbandman was baptized the 25th of March.
> And he was buried the same day.
> Grace Jacksonn Widdow was buried the 27th of March.
> John the sonne the sonne of Simon Smeeton was baptized the 3th of March.
> Thomas the sonne of Richard Bent blacksmyth and Anne his wife was baptized the 24th of March.
> Elizabeth Bent widd. was buried the 28th of May.
> Anne the wife of Richard Bent blacksmyth was buried the 9th of June.
> Elizabeth Freer the daughter of Willm. Freer miller & Frances his wife was baptized the 6th of September.
>   the sonne of Willm. Chrispers husbandman and Isabell his wife was buried the 24th of September.
> Elizabeth the daughter of Elizabeth Gillam was baptized the 17th of October.

> Elizabeth the daughter of John Buffen vagrant was baptized the 17th of October.
>
> John the sonne of Robert Hastings and Elizabeth his wife was buried the 29th of November.
>
> Francis the sonne of Robert Spencer yeoman and Mary his wife was baptized 15th of November.
>
> Thomas the sonne of Thomas Carr was baptized the 7th of February.
>
> William the sonne of Thomas Sutton was baptized the 7th of February.
>
> Thomas the sonne of Edward Wood was baptized the 26th of December 1652.

Inserted in the margin is the information that 'Thomas Jacksonne sonne of Willm. Jackson was baptized July the viiii 1625'.

It will be seen from this extract that at a baptism sometimes both parents' names were recorded, but occasionally only the father's. A man's occupation or standing might be noted, but not invariably. Two of the entries are not in chronological order, which suggests that the recording of events was sometimes delayed. Thomas Jackson may have found that his own baptism had not been recorded and so insisted on having it written in the margin twenty-two years later. And we are left with the problem of deciding whether or not the two Elizabeths baptised on 17 October were really the same girl.

It ought to be said that this particular extract poses more difficulties than the normal run of parish registers. It dates from the time of the Civil War when many registers were not properly kept; thus, under the year 1647 the vicar of Hooton Pagnell (Yorks.) wrote in his register:

> In this year I was imprisoned and in trouble: and the clerk was negligent.

A droll comment from time to time enlivens the dry information that fills most of the pages of a typical register. After recording the burial of Ann Parrot on 18 June 1736 in the Nottinghamshire parish of Beeston, the vicar commented:

> a dissembling canting hollow presbiterian.

The incumbent of Worsbrough (Yorks.) followed the burial entry of 'Richard Guest, Mason', on 28 July 1765 with the extra information that he was:

> Commonly Called Snivelling Dick

And at Cantley in the same diocese the vicar thought it was worth making some comment on a baptism that took place on 12 October 1754:

> Mary Daugr. of Martha Hazlewood of Cantley born above a year after her Husband left her.

Finally, let us observe the predicament of the minister of Horsley (Gloucs.) on 11 August 1731:

> John Pegler & Ann Thomas were half-married. I proceeded no further, because they paid me but one-half, viz. 2/6d.

The incidence of Nonconformity in any particular parish will obviously affect the reliability of the Anglican registration. However, this does not become a major problem until the late eighteenth century. Apart from the Quakers, and sometimes the Roman Catholics, the Old Dissenting sects did not usually object to the baptism, marriage and burial services of the Established Church and therefore Dissenters appear in Church of England registers like anyone else. Lord Hardwicke's Marriage Act of 1753 compelled Dissenters to marry at their parish church; only the baptism registers give cause for doubt. The spectacular growth of Methodism changed all this; the two generations before civil registration began in 1837 are often the most difficult for a genealogist because of this. The Public Record Office has about 9,000 Nonconformist registers dating from 1775, which were deposited when civil registration began; these are on the Mormons' International Genealogical Index microfiche, and of course other Nonconformist records have been deposited in local record offices. D. J. Steel, *Sources for Nonconformist Genealogy and Family History* (1973), is the essential guide.

On 1 January 1813 the Church of England began to standardize entries on printed forms bound into the register. From that time onwards they are both informative and easy to use. Baptism entries give name, date of baptism, parents' Christian names and surname, abode, and occupation of the father. Marriage registers record both names, parishes of residence, date of wedding, and names of witnesses. Burial entries give name, abode, date of burial, and age at death. A uniform system had at last been achieved.

Wills and inventories

Parish registers are the best example of records that were first kept during the Tudor era and which are now invaluable sources for the genealogist. It is far easier to trace one's ancestors in the second half of the sixteenth century than in the Middle Ages, and the information that can be collected is usually much fuller than before. Under the Tudors the age-old practice of making a will spread down the social scale; far more wills were made than in earlier times, even though the custom was still restricted to a minority of the population. Making a will was partly a question of fashion and prestige, partly a matter of providing for children who were still minors. If children had already married and had been provided for a will was not necessary.

Until 1858, when the state set up a new administrative body at Somerset House, the responsibility for proving wills lay with the church. Testators normally began their will by committing their soul to Almighty God and asking to be buried in the local churchyard (or if they were rich and important enough within the church itself). After making provision for the payment of their debts and funeral expenses, they then proceeded to the disposal of their worldly goods. Wills were normally made shortly before death, as many a shaky signature can testify; some people left it so late that they could only make an oral statement (or nuncupative will), which was written down and sworn to by witnesses. It is common to find that the will-maker was 'sick in body but full in mind', and a clause often cancelled any previous wills. If a person died intestate the court had power to grant letters of administration of his estate to executors.

The strength and nature of a person's religious beliefs are often made clear by a will. Before the Reformation it was common not only to commit one's soul to Almighty God, but also to 'Our Lady St. Mary and to all the holy company of heaven'. Later Protestant wills state a belief in the 'full reemission and forgiveness of all my sinnes, onely by the deathe and bludsheadinge of our Lorde and saivoure Jesus Christe'. But one must beware of accepting such statements at their face value as evidence of deep personal belief, for such phrases are taken from books which advised people how to compose documents, and Dr Margaret Spufford has shown how rural wills in Cambridgeshire were drawn up by only a small number of scribes.

The standard guides on how to locate wills are A. J. Camp's *Wills and Their Whereabouts* (1974) and J. S. W. Gibson's *Wills and Where to Find Them* (1974). Most are kept at the record offices of the ancient dioceses, together with the bishop's transcripts.

Substantial landowners tended to by-pass the administrative system by using the prerogative courts at Canterbury and York. Canterbury was the senior court and for a time during the Commonwealth period – between 1655 and 1660 – all wills were proved there. The researcher must also keep in mind the fact that some parishes were 'peculiar jurisdictions' independent of the usual ecclesiastical courts. The thought and, better still, the taste of Theakston's 'Old Peculier' will help him remember this point, for this special beer is brewed at Masham, which was one of the richest peculiar jurisdictions in the country.

The information contained in wills must be examined as critically as that in any other document. Wherever possible, they should be used in conjunction with parish registers and other sources. The will of Joseph Walker of Stubbing House (1729), a nailmaker-farmer in the Yorkshire parish of Ecclesfield, illustrates the pitfalls for the unwary. After a lengthy statement of faith, he settled his personal estate in the following manner:

> I give unto Joseph Walker my Eldest son the sume one shilling in full Item I give unto Benjamin Walker my second son the sum of one shilling in full Item I give unto Mary Crawshaw my Eldest Daughter the sum of one shilling Item I give unto Ann Walker my Loveing Wife all my Cottage Houses standing and being on Grennowside with all my Right and Titles belong to them Item I give unto Ann Walker my Loving Wife all the Rest of my Goods money and Chattles: and I also do make Ann Walker my Loveing Wife sole Executor of this my Last will and Testament Revoaking all other Wills and Testaments formerly made by mee provided shee keepe her selfe unMarryed but if shee Marry my minde is that all my Goods Chattles money and Cottage houses shall be Equally given amonghts all her Children which is Lawfully begotten of our Two Bodies.

Without the information contained in the parish register, one might reasonably suppose that Joseph and Ann had three children, who were each to receive only a shilling unless Ann remarried, upon which occasion they would inherit the entire estate. In fact, Joseph, Benjamin and Mary were the children of Joseph's first marriage (in 1696 to Margaret Bower) and they had each been provided for upon their marriage. Joseph and Ann had six children, none of whom is named in the will. They were all minors and Joseph was taking the normal step to protect their interests, for if Ann remarried the estate would pass to her new husband. Joseph now appears in a very different light.

From the reign of Henry VIII to that of George II it was the practice of the various probate courts to insist that 'a true and perfect inventory' of the personal estate of the person who had died should be attached to his will or the letters of administration. In recent years tens of thousands of such inventories have been studied by historians and our understanding of the social and economic history of the early-modern period has been deeply enriched as a result. No other class of records provides such a rich vein of information on farming systems, old crafts and industries, household arrangements, furniture, utensils and the provision of credit in the form of bills, bonds and mortgages.

Inventories were normally taken within a few days or weeks of the testator's death. Where delays occurred, the chances of an inventory being incomplete were obviously increased; it has been noticed, for instance, that bequests mentioned in wills are sometimes missing from the inventory. The appraisers were two, three or four local men appointed by the executors; usually they were friends and neighbours (some of whom were illiterate), but they often included someone who had the reputation of knowing how to do the job. They performed their task conscientiously under solemn oath and they placed what they thought was an accurate valuation upon every pot and pan, every piece of furniture, each farm animal and even the manure. These inventories, therefore, give a sound idea of the standard of living of thousands of ordinary people.

Anyone studying an inventory must be aware of their limitations. In the first place, it must be realised that the 'goods and chattels' that comprised personal estate did not include the value of buildings and land, which came under the heading of real estate. Inventories, therefore, do not give a complete picture of a person's wealth. Secondly, goods which a husband enjoyed through his wife were excluded; this could have been anything from beds and linen to the poultry. Thirdly, it is often impossible to tell from the inventory whether a person was poor or whether he was living in comfortable retirement, having already passed on most of his estate to his children; a yeoman with very few possessions is likely to have been in the latter category. Poor people rarely left either a will or an inventory, but thousands of people of moderate means did so; the ordinary farmers and craftsmen are well represented in this class of record. Indeed, wills and inventories tell us more about such people than any other source.

Mastering the handwriting of the Tudor and Stuart eras is

merely the first step in tackling these documents. The old adage 'practice makes perfect' must be kept in mind when one begins to despair. Quite apart from idiosyncratic spellings, lack of punctuation, inconsistent use of capital letters and a widespread inability to add up the total valuation, one is confronted with archaic and dialect words. But many historians have trod this path before and there are now a number of glossaries and explanatory works to guide the newcomer. Some of these are mentioned in the bibliography at the end of the book.

Happy is the family historian who finds an inventory of an ancestor's personal estate. Mr Geoffrey Peace of Sheffield can trace his family back from the foundation of the family firm of Samuel Peace and Sons through several generations of filemakers to Anthony Peace, a Rotherham butcher, who died in 1696. Anthony's inventory, taken on 24 October 1696, is given below (without a glossary) as an illustration of this type of record:

Inpr[imis] his purse & apparrell, £5
In the Kitchen: One Iron range a paire of froggs, a paire of Tongs & a Fire Shovell, 16s. 0d, A Jack, 4 Spitts a paire of Iron racks, 2 dripping pans and a Fire plate, £1.12s.0d, A Brass pan & 2 potts, £1.13s.4d, Two Brass panns an iron pot and a grate, £1.4s.0d, One other pot, one pan and 2 Smoothing irons, 10s.0d, All the pewter, £5, A warming pan, a skillet with other husslement there, 10s.0d, 1 Chair, 1 Table & Stooles, 4s.0d, A dresser and a pewter case, 10s.0d.

Goods in the House: One Iron Range, 2 Froggs a Fire Shovell and a paire of Tongs, £1.6s.8d, Two Tables 2 Formes, £1.5s.0d, One Langsettle, 1 Chaire a cieled Bench and a Dresser, £1, One Carpett 7 Quishions £1.10s.0d.

In the Kitchin Parlour: One Stand Bed, one Cupboard a Prass, with other Husslement there, £4.

Goods in the House parlor: A Chest of drawers, an ovall Table, 6 Chaires with other Husslement there, £3.

Goods in the little Parlor: One stand Bed, one prass with other husslement there, £1.17s.0d.

In the Buttry: One Safe, One Fleshkitt with other things there £1.

In the Cellar: Barrells and Brewing vessells, £5.

In the Kitchin Chamber: 2 Beds with Bedding, £2.

Corne: Corne in the Great Chamber, £4.

In the Best Chamber: One Stand Bed with Bedding and Curtains & Vallians, £5, 5 paire of Sheets with the rest of the Linnen, £8, One Skreen, 2 Tables, two Chests, 4 Chaires, & Two Buffetts, £4.

Goods in the House Chamber: One Bed with Bedding, One Ark with other husslement there, £1.17s.0d.

In the Garret: 20 Stone of Wooll, £6.10s.0d.

In the Chamber over the Entry: One Trundle bed, with other huslement there, £1.10s.0d.

In the Closet: Wooll & Teare with other husslement there, £10.

Goods in the Fold: Two Sowes & 6 holdens, £3.6s.0d.

Silver plate in the house, £1.15s.0d, All the husslement about the house, £2.

Goods in Firsby Ground: Two Fatt Bullocks, £12, 2 Heafers & 2 Stiers, £12, 3 Steirs more & one Heafer, £17, Seventy Eight Sheep, £27.6s.0d, Seventy nine Sheep more, £27.6s.0d, Sixty Foure Sheep more, £20.16s.0d, One hundred Thirty three sheep more, £46.11s.0d, Eleaven Lambs, £2.4s.0d.

One Shelfe waine, 2 ropes, 2 paire of Geares, 2 yokes, 1 paire of Buckles. 2 stand hecks & an old Trindle bed, £3, Two pickforks, 1s0d, 2 Stand Hecks, one Slead, a rope, a rope a Buckett and a Grindlestone, 8s.0d, One hundred Loads or Hay, £55.

In Oldwark Grounds: One hundred Thirty nine Sheep, £52.2s.6d, 60 Sheep In the Carr, £24, 3 Oxen, 2 Cowes & a Bull, £24, 4 Cowes, 1 Oxe & a Segg, £23.15s.0d, 21 Sheepe, £10, 3 Seggs, 2 Bullocks and an Heafer, £21.5s.0d, 72 Sheep, £19.16s.0d, A Foale, £2, Eighty Loads of Hay, £52.

Goods in the Barne: a shelve waine 1 Plough a Sledge, 2 Yoaks and 2 paire of Horse Geares, £2.

Goods in the Wood Closes: Sixty Five Sheep, £20, 20 Sheep more, £6.10.0. Two Cort waine bodyes, 2 Stand Hecks, One Oxe harrow, 2 Horse harrows, a Fan, a waine tier, a Swith rack and an Iron Teame, £3.10s.0d.

Certaine Corne in the Barne: (blank)

One acre of Oates and Beans £2, Foure horses, £8, One Cow, £1.10s.0d. Book Debts, £232.15s.11d.

	Summe Totall,	815.12s.5d.
Debts Outward due to paid out of the said Inventory		415. 9s.0d.
	The Remainder is	400. 3s.5d.

Prizers: Daniel Barnard, William Wilson, Charles Stainland, Christoph: Wriggelworth.

Inventories such as this have been used in bulk by agricultural historians to show how varied were the regional farming practices of England long before the Agricultural Revolution. Indeed, that term is no longer used as confidently as it once was. Inventories

Plate 2.1 Highlow Hall, Derbyshire

Highlow Hall commands spectacular views in the northern part of the Peak District. Built of local stone in the Elizabethan or early-Stuart period for one of the younger branches of the Eyre family, it stands alone on the hills a couple of miles west of the Eyres's medieval hall at Padley. Robert Eyre of Highlow Hall paid tax on nine hearths in 1670.

The probate inventory of Thomas Eyre of Highlow, taken on 12 December 1633, names the rooms and demonstrates the uses to which they were put. The principal rooms downstairs were the hall, dining parlour and two other parlours which served as bedrooms; the service rooms comprised the kitchen, buttery, dairy, brewhouse and larder. Upstairs were three more bedrooms named the great chamber, white chamber and chamber over the buttery, together with the middle chamber and 'wynde' chamber which were used for storage. The last rooms to be recorded by the appraisers were the entry between the hall and kitchen and the servants' chamber, two small rooms which were probably located within the projecting porch. The outbuildings consisted of a great barn, cowhouse and workhouse (where farm equipment was stored). Eyre also had two barns elsewhere, a corn mill and a lead smelting house. His '14 score and 18 sheepe' were valued at £80.

prove, for example, that turnips were a successful field crop long before Viscount Townshend, that the Cheshire cheese industry was flourishing by the seventeenth century, that Lancastrian and Cumbrian farmers were the first to grow potatoes on a significant scale and that many Pennine hill-farmers relied upon the local markets for their bread corn and malt, for they grew no cereals at all. Historians working on the history of crafts, trades, housing and furniture have also made significant advances in their subject by using probate inventories. A broad picture is obtained through the analysis of a large collection, while specific features can be vividly illustrated by single examples.

A skilled historian is able to entwine his inventory material with evidence gathered from a variety of other sources. In order to illustrate how this can be done, let us start with the inventory of Abigail Pilmay (1698), a Silkstone (Yorks.) widow who left personal estate valued at just over £300:

A true and perfect Schedule of all & Singuler the goods & chattells of Abigail Pilmay late of Silkstone in the County of Yorke widow deceased, Vallued & apprised by us whose names are hereunto subscribed the Twentieth day of December Anno D[omi]ni 1698.

Impri[mi]s her purse & apparrell, £30.
In the Kitching: one range, 1 pare of tonges, 1 fire shovell, 8s.6d, one grate, 1 pare of briggs, 1 toasting Jack, 2 Iron potts, 14s.0d, one brass pott 3 brass pans, 3 priggs, 2 laddles, one Candlestick, 1 Chafeing dish, 1 Kettle & 1 Sause pann, £1.4s.0d, Six Spitts, 1 Jack, 1 frying pann, 2 Smoothing Irons, 2 Standards & one beef forke, 15s.4d., one dripping pann, 4s.0d., 22 pewter dishes & 3 plates & other Small peices of pewther, £3.12s.6d, Tinn ware, 6s.8d, one long Table & Forme, 1 Long Settle, 3 chairs 3 buffetts, 13s.6d.

In the little parlour: two tables, 7 Chares, 5 Coverd buffett Stooles, £1.12s.0d, 16 holland plates, 2s.8d, some Bookes & a Standidge, 16s.4d.

In the farr parlor: one Clock, £2, one rainge, 1 pare of tongs, 1 fire Shovell, one pare of racks & one pare of briggs, 10s.0d, A warming pann, 5s.0d, 4 Silver Spoones, £1.12s.0d, 3 Stand bedds & bedding, 1 trunle bedd & beding, £6.10s.0d, one press Cupboard, one Long Settle, 1 Counter, 1 close Stool, 15s.0d, 2 chares, 1 chest of Drawers, 1 Desk & a box, a little Chest & one Joynt Stooll, £1.5s.6d, one lookeing glass, 2s.0d, & one Screen, 6d, 2 glass cases & 10 plates, 6s.0d, 1 case of knifes, ls0d, one long Coffer, 8d.

In the Chamber over the Kitching: one range, 1 pare of tongues, 2s.0d, 1 Standbed & bedding, £4, Five Chests, £1, one Chare, 1 deske, a little Trunk a little Table 2 little buffetts, & 12 Cussons, 15s0d, 13 Sheets, & 5 pillow beeres, £4.4s.0d, Three table cloths, three doz. & eight Napkins, £1.12s.6d, 15 yards of bleached Linnen £1.2s.6d, 13 yards more not bleached, 15s.2d, 16 yards more, 16s0d, one pare of new harden sheets, 6s.0d.

In the little Chamber: one Standbed & bedding, £1.10s.0d.

In the Flinte Chamber: one chest & a box, 6s.6d.

In the best Chamber: one rainge, 1 pair of Tongs & a fire Shovell, 6s.0d. ono Stand bed & bedding, £4.5s.0d, a paire of Cortings & vallons & 4 Carpitts £5.6s.8d, a paire of new fustian, 12s.0d, 11 Chares & 4 Covered buffetts, £1.8s.0d, 10 Cushons, 13s.4d, one table & a Cheste, £1.6s.8d, one Large Lookeing glass, 15s.0d.

In the little Chamber goeing to the best: one chest & 12 boards, 12s.0d.

In the green ware house Chamber: one Stand & bedding, £1.6s.8d, one chest, 4 Chares a little table & a long Settle, £1.1s.4d.

In the other green ware house Chamber: one Stand bedd & bedding, £1, two little tables, 1 chest, & 3 buffett Stools, 9s.4d.

Corne, Straw & other things in the barn, £6, one hay Stack, 1.1Ss.0d, one mare Saddle & girth, 2 Cows, 2 heaffers & 1 Steer, 11.10s.0d, Two Swine, £1.8s.0d,

In the buttery: one Cubbert & one table, 5s.0d, Severall barrells, kitts, Flasks, a churne & all other Tubbs & brueing Vessells, in the buttery & tubhouse, £1.15s.0d.

In the glass houses: 11 Greenhouse pipes, 11s.0d, 10 white house pipes, 8s.0d, Tools belonging to both houses & all the old Iron, £2.10s.0d.

In all the warehouses: Stock of glass both flinte, Green ware & ordinary, £40, Rape ashes, £20, Salte peter 10 Stones, 4 poonds, £4.9s.0d, Fretting Clay, Maganeese, Breeley Sand, Red lead, blew powder, Moolds with all other huslements In about & belonging to the dwelling house Glass house ware houses & foldsteads, £28, Vyall metall, £3.

£300.19s.10d.

Vallued & Apprised by us, the day & year above written: John Burdett, John Lindley, Richard Walker, Joshua Bingley.

The information contained in this appraisal provides fascinating insights into seventeeth-century methods of manufacturing glass. Abigail Pilmay's craftsmen were making pure lustrous 'flint glass' and a variety of coloured wares. Several items in the inventory require a technical explanation. 'Breeley sand' was imported from Brierley, near Dudley (Staffs.), as a very high quality component of crystal glass. Rape ashes were a source of alkali, necessary in the manufacture of bottles and green ware. Saltpetre was added to prevent amber coloration when making crystal glass. Red lead added sparkle, and manganese and blue powder (cobalt) were used as colouring agents. 'Fretting clay' was for making the crucible in which the glass was melted, and the 'moolds' were wooden moulds lined with wax. Finally, 'Vyall metall' referred to the unfinished production of small glass containers or vials. On reading this inventory and understanding its meaning one is left with the firm impression that seventeenth-century glassmaking was a sophisticated business.

Abigail's will provided for numerous relatives, i.e. a married son, his wife and 4 children, a married daughter, her husband, 6 children and 1 grandchild, and a brother, a sister and 2 brothers-in-law. Her son was named John Scott, so he was presumably the child of an earlier marriage. The information contained in the will prompts a search of the Silkstone parish registers and a visit to the church to look for tombstones. The Pilmay and Scott graves are found grouped together on the floor of the north aisle of the fine Perpendicular church, a position which suggests that these two families were of superior standing within the community; only the better-off were buried within a church. The tombstone inscriptions and the parish register entries reveal that Abigail had married a Wiliiam Scott, who died in 1655, and that three years later she had taken John Pilmay as her second husband. John Pilmay died in 1676, but his brother Peter was still alive when Abigail made her will twenty-two years later. Abigail did not have any children by her second marriage.

Pilmay is an unusual name; it is the English way of pronouncing the French name Pilmé. The family appear to have come to England during the reign of Queen Elizabeth when several glassmakers from Lorraine were invited to practise their skills in this country. Later generations gradually spread from the South to build new glasshouses on the Midland and Northern coalfields. During the reign of James I and Charles I the Pilmays married into the Du Houx family, Lorraine glassmakers who had settled in Lancashire. John Pilmay had arrived in Silkstone by 1658, when he married Abigail Scott. In November of the following year the memorandum book of Dr Henry Power of New Hall, Elland (British Library, Sloane ms. 1354), recorded the payment of 2s.6d. to his man, John Wilson, 'for fetching glasses from the glasse house at Silkstone', some 16 miles away. Five years later, John Pilmay, glassmaker of Silkstone, was indicted at the West Riding quarter sessions. In 1682 Ralph Thoresby, the Leeds antiquary, 'saw the glasshouses' as he passed through Silkstone, and when John Warburton came that way in 1718–19 while preparing his map of Yorkshire, he pinpointed the position of the glasshouse to the right of the road that crossed the stream just to the south of Silkstone church.

The will of John Scott 'of Silkstone, gentleman' (1707), refers to the 'Messuage Wherein my mother Pilmay lately dwelt with the Glasshouse', together with the nearby water corn-mill. His inventory provides further technical details of the art of glass-making and also reveals the extent of his coal-mining interests. The Scott family deeds, now housed in Sheffield Central Library, record the changing ownership of the Silkstone property and provide clues as to when the glassmaking enterprise came to an end. A mortgage deed of 1748 refers to 'the old Glasshouse' and 6 years later another deed deals with the sale of 'One Corn Mill with the Pott Ovens'. The glass works had been converted into a pottery, just like some of the other south Yorkshire sites during the course of the eighteenth and early nineteenth centuries. The home that Abigail Pilmay built in 1682 has now been demolished but it was remembered in the 1920s as having the name Pot House. A local tombstone recording the death in 1806 of John Taylor, potter, is apparently the last reference to pot-making at Silkstone.

That is the bare outline of the Pilmay and Scott story, a tale that could be told in much more detail. It is a family history that becomes much more interesting when set against the wider background of the local history of an important industry. From Silkstone we need to branch out to other parts of the Yorkshire coalfield. The first glass works in south Yorkshire had been erected in 1632 at Glasshouse Green, Wentworth, on the estate of Sir Thomas Wentworth, the great Earl of Strafford, but it had ceased production before the Civil War. John Pilmay's glasshouse at Silkstone may have been the first successful venture in the district. Quite a lot is now known about the history of glass-making in this region, for the nearby site at Gawber has been excavated and Sheffield City Museum has a collection of local ware. Most importantly of all, one of a pair of cones erected at Catcliffe in 1740 still stands to its full height. It was built by William Fenny, the descendant of another immigrant family whose name was gradually Anglicized. The history of certain key families is obviously crucial to an understanding of the growth of this particular industry. This example could be multiplied many times in all the industrial regions of England.

Manorial records

The manor did not disappear when the Middle Ages drew to a

Plate 2.2 The Catcliffe glassworks
The cone of the old glassworks at Catcliffe in south Yorkshire is the
oldest surviving example of this type of structure in the whole of Europe.
It is one of a pair that were built upon this site in 1740 by William Fenny,
the former works manager of the Bolsterstone glasshouse and a member
of a family of Huguenot origin who were glassmakers in various parts
of Lancashire and Yorkshire. William Fenny had gone to Bolsterstone
in 1718 upon his marriage to Mary Fox, whose ancestors had founded
the glassworks there.

It was during William Fenny's time as works manager that Bolster-

close, nor when the Tudors made the parish the administrative unit that was responsible for maintaining the poor and the highways and for petty law and order. Manorial courts continued to meet regularly throughout the the early-modern period and in many places the quality of record-keeping remained high right through to the eighteenth century and sometimes beyond. In 1731 the old custom of using Latin for legal records came to an end, but in practice many manorial records were written in English from much earlier times. These records are widely scattered now, but most county record offices have collections of local rolls and estate papers and can advise on the whereabouts of others.

A distinction that must be borne in mind is that between the Court Baron (which registered the transfers of copyhold lands) and the Court Leet (which saw to such practical matters as scouring ditches, mending hedges, muzzling dogs, etc.). The records of both these types of court are of use to the local and family historian. The descent of property can sometimes be traced over several generations through the archives of the Court Baron, while individual names can be picked out from the lists of freeholders and customary tenants at the beginning of each meeting of the Court Leet. The tenants of the manor comprised the 'homage' or jury that decided the by-laws for the coming months; even if a man was not present, his absence would be recorded. We are presented therefore with a list of all the owners of land in the manor. Very often we shall also have the names of the major part of the actual occupiers, though we have to remember that sub-tenants were not usually recorded. When I was researching the history of the Shropshire parish of Myddle I was able to trace some of the farming families back beyond the beginning of the parish register by using lists of manorial court jurors

---

stone ware reached its finest quality. His mother-in-law, Mary Blackburn (formerly Fox), added a codicil to her will shortly before her death in 1738, instructing her executors that, 'Whereas my Son in Law William Fene has given mee such an aprehencion of beeing troublesom by his design of setting up a Glashous at boulsterstone made me allter my will for I would loath have it that what I leav shoud be the caus of breach of Charity soe I have alltred my will that if will: fene does prove letigous his children shall loos what I have given them in my will'. Fenny was forbidden to establish a new glasshouse within 10 miles of the one he had managed at Bolsterstone. In 1740, therefore, he moved to Catcliffe, 10½ miles away, accompanied by some of his workers. Glass was made at Catcliffe until the early years of the twentieth century.

dating from 1528. It is not always possible, of course, to see how many of the homagers actually resided within the manor, nor how much land they might have held elsewhere. Moreover, one must always bear in mind England's complicated manorial structure. A manor did not necessarily cover the same area as a parish; indeed, parishes sometimes contained two or more manors and the boundaries between the two institutions often overlapped. Despite these problems, manorial court rolls provide a great deal of information that is of use to the genealogist and they enable the family historian to gain insights into how the local society in which his ancestors lived was administered and to see what disputes arose.

Mr Frank Tyack of Sheffield knew that his ancestors must have come from Cornwall, for Tyack is a Cornish word meaning 'farmer'. While pursuing his family tree he found two Tyacks amongst those who held land in the Cornish manor of Binnerton, one of whom held the office of manorial reeve. The record of the court proceedings on 7 October 1700 begins as follows:

Mannor of Binnerton.
The Law Court of Sir John St Aubyn Barronett held this 7th day of October 1700 att the house of Tho. Prosser in Breage Church Towne for his said mannor.

Fre Tenants

Sir Wm. Godolphin Barronett / The Lord Godolphin
The heires of Kellway / The Heires of Ezechiell Arundell Esqr
Sir John Arundell Knight /
Hen. Rogers & the heires of / The heires of Chenoweth
Jno. Thomas & Tanner / The heires of Tanner & Cooke
Fra. Paynter Gent / Hugh Jones Esqr
Char. Earle of Radnor / The heires of hugh Lanellis
Jonathan Rashleigh Esqr / Wm. Harris Esqr
James Keygwin Esqr / The heires of Wm. Frewren Gent
The heires of Rich. Bennets / The heires of Rich. Lanyon Gent
Cha. Trevanyon Esqr /
The heires of Grosse & paynter / John Burlaw Esqr
Jno. Vyvyan Esqr / The heires of Wm. Diggens Gent

Convencionarye Tenants
Mr Jno. Row
Mr Rich. Tyack / Jno. Williams
the Executors of Susan Eatherne / Abraham Scollar
Tho. Prosser / Leonard Stephens
Mr Tho. Row / Jane Rogers
Wm. Tyack / Widdow Hixt
Ely Sampson / John Rodda
/ Rich. Courtice

Imprimis The homage doe present the defaults of all the Free and Convencionary Tennants of the said Mannor who were Lawfully Summon'd to appeare at this Court and have not as they ought to doe.

They Likewise present Richard Tyacke to be Reeve of the said Mannor for the Ensueing yeare.

They Likewise present John Rowe & John Rodda to be veiwers of repayracions of the said Mannor for the Ensueing yeare.

They Likewise present Mr. John Williams Mr. John Lanyon and Mr. John Grosse to serve the office of a Tithingman for the Ensueing yeare . . .

It is perhaps worth making the point (for readers who are just beginning their enquiries into the history of this period) that a lord did not usually own all the land on his manor but had certain defined rights, which differed from place to place and even between neighbouring settlements. Binnerton manor obviously had a large number of freeholders, including some members of the nobility and gentry who probably never set foot in the place let alone attended the manorial court. Some of this freehold land was no doubt held in small parcels but in the absence of a survey and map its full extent cannot be known. The conventionary tenants were much more likely to live locally. Their system of tenure was peculiar to Cornwall and parts of Devon; it did not provide hereditary security but consisted of a seven-year lease at a negotiated rent with no automatic right of renewal. The tenants were the people who knew the district intimately from years of experience living and farming there and they were the ones who made the decisions in the manor court. The roll that is quoted above records the election of officers for the coming year and then goes on to note the making of by-laws and the fining of defaulters. The deliberations of such courts are often full of minor points of interest.

In addition to court rolls the family historian may come across rentals which give the names of tenants and the rents that they paid each year at Ladyday (25 March) and Michaelmas (29 September). With luck he may also find surveys that provide a much fuller description of properties and the nature of tenancies, including sometimes the names of previous owners. A survey of lands belonging to the manor of Sheffield in 1611 describes the farmsteads and gives the names and measurements of all the fields. One item reads:

Nich. Sampson: One house one bay, one parler above the house, 2 baies beneath the house for beast houses, 2 parlers newly builded,

2 chambers over the parler, one Barne 4 baies 2 outshutts one
Beast [house] 2 baies 1 hay house 2 baies.
One orchard a garden & Fold 0 [acres] 3 [roods] 20 [perches]; One
Croft near the house 1.1.0 prat [=meadow]. The Well Field 5.0.0.
past[ure], The Fox hill Inge, 4.0.0 prat, The narr over Feild 12.0.0
past, The farr over Feild 12.0.0 past, The little pasture Close 3.3.0
past, The over Nick Stubbing 5.3.0 past, The nether Nick
Stubbing, 5.0.0 past, Dowe Royde 13.0.0 prat, Nicke Wood 8.0.0
past, The nether bromefield 10.2.0 prat & past, The nether Inge
5.2.0 prat, The midle Close 11.0.0 past, The Wheate Feild 9.0.0
past, The Pingle adjoyning to the house, 1.3.0 past. Total prat.
29.0.0, past. 79.1.20. Rent per ann. £8.5s.10d.

This farm can be identified with Fox Hill, about 3 miles north-
west of the centre of Sheffield.

On the various types of tenure by which people held their
farms and cottages the reader is referred to Dr Christopher Clay's
lucid account in Joan Thirsk (ed.), *The Agrarian History of England
and Wales, vol. V. 1640–1750* (1985), pp. 198–230. Dr Clay writes
that during the middle years of the seventeenth century customary
tenures were still widespread and important, especially for the
smaller properties, but that much less land was held in this way
than was the case 100 years earlier. During the sixteenth and early
seventeenth centuries tenants throughout the realm had found that
custom did not always give them the protection that they believed
they had. Some won their battles, but many others discovered
that in law they were merely tenants-at-will and that as a consequence they had to pay much higher rents than before. In an
inflationary age those who had sound customary tenures reaped
the benefits of fixed annual rents, but those tenants who were
successfully challenged by their lords had to meet demands for
considerable increases.

The incidence of customary tenure varied from region to
region and from manor to manor. In Surrey and Sussex, for
example, customary tenures were still common in the seventeenth
century, but just across the border in Kent they were rare; Kentish
families were either freeholders or else they held their land on a
yearly basis or by a lease for a term of years. In the country at
large copyhold was by far the most common form of customary
tenure. Under this system tenants paid low annual rents and a
large entry fine at the beginning of their tenancy. This fine was
either 'certain', i.e. fixed by local custom, or 'arbitrary', i.e.
negotiable. Otherwise, the main burden was the payment of a

heriot at death, usually in the form of 'the best beast' or money in lieu. Copyholders were obliged to attend meetings of the manor court, and any changes in tenancy were recorded in the court rolls.

During the sixteenth and seventeenth centuries many copyholds were converted into leaseholds. Local practice varied enormously, but a general picture may be obtained by dividing England into two halves. In the western half the common system of tenure was the lease for three lives, whereby the tenant entered the names of any three people, and as long as one of them remained alive the lease held good. It was common for a man to enter his own name, that of his wife, and that of his intended successor, usually the oldest son. Such leases are therefore a useful source of genealogical information. Obviously, this method of holding was a chancy business, but on the whole leases for three lives were considered slightly superior to leases for twenty-one years. A tenant could insert a new name in his lease upon payment of another entry fine, and he had the power to sub-let all or any part of his property if he wished. The terms were not onerous and few restrictions were placed on the tenant's actions.

Leases for lives were sometimes used in the eastern half of the country, but here the normal method of tenure was the lease for a restricted period, from one to twenty-one years. Yearly tenancies held at rack rents (i.e. rents that were not fixed by custom but which were negotiated by the landlord and tenant) were common for the smaller farms and cottages and in the Midlands in particular they were usual for any property other than a freehold. These 'tenants-at-will' had no written agreements, but that did not mean that a landlord could eject them whenever he liked. Custom granted a tenant-at-will a full quarter's notice and compensation for his crops and the work he had put into the farm if he went before the harvest was gathered in. Moreover, landlords were restrained by the knowledge that they would attract good tenants only if they had a reputation for fairness. Given the fact that much of the property in the western half of the country was sub-let to under-tenants at rack rents, it is doubtful whether regional differences were as pronounced as they appear at first sight. Having considered the conflicts that might arise between a landlord and his tenant, Dr Clay concludes that:

> In practice it probably did not make a great deal of difference to either party whether or not leases existed, unless or until a serious

dispute between them arose. In fact, it must be very doubtful whether in any given district tenants-at-will, yearly tenants, and tenants with leases for years held their land on significantly different terms.

Hearth tax returns

The most important tax levied upon the people of seventeenth-century England – as far as the local and family historian is concerned – was that based upon the number of hearths or chimneys that each house contained. The first assessment was made in 1662, but the tax proved deeply unpopular and was finally abolished in 1689. Returns are kept in the Public Record Office at Chancery Lane, London, under the classification E179, but an enquirer should first check the availability of those which have been printed on a county basis or have been copied on to microfilm. The tax was paid by the occupier (or if a house was empty by the owner) at the rate of two shillings per hearth in equal instalments at Ladyday and Michaelmas. A number of people were granted exemption on the grounds either that they were too poor to pay taxes and rates or that they had a certificate signed by the minister and parish officers to the effect that their premises were worth not more than £1 per annum or that their personal property was worth less than £10 per annum; however, no exemption was allowed anyone possessing more than two hearths. Some collectors listed the exempted poor in their returns – in which case the names of all the heads of households of a particular parish or township were recorded – but others did not bother to name them. The number of exempted people often amounted to 30–40 per cent of the community, and sometimes even more, so if the proportion is much lower than that the historian is left wondering whether his list is complete.

An individual's wealth tended to be reflected in the number of hearths he had in his house. A full return will therefore allow the local historian to reconstruct the social structure of his community. He will normally find that this assumes the shape of a pyramid, with a broad base of people who had only 1 or 2 hearths tapering to a few persons or a single individual who owned a disproportionate share of the wealth. In an extreme case such as the Yorkshire estate village of Thrybergh the squire's hall was in a class of its own and the parsonage was far superior to

Plate 2.3 Offerton Hall, Derbyshire

Many a seventeenth century gentleman's hall can still be found on the fringes of the Pennines, either standing alone or dominating a hamlet. They are built of local stone and roofed with heavy, local slates. Their gables and their mullioned windows give them a robust, independent character.

The inscription on the door lintel of Offerton Hall reads RG 1658 with the initials MG above. Local records enable us to identify this couple as Robert and Mary Glossop. In the 1670 hearth tax return 'Widdow Glossopp' had six hearths in this house.

the rest. The 1672 returns list the following heads of households and number of hearths there:

Sir Jo. Rearsby	22	Jos. Nantcliffe	1
Robt. Steele	2	Willm. Smith	4
John Cross	1	Tho. Lyster & Smithy	2
Tho. Milne	2	Stephen Liversidge	1
Sir Jo. Rearsby per lodge	2	Robt. Yates	1
Abr. Aynelay	1	Abra. Holden	1 poore
Ralph Clarke	1	Widd. Tyas	1
Gregory Bower	1	Edwd. Ratcliffe	2
Widd. Leach	1	Wm. Carr	2

Godfrey Wigfeild	2	Tho. Nicholson	1
Wm. Watterhouse	3	Widd. Poole & Jo. Frost	2 poore
James Haworth	1	Sir John Rearsby	1
Edwd. Roebuck	2	Fran. Fowler	3
Tho. Roebuck	1	The parsonage	7
Robt. Chapell	1		
John Smith	2	Robt. Bennett, Coll[ector]	
Tho. Holmes	1	Thos. Chappell, Const[able]	

The fact that only two poor people were recorded makes one question whether the return provides a complete list of households, but then Thrybergh was an estate village that did not allow poor immigrants to settle within its bounds. It is worth noting that Sir John Reresby appeared twice after his first entry, presumably as the owner of empty houses, and that women who were heads of households were often described as widows rather than given their Christian names.

Occasionally, and especially in an area of scattered settlement, buildings which still survive can be identified in the tax returns. The number of recorded hearths may even be a clue as to whether or not a house had been completed by a particular date. For the genealogist, however, the principal value of the returns lies in the help they provide in tracing elusive ancestors. A thorough examination of all the available hearth tax returns on a county basis will enable him to identify which parishes had someone with the appropriate surname living there during the reign of Charles II. This information will enable him to concentrate his search on certain parish registers.

The returns also show how far those surnames which are peculiarly local in origin had ramified by the second half of the seventeenth century. A good example is the Derbyshire surname Bagshaw or Bagshawe, which is derived from a minor place-name near Chapel en le Frith, high in the hills of the Peak District. The hamlet, whose name probably means 'badger-copse', was recorded in 1251, though of course it may be much older in origin; the surname had no doubt become hereditary by the following century. Fifty-two Bagshaw households were recorded in the Derbyshire hearth tax returns of 1670, including that of Mr Bagshaw, who had 5 households in the original township of Bowden chapel, and his neighbours Robert and Thomas Bagshaw, who had 2 and 1 hearths respectively. The name was found most commonly in its ancient heartland and surrounding parishes, though a few branches had ventured off the hills to settle

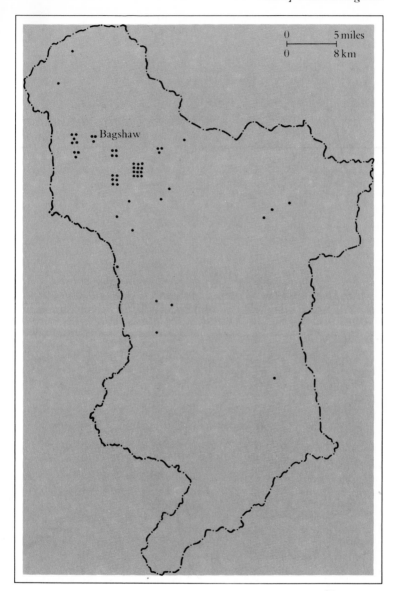

Fig. 2.2 Distribution of Bagshaw(e) households in the Derbyshire Hearth
Tax returns, 1670

in and around Chesterfield. The gradual way that the family
spread into neighbouring parts is entirely typical of the pattern
of movement of most English families.

THE FAMILY, POPULATION TRENDS AND MOBILITY

Anyone who has read Richard Gough's *History of Myddle* (1701–2) is left in no doubt that the basic unit of English society in the Tudor and Stuart period was the family. The inhabitants of his Shropshire parish had a clear sense of belonging to a local community within a wider neighbourhood – hospitality and neighbourliness were common ideals – but it was the family that was of prime importance. With the help of his neighbours and by studying every relevant historical record that he could lay his hands on, Gough was able to trace the personal history of every family in his parish – often through several generations – and to show, incidentally, that intermarriage between the long-established families strengthened the bonds that made people think of themselves as a special community somehow different from all the others. To Richard Gough local history seemed a natural extension of family history. His purpose in writing was to recount the human stories of all his fellow parishioners and their ancestors and to set them against the physical environment and administrative framework of the place where they lived.

The typical English household in the Tudor, Stuart and Hanoverian era was not very different from that of today, except in its age structure. It was rare for more than one married couple to live together in the same house. The occasional listings of inhabitants that survive for places up and down the country make it clear that older married people did not live with their married children, though they were often housed nearby. Even when they were old and widowed, grandparents often preferred the independence of living on their own, within daily reach of their offspring, as long as they could manage. The size of each household depended upon the stage of the life cycle that the occupants had reached and upon whether or not adolescents were living-in as servants or apprentices. On average, 4.75 seems a reasonable multiplier to use in order to estimate the total population of a community from such listings of households as the hearth tax returns. The modern, nuclear form of family was the norm; large households with an extended range of kin were unknown.

Marriage was delayed until the young couple could afford to set up a home of their own. Precise average figures are rather meaningless, for the range might be wide, but it is useful to think in terms of an average age at marriage of twenty-seven to twenty-nine for men and of about twenty-six for women; the nobility and gentry usually married a little earlier. A higher proportion of the population than today never married at all; throughout the period at least 1:6 people remained unmarried and sometimes the proportion reached 1:4. Parents tried to help their children set up home with the aid of a 'marriage portion', but most couples had to rely mainly on their own savings. Young people were normally allowed many opportunities to meet members of the opposite sex, and though examples can be quoted of disinheritance because parental wishes had not been met, the prime consideration in choosing a wedding partner was undoubtedly mutual love.

Family historians need to be aware that long after the Reformation people contined to observe the prohibited periods of Lent and Advent when arranging their wedding day. Harvest time was also avoided for obvious reasons. By far the most popular months for marriage were October and November, when harvest was safely gathered in and the annual period of service for farm servants in the corn-growing regions had come to an end and wages had been paid. May and June were the peak months for marriages in pastoral districts for that was when the annual farm cycle and period of service ended there. Other peaks came during the months following the prohibited times of Advent and Lent.

The intensive study of demographic records through the technique of family reconstitution has dispelled many myths. It is now clear, for instance, that before the nineteenth century illegitimacy rates were low and that bastardy was disapproved of by all sections of society, not just the church authorities. On the other hand, bridal pregnancy was widely tolerated despite the exhortations of the professional moralists. This in no way implies a relaxed attitude towards sexual liaisons. Marriage was expected to last for life and adultery and fornication were punished in the ecclesiastical courts.

Whether or not they were legitimate, many children failed to survive their early critical years. They were particularly vulnerable during their first 12 months and about a third of them did not live to reach the age of 10. Nevertheless, high birth rates ensured that society was far more youthful in its composition than it is today. At any one time about 40 per cent of the population were children who were living at home with their parents. During their mid teens many adolescents left home to enter farm service or to begin an apprenticeship. Dr Anne Kussmaul has estimated that between the fifteenth and the nineteenth centuries about 60 per cent of the population aged between 15 and 24 were farm servants and that between a third and a half of the country's hired labour force was supplied in this way. Many small farmers, of course, did not hire any outside labour but relied entirely on the combined efforts of each member of their family. One has always to bear in mind that for very many people in early-modern England – in the towns as much as in the countryside – the home was also the place of work.

Only a minority of people lived to be grandparents. Children very often lost one or more parents before they reached adulthood and the chances of a husband or wife losing his or her partner before old age were far greater than they are today. Second marriages were therefore common, as anyone who has tried to construct a family tree for this period will know. The Cambridge Group for the Study of Population and Social Structure (CAMPOP) have shown that in seventy communities where total lists of inhabitants were made at some point between the late sixteenth and the early nineteenth century the proportion of householders who were widowed was about 1:5; at Clayworth (Notts.) in 1688 it was higher than 1:4.

The earliest surviving parish registers consistently record a greater number of baptisms than burials. By the last decade of Henry VIII's reign, if not before, England was beginning to recover from a long period of population decline. All over western Europe the trend was towards moderately fast growth up to about 1640. CAMPOP's researches have shown that during the 100 years after 1540 England's population rose from about 2.75 millions to roughly 5 millions. Thereafter, the country experienced sixty years of stagnation, and during the period 1656–86 the national total declined slightly. At the close of the seventeenth century, however, towns and villages in certain industrial regions started to grow, and despite a setback in the 1720s they continued to expand at an astonishing rate throughout each decade of the eighteenth century. The enormous growth of population in the rest of England began in the 1740s. It has never stopped rising since.

This general pattern of growth was subject to regional variation and was punctuated by devastating epidemics – of which bubonic plague was only the most notorious – and by harvest failures that were so catastrophic that people died of starvation. In 1551, for example, a virulent form of influenza known as 'sweating sickness' killed thousands throughout the land. In 1555 and 1556 continual heavy rain ruined the harvests and brought famine, thus weakening human resistance to the epidemics which struck in 1557–59. Bubonic plague was endemic in the towns, less so in the countryside. In 1563 it killed one in every five Londoners. Other places were also hit savagely from time to time, but it is often difficult to tell from the registers which particular disease was responsible for an unusually high number of deaths. The word 'plague' was used loosely in an era when medical knowledge was rudimentary. Genuine bubonic plague can be detected by the seasonal pattern of deaths, which were extraordinarily high in the summer months but low in winter when the pestilence lay dormant. Thus, there seems little doubt that it was bubonic plague which struck Chesterfield in 1586–87. During the previous twenty-five years Chesterfield's burial totals never rose to more than seventy per annum and were usually at a much lower level, but in 1587 the number of recorded deaths reached a staggering 313. At this time the whole of England was suffering from the effects of the disastrous harvests of the previous two summers. Elsewhere, typhus carried off many who had been weakened by starvation; in Chesterfield the pestilence was almost certainly bubonic plague. A comment inserted in the register for October 1586 reads: 'Here began the great plague of Chesterfield'. Few died during the winter but the plague reappeared in the spring and killed 154 people in the summer months of June, July and August, before disappearing with the onset of a new winter.

Local historians should be aware that the high number of deaths that they may find during certain years in their own register could fit the experience of the nation at large. The worst years for deaths caused by epidemics following in the wake of harvest failure were 1586–87, 1591–2 and 1596–98; these were times of acute distress. In northern parts 1623–24 was equally bad and all over England 1630 was long remembered as a year of dearth. Even so, the national population continued to rise steadily during the reigns of Elizabeth and the early Stuarts. Bubonic plague struck London again with devastating effect in 1665 and during the following year even penetrated the Peak District at remote Eyam, but then it mysteriously disappeared. Restoration England's improved agriculture made famine a thing of the past, though temporary shortages still caused suffering. The last period during which the country suffered from the combined effects of disastrous harvest and epidemic diseases was from 1723 to 1730, particularly the later years. Lancashire burial registers, for instance, refer to fever, ague fever and pleurisy, but several diseases rather than a single culprit appear to have been responsible. Imported corn staved off the worst effects of harvest failure and some communities appear to have escaped altogether. In the Yorkshire parish of Arksey, however, the vicar wrote in the register for 1729: 'The greatest mortality that ever can be remembered, or made out to be', and many other accounts speak of considerable distress.

The sixteenth and seventeenth centuries saw some redistribution of the population, for the towns grew faster than the villages because of immigration from the countryside. London grew at an astonishing rate, from about 60,000 in 1500 to approximately 200,000 in 1600 and to an enormous 575,000 in 1700, by which time it was probably the largest city in Europe. It has been estimated that between 1580 and 1650 London probably absorbed half the national increase of England's population and that about one in every eight English people lived in London at some stage of their lives; after 1650 the proportion was as high as one in six. The leading provinical cities were tiny in comparison with the capital. By the end of the seventeenth century Norwich had about 30,000 inhabitants, Bristol 20,000 and Exeter, York and Newcastle even less. England was still overwhelmingly rural; 75 per cent of the population lived in small communities of less than 450 people, and many of those who lived in more urban surroundings nevertheless had only 1,000 to 2,000 neighbours and often even fewer. England was still an underpopulated country by later standards.

One of the most popular misconceptions about the past is that our ancestors were rooted in one particular place, that they rarely ventured beyond their restricted horizons and that consequently they were limited in their outlook and in their knowledge of life beyond the parish. Now it is perfectly true that some families remained in the same district for hundreds of years. When I traced my own family tree I found that the Heys had come into the parish of Penistone (and more particularly to that part known as the township of Thurlstone where I lived) about the year 1800 and that during the previous three centuries they had resided in Kirkburton parish immediately to the north. Many other English families remained localized in this way, but even they usually moved short distances beyond their parish boundaries from time to time and younger branches of the family ramified the surname

Within the image, the following text labels appear: St Laurens Powltry, the Dutch Churche, St Michels, St Peters, the Loon Steeple, Leaden hall, Old Swan, Fishmongers hall, FLUVIUS, South, Winchester house, Warke

Plate 2.4 Visscher's view of London, 1616 (detail)
Nicholas John Visscher was a Netherlands artist who engraved this view
in 1616, possibly from earlier maps and pictures. This detail shows part
of the City of London as seen from the southern bank of the river
Thames.

The river was an important highway and boatmen competed fiercely
to take passengers up or down stream or across to the other bank. Along
a 1-mile stretch about forty sets of steps led down to the waterfront; the
Swan stairs and the Fishmongers' Hall steps can be distinguished in this
section of the view.

At this time London had about 100 places of worship, whose towers
and spires (including that of the Dutch Church) pierce the skyline. The
Royal Exchange and Leadenhall were two of the important commercial
centres. The south bank was known for its taverns, theatres and other
places of entertainment. Winchester House was the palace or town-house
of the medieval bishops of Winchester; in 1642 it was converted into a
prison like its neighbour, the Clink. The Globe Theatre, opened in 1599,
stood nearby, a little further west.

77

far and wide. We have already noted the prevalence of this sort of small-scale mobility during the Middle Ages. In the Tudor and Stuart era, judging by the evidence of parish registers, court depositions and diaries, most people moved at least once in their lives. Dr Peter Clark has called this 'betterment' migration, the movement particularly of apprentices, servants and young married couples within an area bounded by the local market towns. Seventeenth-century people referred to such an area as their 'country'. In the Shropshire parish of Myddle between 1541 and 1701 nearly everyone found a husband or wife within a 10-mile radius of his or her dwelling and most partners came from within the neighbourhood that was centred upon the market towns of Shrewsbury, Ellesmere and Wem; only the gentry sought wives or husbands from a slightly wider area. Several young couples took up residence in a neighbouring parish at the start of their married lives but returned later to inherit the family property. The great majority of English people seem to have moved short distances at some time or other. Such mobility was not only common, it was the usual way of life.

Recent demographic work has made this point time and time again. It is brought home sharply when we look at the two lists of the inhabitants of the Nottinghamshire village of Clayworth that were made by the minister in 1676 and 1688, for we find that no less than 61.8 per cent of those recorded in 1676 were not there twelve years later; only one-third of those who had disappeared had died. In the Northamptonshire village of Cogenhoe half the villagers recorded in 1618 were not there ten years later, and in the Suffolk parish of Horringer only two of the sixty-three family names recorded between 1600 and 1624 were still found in the parish register between 1700 and 1724. Much of this mobility was accounted for by adolescent farm servants who regularly changed jobs every year; they moved from farm to farm regardless of parish boundaries but rarely went very far. Once they were married adults they settled down for longer periods. There is every reason to believe that this degree of movement was typical of the corn-growing regions, but we have to constantly bear in mind that one part of England may have very different experiences from another and that even neighbouring communities might have contrasting stories to tell. Myddle parish saw nothing like the same rapid turnover of personnel. Some of the tenement farmers there leased a family holding for five, six or seven generations under the Tudors and Stuarts, and old-established surnames accounted for four out of every five entries in the Myddle parish register. Even so, the younger children of yeomen and husbandmen moved on elsewhere and the labouring families were far more volatile than the stable core of farming families.

Generally speaking, people did not move very far. Settlement certificates granted by parish authorities in Kent between 1691 and 1740 show that well over half the immigrants into Maidstone travelled no more than 10 miles and that only 15 per cent journeyed more than 40 miles. Nearly three-quarters of the boys who were apprenticed to cutlers in and around Sheffield between 1650 and 1724 came from within a 15-mile radius of their new homes and only 4 per cent migrated more than 40 miles. They were typical of apprentice lads all over England. After studying the detailed entries in the parish registers of a group of farming settlements in the Vale of York from 1777 onwards, Dr B. A. Holderness has concluded that, 'The picture which emerges is of village communities refreshed by an influx from similar settlements lying at a comparatively short distance away.' The ebb and flow of personnel in these agricultural communities was notable in all occupational groups, though here too the farmers were the most likely to stay put and the labourers to move on. The examples that have been quoted above could be multiplied by case-studies from all over England and from widely-separated periods of time. Short-distance mobility was a normal feature of provincial life.

Dr Clark distinguishes this type of 'betterment' migration from longer distance 'subsistence' migration, which occurred on a significant level in the century before the Dissolution of the Monasteries and the Civil War. During those decades bands of pauper migrants went on the tramp in search of food and a living. They caused public alarm wherever they went; the words of the nursery rhyme, 'Hark, hark, the dogs do bark' succinctly describe the mixture of fear and charity with which they were greeted. The Elizabethan poor law acts of 1598 and 1601 threatened beggars with a whipping and placed the responsibility for maintaining the poor on 'the Churchwardens of every parish and four substantial householders there . . . who shall be nominated yearly in Easter week under the hand and seal of two or more Justices of the Peace . . . [and who] shall be called overseers of the poor'. These overseers were empowered to levy local rates, to set the poor on work, to apprentice poor children and to provide relief in the form of clothes, food, fuel and rents for the 'lame, impotent, old, blind, and such other among them being poor and not able to work'. Pauper migration was also limited by the settlement laws. From the early seventeenth century onwards some towns erected barriers against incoming vagrants, and though parish officers were sympathetic to their own poor they were hostile to outsiders. The 1662 Act of Settlement turned this widespread local practice into the law of the land. It stated that anyone who moved into a property valued at less that £10 a year could be sent back to the place where he or she was last legally settled if they were likely to become chargeable to the poor rates. Anyone seeking temporary work beyond his own parish had to have a certificate (signed by the minister and an overseer) which acknowledged legal responsibility. Disputes between parishes were settled by the justices of the peace at quarter sessions.

The settlement laws help to explain why long-distance 'subsistence' migration declined rapidly after the Restoration. Most poor folk now moved only short distances away from 'their' parish. The plight of the poor was ameliorated by the slowing down of population growth during the second half of the seventeenth century and by simultaneous improvements in agricultural production techniques and employment opportunities offered by rural industries. Farming became geared to the demands of regional and national markets and harvest crises eventually became a thing of the past. During the century after the Restoration rural industries such as framework knitting and nailmaking grew at an unprecedented rate and the industrial towns flourished as never before. A greater gross national product meant that local authorities could be more generous towards the poor. Parishes were able to cope with their pauper problem until England's population began to soar dramatically during the second half the eighteenth century. Meanwhile, another option became available to the poor as they joined the growing number of emigrants to the New World. It has been estimated that during the last forty years of the seventeenth century between 100,000 and 150,000 people crossed the Atlantic Ocean to start a new life in America.

London was the great magnet, the one place that continued to attract immigrants from all over the country, not just the poor but people from all classes of society. London depended upon its immigrants to sustain its increase, for until the later seventeenth century its death-rates were higher than its birth-rates. Professor E. A. Wrigley has estimated that between 1650 and 1750 London needed 8,000 immigrants per annum to account for its phenomenal population rise. The surplus population of England, especially that of the Home Counties and the Midlands, was siphoned off to the capital. The Shropshire parish of Myddle lies some 160 miles away from London but at least fifteen of the ninety-one families that paid the hearth tax there in 1672 had one member or more who had been to the capital city. As we noted earlier, perhaps as many as one in six of the adult population of England had lived in London for part of their lives.

To a much lesser extent other towns also depended upon an inflow of migrants to maintain their numbers. The drift to the towns from the countryside was not merely associated with the Industrial Revolution. Dr Alan Dyer has estimated that the doubling of Worcester's population between 1563 and 1645 was due in equal part to natural increase and to immigration. Peter Clark has shown that at least half the Gloucester men and women who were called as witnesses in church courts during the early seventeenth century were first generation immigrants. All towns drew the great majority of their recruits from their own hinter-lands, though a significant minority came from further afield, especially to the larger towns.

In tracing that elusive ancestor the family historian therefore needs to be aware that long before the age of the railways people did sometimes travel long distances and that it was very common for men, women and adolescents to move within a few miles radius of their birthplace. It is necessary for the researcher to become familiar with a whole neighbourhood, to become aware of the different types of community that formed such a 'country' and to search the parish registers of neighbouring settlements in ever increasing circles. Every small clue should be noted. For example, when John Hey of Birkhouse in the West Riding parish of Kirkburton died in 1719, the executors of his estate were his widow Susannah and a John Halstead, who lived at Thornhill, some 10 miles or so away. I knew of no previous family connec-tion with this place, but the information was sufficient to prompt a search of the Thornhill registers. I was rewarded with the discovery that on 21 July 1718 John Hey and Susannah Hepworth were married there.

How did people travel such long distances around the country? Many of them walked. On 10 March 1736 the Revd James Clegg, a Nonconformist minister and apothecary from Chinley in the heart of the Peak District, noted in his diary: 'An ancient man came for advice and brought a water [a urine sample?] from beyond Southwell in Nottinghamshire, on foot, about 36 miles'; no doubt he returned the same way. Otherwise, the cheapest way of travel was by the carrier's cart which trundled slowly but regularly to the market towns, where another carrier offered a service to the next destination. The whole of England was linked by a network of carriers' routes. A 1787 directory of Sheffield, for example, shows that local people could take advantage of forty-two different services leading directly or through connections in distant towns to most parts of England, Scotland and Wales.

London was linked to all parts of the provinces by weekly services as far back as the reign of Charles I and probably earlier. In *The Carriers' Cosmographie* of 1637 John Taylor named the usual lodgings of provincial carriers in London, together with their times of arrival and departure. For instance:

> The Carriers of Manchester, doe lodge at the Beare in Bassingshaw, they doe come on Thursdaies or Fridaies.
> The Carriers of Manchester, doe likewise lodge at the signe of the Axe in Aldermanbury.
> The Carriers of Manchester, doe also lodge at the two neck'd Swan in Lad Lane (betweene great Woodstreet, and Milk-street end) they come every second Thursday: also there do lodge Carriers that doe passe through divers other parts of Lancashire.

Nottinghamshire travellers could no doubt use the services of carriers coming from further north as well as their local men:

> The Carriers of Nottingham, doe lodge at the crosse-keyes in Saint Johns street, he commeth every second Saturday.
> There is also a footpost doth come every thursday from Nottingham, he lodgeth at the swan in Saint Johns street.

Travelling was a slow, tedious business but the difficulties were not insuperable.

RURAL COMMUNITIES

Each local community has its own individual character and does not conform in all its particulars to a general type. Nevertheless, the local historian will find it useful to think of his chosen parish or neighbourhood in terms of broad categories such as 'open-field arable' or 'wood-pasture' or 'fenland edge' and to set himself the

fundamental task of understanding how people adapted themselves to their physical environment. It is sometimes hard today
for us to grasp how much people's lives were governed by the
nature of their everyday surroundings. The physical setting of a
parish influenced not only the ways in which a family might farm
their land or work at a particular craft but also such basic matters
as whether they lived in a village, a hamlet or an isolated farmstead, whether or not they had valuable rights of common to go
with their farms or cottages, and sometimes the type of tenure
by which they held their land. The local topography helped in
many subtle ways to shape their attitudes and whole outlook on
life. Thus, the dairymen who farmed the lush meadows of the
Dove Valley geared their husbandary to a different system from
that followed by the sheep-and-corn farmers on the Lincolnshire
Wolds, and the range of opportunities for earning a living and for
gaining some measure of independence from a lord or squire was
much greater for a cottager living on the edge of a moor, forest
or marsh than the scope available to his counterpart in one of the
nucleated, corn-growing villages of the Midland Plain.

Recent local studies have emphasized how different the
fortunes of neighbouring parishes could be. It is often more useful
for the historian to compare types of local community which are
widely separated from each other than to make comparisons with
nearby settlements. For example, the historian who is studying
a parish in the Sussex Weald might get more enlightenment from
an analysis of the economy and social structure of a wood-pasture
community in the Forest of Arden than from a comparable study
of a nearby parish on the South Downs, which might offer some
rewarding contrasts but few points of similarity.

Cambridgeshire examples

Dr Margaret Spufford has examined the varying fortunes of three
different Cambridgeshire parishes – Chippenham, Orwell and
Willingham – in *Contrasting Communities: English Villagers in the
Sixteenth and Seventeenth Centuries* (1974). Cambridgeshire has
never been a county dominated by the nobility and gentry, for
the degree of manorial fragmentation found there from Domesday
Book onwards did not encourage the development of strong lordship. The county was characterised instead by numerous small
farmers and cottagers. By the time of the 1524–25 lay subsidy

over half the rural population of Cambridgeshire were already dependent upon wages to supplement earnings from their own holdings, a proportion that had not quite been reached in the country as a whole at the end of the seventeenth century. Only a little further up the social scale, another quarter or more of the rural inhabitants had tenements varying in size up to a yardland, which in Cambridgeshire seems to have been about 30 and 40 acres. What happened to all these small owners in the next century and a half?

In general terms, renewed population growth and the corresponding rapid rise in the price of foodstuffs during the sixteenth century benefited the larger farmers (for they were able to produce a surplus for the market) and worsened the purchasing position of farm labourers whose relative wages sank as prices rose. That much is clear, but how did the small landowner of a yardland or less fare in these circumstances? Historians agree that the size of this group was certainly much reduced in number by the middle of the eighteenth century, but the chronology of this decline is debatable for it varied from region to region. Dr Spufford's book has successfully demonstrated that the timing of this change depended in large measure upon the farming system and the social and economic structure of the communities that were affected.

Chippenham lies on the chalk ridge that forms the northeastern part of the county. It provides a classic example of the way that engrossers in the corn-growing regions enlarged their farms when small-holders could no longer cope and were forced to sell. A detailed examination of the manorial court rolls reveals that the characteristic medieval holding, ranging from 15 to 45 acres, disappeared from the local scene between 1598 and 1636. By the middle years of the seventeenth century Chippenham had a much higher proportion of farms with more than 50 acres and also more cottagers who were dependent upon their earnings from their work on these bigger farms. Local society was becoming more polarised as smallholders sold up and moved elsewhere.

On the western clay plateau at Orwell the number of customary tenants who held yardlands or half-yardlands declined during the first thirty years of the seventeenth century. Here again, both the size of larger holdings and the number of cottagers at the bottom end of the social scale increased as the Stuart era progressed. The seventeenth century witnessed a tremendous expansion of the lord's demesne at the expense of some of the

Plate 2.5 'Newlandes Ende' (Essex) in 1609

This detail of John Walker's map of Matching (1609), now kept in the Essex Record Office, is a marvellous example of the seventeenth century surveyor's art. It depicts one of the hamlets in Matching parish. Not only does it name the owners of tenements and note the size of the fields in acres, roods and perches, it shows the irregular arrangement of the settlement and even marks the hedge-timber and gates.

Most interestingly of all, it has sketches of the houses, barns and other farm buildings. The houses are all of the lobby-entrance type with a doorway opening onto a central chimney stack in accordance with the fashion of the times. The drawings show six single-storey houses, a more substantial dwelling with a gabled, two-storey cross wing, and a four-bay, jettied house of two storeys. It is likely that all of them had been built or remodelled during the previous forty years. They are likely to have been timber-framed structures, plastered over, though Essex does have some brick barns from that period.

tenants' arable and possibly at the loss of their commons as well. The population level remained stable despite a surplus of baptisms over burials. Orwell had fifty-two taxable adults in the 1520s and between fifty and fifty-four households 150 years later. The surplus recorded in the parish register must have been lost through migration to other places.

The fortunes of the inhabitants of the fen-edge parish of

Willingham, where stock farming and dairying rather than cereal production were the mainstays, were rather different. At the beginning of the sixteenth century the fens were less thickly settled than the clay plateau, but 200 years later they were amongst the most populous districts in the county. The transformation and expansion of the fenland villages was one of Cambridgeshire's most significant and marked developments during the Tudor and Stuart era. In Elizabethan Willingham the typical holding was no more than half a yardland, a size which in practice varied from 14 to over 20 acres. On the main manor twenty-eight of the forty copyholders were half-yardlanders; as a group the copyholders were distinct from the thirty-one freeholders, for only three men held land by both methods of tenure in any significant quantity. In a survey of 1575 between 40 and 50 per cent of the Willingham villagers held only a house or a house with a couple of acres of land. In all, sixty-seven of the tenants named in this manorial survey held less than a half-yardland. This does not mean that they were necessarily poor. In fen and fen-edge parishes such as this a half-yardlander was quite a wealthy man, for the generous nature of his common rights completely changed the value of his holding. The local historian who is trying to build up a picture of the social and economic structure of his own parish must always take into consideration the extent of the common and the value of the rights over it.

By the time another survey was made in 1603 the signs of change in Willingham were apparent. The number of half-yardlanders had declined from twenty-eight to twenty, for three had enlarged their holdings and five had relinquished some of their property. Furthermore, a quarter of the freeholdings were in the hands of completely different families from those which had held them in 1575. On the other hand, over half the holdings remained intact and in the same family possession. The breakdown of the old holdings continued through the next five generations between 1603 and the 1720s, and although the rate of change was no faster than before, in the end the results were dramatic. By the Hanoverian era the half-yardland was no longer a recognizable unit in Willingham. The total number of tenants had risen from 125 to 153; the number of wealthier farmers remained steady, but the poorer section had increased considerably. Moreover, since the end of the sixteenth century incoming cottagers had no common rights and were dependent entirely upon their labour for their living.

Dr Spufford's study deals with many important themes which cannot be considered here, but the attention of the family historian is drawn to her conclusions about mobility into and out of the parish during the six generations between 1575 and the 1720s and to her remarks on the provision of education. The fifty-eight separate surnames recorded in Willingham in 1575 had risen to ninety by the 1720s, but only a hard core of twenty-two families remained. In other words, thirty-six (or about two-thirds) of the families that were resident in Willingham in 1575 had either moved or died out in the male line during the course of a century and a half. Whether or not a family moved depended in large measure on the amount of land that they held and on the number of landholding branches. Of the eleven families who had more than one member holding land in 1575 no less than nine were still in the village in the eighteenth century. In contrast, all but one of the eighteen cottagers who had some common rights but no land in 1575 had disappeared altogether and had been replaced by others. Immigration into the fens during this period outstripped emigration to other areas. Sixty-eight of the ninety family names recorded in the 1720s, that is three out of every four, were those of families which had come into the parish since the Elizabethan period. Under the presssure of population growth the fenland holdings were broken down into smaller and smaller fragments.

As for education, Dr Spufford showed that about a fifth of Cambridgeshire's villages and minor market towns had a schoolmaster licensed continuously between 1570 and 1620. Some sort of teacher was almost always within walking distance of a rural child. The same sort of picture emerges from the study of other parts of the country. During the sixteenth and seventeenth centuries England became a semi-literate society in which even some of the agricultural labourers could read. A study of the signatories to the 1642 Protestation Returns shows that the proportion of illiterate males varied from 53 to 79 per cent across the country and averaged 70 per cent. Looked at the other way this means that at least 30 per cent of Englishmen in the mid seventeenth century were able to read and to sign their name.

Terling

Terling, a small parish on the Essex boulder clays, has been the subject of an intensive study by K. Wrightson and D. Levine entitled *Poverty and Piety in an English Village: Terling, 1525–1700* (1979). Terling (pronounced Tarling) was an almost wholly agricultural parish, anciently enclosed, and for the most part devoted to mixed farming, with some emphasis on wheat and dairying. When a lay subsidy was collected in 1524–25 Essex was one of England's richest counties and Terling was one of the wealthier villages, both in terms of total tax and the average amount paid by each person assessed. About seventy Terling households and eighteen non-residents were taxed, ten on their land, forty-nine on their goods, twelve on their wages and seventeen on their earnings; the two latter categories are best explained as living-in farm servants and agricultural labourers.

A point of contrast a century and a half later is provided by the 1671 hearth tax return, by which time the seventy householders had grown to 122. By that time the living standards of the middling sort of English countrymen had improved significantly. In the 1570s William Harrison, an Essex parson, had commented on the new comforts provided particularly by chimneys, bedding and tableware. A 1597 map of Terling depicts the village houses as mostly single-storey dwellings, though some had an upper storey at one end and many had chimneys. By the middle of the seventeenth century references in inventories to parlours as well as hall and chambers were commonplace, and by 1700 a wide variety of rooms were being listed. In 1671 8.2 per cent of the householders had at least six hearths (the squire had twenty), 23.8 per cent had three to five hearths, 17.2 per cent had two hearths, and 50.8 per cent had only a single hearth. Forty of the 122 households, that is 32.8 per cent, were exempted from paying the tax on grounds of poverty. In Essex as a whole the number of exempted poor in a parish ranged from 23.2 per cent to 53.2 per cent and averaged 38 per cent. The broad structure of Terling society in 1671 remained similar to that in 1524, except that numbers in the poorest section had increased enormously.

Terling's population grew steadily during the sixteenth century and the first quarter of the seventeenth. The only severe check came in 1625 when plague killed one in twelve people and raised the death rate to three times the annual norm; after that the population remained stable for almost 150 years. Terling was a well-defined social unit, its villagers well aware of their special identity, yet it was in no way isolated from the surrounding parishes, for a majority of the adult population of the village had experience of living in other communities. The composition of the village was constantly changing as a result of short-distance mobility. Keith Wrightson and David Levine were able to trace the ownership of about half the freehold and a quarter of the copyhold properties during the course of the seventeenth century. They established that 6 copyholds changed hands a total of 36 times and 21 freeholds changed ownership a total of 118 times. In both types of tenure sale was almost as frequent as change through inheritance. Not a single holding in their sample remained in the same family name between 1600 and 1700 and only 2 freeholds and 1 copyhold stayed in the possession of the same family during this century even if allowance is made for inheritance through a female line.

Inheritance customs in Terling were far from rigid. Children received portions of the family property on different occasions over long periods of time. They did not delay their marriage until they had received their inheritance, and younger sons and daughters were provided for even though the formal system was primogeniture. Kinship networks were loose but might extend far across the social scale of the village, and though Terling was riddled with petty conflicts, good neighbourliness was regarded as a virtue and a crucial social bond. Nevertheless, Terling society was highly stratified; by the later seventeenth century the 'better sort' were becoming increasingly set apart from the labouring poor. During the eighteenth century the word 'class' would be coined to differentiate the different social groups.

Leicestershire examples

The type of farming system that was followed was an important determinant of the character of a local community, but it was not the only one by any means. Adjacent parishes on the Midland clays sometimes had very different histories from each other because of the varying ways in which the ownership of land was divided. These divisions run very deep and go back as far as the available documents provide information on such matters. Leicestershire lay at the very heart of open-field England. Its cornfields were farmed in common and the individual strips were demarcated by the gently undulating patterns of ridge and furrow that stretched from village streets to the very edge of each parish.

Until these fields were enclosed by private agreement or by act of parliament hardly a building was erected beyond the nucleus of the settlement, for every piece of land was precious. Yet Leicestershire also has many parishes where the village has disappeared from the landscape, leaving perhaps only the manor house or squire's hall and sometimes a forlorn and decaying church. Of Leicestershire's 370 medieval settlements no less than sixty have been deserted and many others are now much smaller than they were in their heyday during the thirteenth and early-fourteenth century. The Black Death began the long process of decline for many, but it rarely wiped out an entire village at a single blow. Many settlements withered during the late Middle Ages but did not die until the Elizabethan or Stuart era when a local lord decided that corn production was no longer economical and that the arable land must be given over to cattle and sheep pastures. An enquiry of 1607 claimed that in Leicestershire at least 8,245 acres had been enclosed and converted in seventy-one different places since 1578. This figure understated the case; much more land had been put down to pasture and the tenants had been forced to leave. Many of them fled to neighbouring parishes where the manorial structure was far weaker and poor immigrants were not prevented from setting up home. By the nineteenth century these contrasting types of community would be categorized as being 'open' or 'closed' to migrants who might become a burden on the poor rates.

A perfect example of a site that was deserted in the middle years of the seventeenth century can be examined on the ground at Great Stretton, a few miles south-east of Leicester. The village took its name from the Roman road or *straet* known as the Gartree Road which passes close to the little limestone church of St Giles that now stands all alone on the skyline. All around the oval churchyard can be found the sunken tracks that were once the village streets and paths and raised above them are the grassy mounds that cover the foundations of houses and cottages long since gone. The deeply moated site of the former manor house marks the edge of the old settlement; sheep now graze peacefully over the remains of the village and over the ridge and furrow patterns of what were once the communal arable fields. By the nineteenth century the church was almost in ruins, for only its sturdy medieval tower remained intact; the whole building was restored in 1838 when fragments of the ancient structure were patched together in new walls. Like most deserted villages Great

Stretton was always on the small side, but in 1563 it still contained fifteen families. By 1670 this number had fallen sharply to five. The number of entries in the parish register dwindled in the middle decades of the seventeenth century, suggesting that many villagers moved elsewhere once the arable fields were enclosed. By 1801 Great Stretton consisted only of a hall, a church and two farmsteads.

A similar story can be told about Foston parish not very far away. A narrow lane, unenclosed by the usual hawthorn hedges of the Midlands, heads across open, pastoral countryside to the hall and the restored church dedicated to St Bartholomew. Cattle and sheep move at a leisurely pace over the earthworks that mark where men once lived and worked. In 1563 this small parish contained twenty-one families but by 1670 only eight households remained. Soon there were even fewer. When William Faunt bought the manor in 1549 half the land was already enclosed. A quarter of a century later Anthony Faunt enclosed another 250 acres. The arable side of the local economy had been destroyed and whereas many had once found employment in growing corn only a few people were now needed to tend the flocks and herds. Burton's *History of Leicestershire* (1622) noted that Foston had some of the finest sheep pastures in the county and that the village community consisted only of the squire, the parson and three or four labouring families.

But on the near horizon, immediately beyond Foston's sheep pastures, stands Wigston Magna, the most populous village in Leicestershire since at least the time of the great Domesday Survey and a world apart from Squire Faunt and his shepherds. In 1670 Wigston contained 161 households, including forty-seven that were exempted from payment of the hearth tax on the grounds of poverty. No rich family dominated their neighbours. The majority of the inhabitants were still the middling farmers of old, but the number of landless cottagers was on the increase. Framework knitting offered a lifeline to such people in 'open' parishes all over Leicestershire. At the top of the social scale the five largest houses in 1670 had five hearths apiece, which was hardly grandiose but was sufficient to set them apart from the rest. For the first time in Wigston's long history a class of gentry was beginning to appear; moreover, substantial holdings were passing into the hands of absentee landlords. As in Cambridgeshire and Essex, the gulf between the richer families and the very poor was getting wider.

Professor Hoskins has written that the 161 households recorded in the 1670 Wigston hearth tax return represent eighty-two different family names. Thirty-six of these families (44 per cent) had lived in Wigston for at least a century and fifteen or sixteen (20 per cent) had been there for 200 years or more. During the later Middle Ages the turnover of names had been rapid, but afterwards an important group of middling farmers had put down roots in the parish and had given the community a sense of cohesiveness and continuity. The most remarkable of these long-established families were the Boulters who had established no fewer than eight different households during the 100 years or so that they had lived in Wigston. The Freers were equally prolific but at a slower rate, with eight branches after 200 years of residence. The Smiths, Vanns and Wards each had six branches, the Johnsons five, the Langtons, Holmeses, Noones and Abbotts four and several others had three. Kinship links through frequent inter-marriage and numerous personal friendships cemented the bonds that gave Wigston and similar places a real sense of belonging to a community. The old agrarian basis of the economy survived well into the Georgian era but the enormous growth of population made a new form of local society unavoidable and the Enclosure Award of 1766 put the final seal of approval on changes that had long been underway. Prior to these changes, Wigston was typical of many Tudor and Stuart parishes where small-holders managed to hang on to their property for generation after generation. A few rich families began to emerge at the top of such societies and the numbers of poor cottagers grew significantly, but the old-established middling families long remained the backbone of many a rural community.

Myddle

The pressure of population caused much less concern in the Welsh Border counties where there was still sufficient land available to allow poor immigrants to erect cottages on the wastes and to claim common rights to go with the few acres that they had cleared from the woods or the moors. By draining meres and felling trees the inhabitants of the north Shropshire parish of Myddle were able to clear at least 1,000 acres of land between the late fifteenth and the early seventeenth century. The signs are that other parishes in this region were equally active in increasing their supply of pastures and meadows. Some of these new 'leasows' were added to existing farms or smallholdings, but elsewhere in the parish entirely new units were created; then from the reign of Elizabeth onwards poor families who wanted a little land to go with their cottages encroached further into the remaining woods and wastes. The landless cottagers of Midland and Eastern England had no counterparts here.

Richard Gough planned his *History of Myddle* (1701–2) to follow the arrangement of the seats in the parish church. The social structure of the parish – in common with other contemporary communities – was formalized by the hierarchy of the pews. The most sought after positions were at the front, where the gentry families had their seats. Behind them came the yeomen and husbandmen and the better-off craftsmen, and at the rear and along the south wall sat the cottagers. Pews were not personal possessions that could be sold or bequeathed but were part of the property of each farm, tenement or cottage, they passed to the new owner or occupier once the property was sold or transferred.

The topography of the parish of Myddle was very different from that of the open-field village of Wigston. Excluding the chapelry of Hadnall, it was divided into seven townships and covered 4,691 acres. It included several hamlets and scattered farms within its bounds as well as the village that was clustered close to the church and the ruined castle. The lord of Myddle was a great figure who never visited the parish, so no one family dominated the others from an ostentatious pew at the front of the church. Instead, the occupants of the best seats held twelve farms between them, ranging in size from 100 to 650 acres. These parish gentry were conscious of their elevated status but they were not sharply separated from the rest of the community, for it was quite common in the Tudor and Stuart era for such a family to contain men and women of various occupations and lower social standing. Younger sons did not at this time seek to maintain their gentility by going into the church or the army or by living off an annuity that allowed them to pass their time in respectable ease.

The fortunes of this richest group in the parish of Myddle varied according to the individual qualities, decisions and luck of the heads of each family. Only the Gittinses and the Hanmers were resident gentry from the second quarter of the sixteenth century through to the early years of the eighteenth century.

Plate 2.6 Interior of St Mary's Church, Whitby
Every possible space inside St Mary's church is taken up with a profusion
of pews and galleries to accommodate a congregation of 2,000 people.
This is the best preserved and most lovable of all the Georgian church
interiors that were left undisturbed by the Victorian High Church move-

Richard Gittins I, a rich Shrewsbury tanner, had arrived as tenant of Eagle Farm by 1528, when he was one of the jurors of the manor court. His great-grandson, Richard Gittins IV, married an heiress and added the lease of Castle Farm, thus amassing an estate of some 650 acres, the largest in the parish. However, the family were unable to hang on to both properties, for Richard Gittins V stood surety for a friend, lost a lot of money and had to relinquish the lease to Eagle Farm. Nevertheless, the male line continued to thrive and two strong branches continued the family name in Myddle well into the eighteenth century.

A complete contrast to this story of stability and continuity is provided by the successive owners of Balderton Hall, an Elizabethan timber-framed dwelling that still stands a mile or so to the east of Myddle village. Here, the Nicholas family held some 500–600 acres of land by the later years of the sixteenth century and ranked with the Gittinses as the largest landowners in the parish. John Nicholas was not amongst the Balderton men who paid the 1524 lay subsidy but he was a manorial court juror four years later. His son, Roger, may have been the richest man in Myddle upon his death in 1572, and his grandson, William, was responsible for building the hall. Gough's comment on William Nicholas was that:

> by his greate charges in building, hee contracted much debt. Yet beeing addicted to projects, hee became a timber man, and purchased all the timber in Kenwick's parke, thinkeing to enrich himself by it, but it proved his ruine.

---

ment. Each quarter of the parish had its own part of the church and the Cholmleys, lords of the manor, sat in a pew supported by four 'barley sugar' columns where once the rood screen had stretched across the Norman chancel arch. From this elevated position they were able to survey the congregation assembled before them and to breathe down the neck of the minister in the three decker pulpit.

The Norman church had been built on the cliff top overlooking the town in the shadow of St Hilda's Abbey. Population growth necessitated the enlargement and adaptation of the church during the eighteenth and early nineteenth centuries. Dark brown box pews stand shoulder high in the nave and aisles and white-painted galleries with numbered seats were fitted to the walls above them and in the transepts. A stove whose flue reaches up through the ceiling, a baroque brass chandelier, commandment boards and Gothic windows help to create a period flavour from the time when church seating arrangements formalized the social structure of the parish. The whole of the interior had been re-designed to make it a preaching area focussed on the pulpit.

He was forced to sell the freehold of Balderton and his lease of the adjacent Broomhurst Farm and to leave the district. Gough's account of the changing ownership of the Balderton estate over the next 100 years shows how varied the fortunes and personalities of the parish gentry could be. Michael Chambre, the next owner, was 'a person of noe accompt . . . wholly addicted to idlenesse' and debauchery, who frittered away his partrimony and had a spell in prison for debt. Having sold Balderton Hall, he went to live on the smaller farm at Broomhurst. The next two owners were wealthy Shrewsbury drapers, each of whom lost a great deal of money when their London connections went bankrupt and were forced to sell again. The virtuous and pious rector of Hodnet purchased the estate but died soon after his arrival; his widow, however, lived at Balderton for many years. Upon her death the property was bought by Matthew Lath, a man who had risen from humble origins through hard work and good fortune. He had only a daughter to succeed him and his son-in-law turned out to be a second Michael Chambre, who after Lath's death 'let loose the reins to many disorderly courses, as cocking, raseing, drinking and lewdnesse', so that he too finally lost all and sold Balderton to Robert Hayward, a local yeoman. The contrast between the continuity of the 'charitable, meeke and comendable' Gittins family at Castle Farm and the rapid turnover of contrasting personnel at Balderton could hardly have been more marked. The stability of the Gittins family could almost be matched in other parts of the parish by the Hanmers and the Atcherleys of Marton, the Watkinses of Shotton and less wealthy farmers such as the Downtons of Alderton. In contrast, during the last quarter of the seventeenth century Bilmarsh Farm had six successive tenants and Webscott had five. The chances of a local gentry family holding on to its farm through three or more generations were about 50:50 during the Elizabethan and Stuart era.

Gough was careful to distinguish between the twelve farms, the forty-eight tenements and the growing number of cottages. The tenements varied in size between 10 and 90 acres (depending in part upon the quality of the land), though their value was increased by generous common rights. A quarter of the tenements were freehold; the rest were held by the normal Shropshire tenure of leases for three lives, with a large entry fine and a nominal annual rent. The yeomen, husbandmen and craftsmen who lived in these tenements had mostly just a single fireplace in their timber-framed houses at the time of the hearth tax return of 1672. As farmers who concentrated on stock-rearing and, increasingly, on dairying, they had sufficient resources to survive but rarely had the means to expand their activities. Like the middling farmers of open-field Wigston, they formed the backbone of the community. From 1541 to 1701 the parish registers, with remarkable consistency, show just how important the long-established families were. At any one time only two out of five surnames in the parish were those of this hard core of families, but four out of five of the total entries belonged to this group. Some yeomen families were there for five, six or seven generations, and in some other cases the turnover of names is explained by inheritance through a female line in the absence of male heirs.

Richard Gough himself came from one of the most ancient families in the parish of Myddle, and one that had branches in several parts of north Shropshire. His ancestors came from Tilley, just across the parish boundary, where the first Richard Gough of that name died in 1538 at the age of eighty-three. Next year, the younger son of this old man became the first of five Richard Goughs to live at Newton on the Hill, a mile or so from Myddle church. As in Wigston, few of the families that put down roots in the parish of Myddle during the sixteenth and seventeenth centuries had been there in earlier times; the turnover of names between the 1370s poll tax returns and the subsidies levied in the reign of Henry VIII was equally remarkable in both parishes. But the new families that came into Wigston and Myddle during Tudor times tended to stay put.

Gough thought that the Lloyds were possibly the most ancient family in Myddle village. They owned a freehold tenement that stood close to the north door of the church and another small tenement in Houlston township, which they normally let to tenants. John Lloyd paid the subsidies in 1524 and 1544 and served as a juror of the manor court from at least 1528 to 1542. Six generations of his direct descendants continued to live in Myddle throughout the sixteenth and seventeenth centuries. The senior members of the family and some of the younger sons were described as yeomen or husbandmen, but the most junior members were craftsmen, such as glovers or weavers.

Some of the leaseholders were also remarkably stable over the generations, families such as the Braynes, the Groomes, the Tylers, the Juxes and the Formstons. The first Brayne to live in a house by the village street in Myddle was William Brayne, a

husbandman who appears in the 1544 subsidy roll. Four successive Williams then three Michaels carried the surname well into
the eighteenth century. Their neighbours, the Formstons, were
a prolific as well as a long-resident family. William Formston was
a tenant at Marton in 1529; by the seventeenth century there were
five branches in various parts of the parish, one of which
continued there till Victorian times. Many of Richard Gough's
contemporaries provided him with information about a wide range
of cousins and about ancestors going back several generations.
Gough was able to give character sketches of relations long since
dead and not directly in his own line, as well as intimate portraits
of the kinsmen of other families. Time and time again families
were identified with a particular farm or tenement, a link that was
all the stronger because the home was also the place of work, the
spot where an individual spent most of his time. Recounting the
history of Bilmarsh farm, Gough observed: 'Nathaniell Reve had
a desire to been tenant of this farme, because his grandfather and
father had been tenants to it before'. Family sentiment linked to
a particular place is not a modern phenomenon.

   The craftsmen were not always recognizable as a separate
group within the parish, for they were often younger sons of
farmers and had land of their own. A few families followed a
particular trade for a few generations, however. The Hordleys and
Taylors were prosperous yeomen-tailors, the Parkeses of Newton
and the Davieses of Myddlewood were poor weaver-cottagers,
the Raphes and Wagges were carpenters and the Chaloners were
the village blacksmiths and coopers. The Chaloners were one of
the most prolific families in Myddle. Their names appear in every
type of record, with five Alans, four Williams and four Georges
to baffle the person who is compiling their family tree. The pain-
staking task is finally rewarded, however, by the detailed picture
that emerges of an 'ordinary' family of farmers, craftsmen and
labourers over a century and a half. This village dynasty was
founded by Alan Chaloner, a blacksmith who married in 1552 and
died in 1601, leaving seven children alive. Two main lines were
carried on by Richard Chaloner, cooper, and George, the
youngest son who inherited the cottage and smithy that his father
had erected on a piece of waste land east of the church, together
with the lease of 3 acres of land enclosed from Myddlewood. The
individuals who comprised the Chaloner family varied as greatly
in their characters as did the members of the parish gentry, from
Alan Chaloner (1603–84), the blacksmith who took pride in his

work, to his elder brother Richard, whom Gough described an 'an untowardly liver, very idle and extravagant, endeavouring to supply his necessytyes rather by stealeing than by his honest labour'. As I wrote in *An English Rural Community: Myddle Under the Tudors and Stuarts* (1974):

> Some of the Chaloners were respected for their craft skills, others through their initiative and hard work earned the name of yeoman, but yet others through idleness or misfortune fell into poverty. There were Chaloners who lived to be seventy or eighty, there were those who died in their youth or early manhood, and many others never reached their first birthday. Some were fortunate in their wives; some were unusually unlucky. Some had children of whom they could be proud; some were ashamed of their offspring. Misfortune was surmounted, and misfortune became too great a burden; virtuous reputations were earned, and scandalous stories were recounted. The family was one of the most prolific in the parish, but in the end the male line withered. In short, the history of the Chaloners reminds one that people living in the sixteenth and seventeenth centuries were as varied and as human as we are today.

During the sixteenth century Myddle was essentially a society consisting of numerous smallholders and a few large farmers, but from the second half of Elizabeth's reign onwards poor immigrants came into the parish in search of labouring work and the opportunity to erect a cottage in the woods or on the manorial wastes. The population of Pimhill Hundred, in which Myddle lay, rose by two-thirds between 1563 and 1672; Myddle's population during that period increased from about 270 to about 450. Between 1541 and 1570 the labourers recorded in the Myddle parish register formed only 7.1 per cent of adult males, but during the next thirty years the proportion rose to 23.4 per cent. Following a subsequent period of stability a fresh wave of poor immigrants arrived between 1631 and 1660, bringing the proportion of labourers up to 31.2 per cent. After the Restoration the keeper of the parish register no longer recorded occupations, but Gough observed that whereas his father paid only 4d. per annum poor rate upon his marriage in 1633, by the end of the century he (Gough) paid almost 20 shillings. Myddle was no doubt typical of many another parish in the Welsh Borders. But the poor were still not the problem that they were in other parts of England. Only 16.5 per cent of the inhabitants of Pimhill Hundred were exempted from payment of the hearth tax in 1672, and though many cottagers remained near the poverty line all their lives others prospered a little and moved up the social scale.

This group of cottagers were the most mobile of all, appearing briefly in the parish register or other records and then moving on. But certain families remained for two or three generations, sometimes more. The Hanmer family were the first of the new immigrants to appear and they were still there 120 years later. The Hanmers were unconnected with the gentry family of the same name at Marton and their surname was not formed until they arrived in Myddle. John Ellis of Hanmer (a small village just across the Welsh border) was presented at the manorial court in 1581 'for erecting of one bay of a house upon the lords waste grounde in Myddle woode'. Seven years later a cluster of names in a rental follows that of Ellice Hanmer, as he was generally known in his new parish. By 1701 Myddlewood had attracted a squatters' colony of fourteen cottages that formed a distinct, new settlement between Myddle village and the hamlet of Marton. A labourer's cottage that still stands at the edge of the former wood was a one bay dwelling, open to the rafters, built by John Hughes in the 1580s and enlarged by the Hanmers during the seventeenth century. It shows that not all labourers' cottages were flimsy hovels and that families in this group could aspire to reasonable comfort. In contrast to the Hanmers, the Chidlows seem to experienced years of relentless poverty. Roger Chidlow was amongst the first group of immigrants, for he appears in a 1590 rental paying 4d rent for a cottage in Newton. He had three sons: James, a weaver, who lived in a little cottage without a chimney at Newton; Jacob, a tailor of Brandwood who died young; and Thomas, a labourer, who set up home in 'a poore pitifull hutt, built up to an old oake' at the side of Divlin Lane. It was later converted into a better dwelling, but while they were rearing their eight children during the 1590s and early 1600s Thomas and his wife must have found life hard and unpromising.

The rise and fall of families depended not only on the circumstances in which people found themselves but upon individual character and temperament. The Protestant ethic was observed by most people in Myddle except in one startling way; many ruined themselves and their families by excessive drinking. We have only Gough to guide us on this, but he has some amazing tales to tell. Thomas Downton's wife 'went dayly to the alehouse. Her husband payd £10 att a time for alehouse scores' and in the end he had to sell his lands to pay off her debts. David Higley of Balderton 'was a good husband by fitts. What hee got with hard labour he spent idely in the Alehouse'. And in Gough's pithy phrase, William Cross of Bilmarsh and his wife 'went dayly to the alehouse, and soone after the cows went thither alsoe'. Historians are rarely able to get to the truth of the matter in this way, but family stories often suggest that drunkenness was the reason for an otherwise inexplicable decline, not just in the Tudor and Stuart era but in much later times. Heavy drinking sometimes went with immorality but many people who were otherwise upright and hardworking ruined themselves by spending all their available money on drink. Thus Thomas Hayward of Balderton:

> 'had little quietnesse att home which caused him to frequent publick houses merely for his naturall sustenance, and there meeting with company and being generally well beeloved hee stayed often too long . . . This Thomas Hayward sold and consumed all his estate and was afterwards mainetained on charyty by his eldest son.

INDUSTRIAL COMMUNITIES

Even in the Elizabethan and Stuart era rural communities in certain regions such as the West Riding of Yorkshire or the West Midlands had an industrial character that marked them off from the societies that have so far been described. In these industrial districts a high proportion of families earned a substantial part of their living from metal crafts or mining or the manufacture of cloth. In the West Midlands, for instance, over a third of the men whose occupations were noted in the Sedgley parish register during 1579 and 1580 were either nailmakers or some other type of metalworker. Until the eighteenth century settlement within the neighbouring parish of West Bromwich took the form of small groups of cottages clustered together in 'ends' around the heaths, where squatters had opportunities to graze a few animals and to build a little workshop. The 212 occupations recorded in the parish register between 1608 and 1658 include those of 122 nailers and 12 bucklemakers. By 1723, ninety-nine cottages had been erected on small pieces of land taken from the wastes.

Before the huge population rise of the eighteenth century English rural craftsmen normally combined their trade with the running of a smallholding. The most substantial of them farmed sufficient land to earn themselves the description of yeoman; the poorest had merely an acre or two and perhaps the right to keep a cow and some sheep on the common. Having a dual occupation

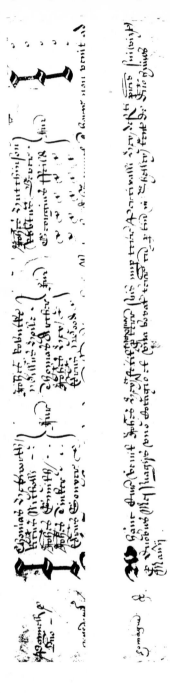

Plate 2.7 Extracts from the Shelley manor court rolls, 1631

These extracts (written in Latin and much abbreviated) name John Hey amongst the panel of thirteen jurors and show that he was admitted to the tenancy of two messuages, one cottage and one bovate of land, property which he had inherited from Percival Hey. John was also recorded as a musketer in a muster roll of 1626. He died in 1633. I am descended from him through nine generations. He lived at Birk House on the southern edge of Shelley township, the family home from at least the reign of Henry VIII until the death of another John Hey in 1719. A nineteenth-century farmstead now occupies the site. The family earned their living from weaving and farming.

Eileen A. Gooder, *Latin for Local History: an introduction* (1976), together with the various guides to handwriting referred to in the Bibliography, is of great help to anyone wishing to read documents such as this. (Yorkshire Archaeological Society, DD 181/1.)

was the typical way of life in many parts of the country, particularly in pastoral zones where farming did not require constant application. Men were described alternatively in the records as yeoman or husbandman or by their craft name, for industry and agriculture were not then regarded as two entirely separate ventures. When John Nobles, a kersey clothier in the West Riding parish of Kirkburton, made his will in 1715 he directed his supervisors to 'chuse such a master for my son where he may learn both the clothier trade and husbandry' when he reached the age of 14. The wills and inventories of the inhabitants of Pennine villages, hamlets and farmsteads show that those described as clothiers had livestock amongst their possessions and that the farmers had stores of wool, spinning wheels and looms.

In her book *Masters and Men in the West Midland Metalware Trades before the Industrial Revolution* (1975) Dr Marie Rowlands emphasizes the role of the family as the unit of production and the source of necessary capital. It did not cost much to set oneself up as a metalworker. Wills make it clear that fathers and sons worked together in the same little workshop, and perhaps the women and girls helped occasionally. Tools, especially bellows, were passed on to the eldest boy, younger sons had the opportunity to rent workshops of their own. Manor court rolls and deeds show that familes possessed small parcels of land on a variety of copyhold, leasehold and freehold tenures and that income from even the smallest holdings was often set aside to provide for dependants. The local historian's problems in tracing the descent of family properties in districts with a high rate of turnover are made even more difficult by the complicated administrative structure and settlement patterns. In the West Midlands detached portions of parishes and manors even crossed the county boundaries. Freedom from the restraining hand of a squire or a parson no doubt encouraged enterprise but it meant that much activity went unrecorded.

By the late-sixteenth century certain trades were already concentrated in particular localities within the West Midlands metalworking region. The scythemakers were found in the north Worcestershire parishes of Belbroughton, Chaddesley Corbett and Clent, the lockmakers worked mainly in Wolverhampton and its chapelries of Wednesfield and Willenhall, and the bit makers were mostly Walsall men. The same sort of pattern, with each parish having a reputation for a certain product, is discernible in the other great metalworking region, around Sheffield. Dr Rowlands observes that the Sedgley parish registers, which give occupations almost continuously from the sixteenth to the nineteenth century, demonstrate the continuity of family involvement in scythe-making, lockmaking and nailing. Newcomers often turn out to be sons-in-law or cousins. Members of metalworking families were far more likely to change their place of residence than their trade.

The importance of the family unit is most evident amongst the scythesmiths, with local dynasties such as the Rayboulds of Lower Gornal, the Waldrons of Clent, the Hill and Lea families of Bloomers End, Cradley, the Badgers of Kingswinford and others whose names constantly recur in local records. The ironmongers also built up their businesses by using the human and material resources of their families. Though the backgrounds of the successful ironmongers were varied, nearly all their families can be traced back in the neighbourhood to the sixteenth century, either through a direct line or through marriage. Likewise, in south Yorkshire, the cutlery factors and nailchapmen started in a modest way from the local ranks of metalworker-farmers whose surnames had long been characteristic ones in the area.

The Booth family were amongst the leading chapmen who organised the nail trade in the rural parishes that lay to the north of Sheffield. They provided rod iron from the local slitting mills at Wortley and Masborough and collected the finished products for sale in country fairs or for distribution down navigable rivers to the capital and abroad. Abraham Booth of Loundside, yeoman, died in 1671, leaving a widow who paid tax on three hearths the following year. Their four sons, Abraham, John, Thomas and George, were prosperous nailer-farmers and so were those of their children who were middlemen in the trade. John Booth was the first of four generations of that name who were described variously as yeomen, nailers, nailchapmen and eventually gentlemen. The third John Booth provided much of the capital for his partners, Samuel and Aaron Walker, when they established the business that eventually made them the leading ironmasters in the North of England. The fourth John Booth founded another major firm in partnership with John Hartop and George Binks, whose own families also had had a long involvement in the local metal trades. From families such as these came men with the knowledge, resources and entrepreneurial spirit that was a vital ingredient in the industrial development of their districts. The individual histories of such families should be a major concern of all those who wish to understand how Britain became the first country in the world to undergo an Industrial Revolution.

URBAN COMMUNITIES

Few English people lived in towns with more than 10,000 people during the Tudor and Stuart period, apart from those hundreds of thousands who dwelt in the capital city. London was a giant that dwarfed the rest into comparative insignificance. It was the commercial as well as the administrative capital of England and the nation's greatest port by far. The enormous number of immigrants who poured in from all over the country congested the old area within the medieval walls of the City and created new suburbs all around. William Cecil blamed the devastating plague of 1563 on the overcrowding of the central area and ordered that each house which had been subdivided during the previous year should be restored to occupation by a single family only and that recently-arrived lodgers should be removed, but such measures did not have a lasting effect. Wealthy families were already seeking more desirable surroundings beyond the walls, particularly in the western suburb that stretched all along the road to Westminster. South of the river, Southwark had effectively become a suburb rather than an independent borough, and to the north and the east of the City walls the immigrant poor clustered together in their cottages. Newcomers often found work in areas that lay outside the jurisdiction of the Lord Mayor and Corporation, in what had once been rural manors; they moved constantly from one district to another. London had well over 100 parishes. My sympathies are extended to those family historians who are trying to locate an ancestor in the capital during this period.

Far below London in size came the provincial capitals, the cities of Norwich, Bristol, York, Exeter, Newcastle upon Tyne and perhaps Salisbury and Coventry, each of which began to recover from the doldrums of the late-medieval recession during the middle years of Elizabeth's reign. Below them in the urban hierarchy came 100 or so towns with between 1,500 to 7,000 people each. Most of them retained their medieval walls and intricate street patterns and they often served as ecclesiastical or secular centres of administration, but their major role was to act as retail,

handicraft and distribution points for wide hinterlands. A simpli-
field version of this role also distinguished the 500 or so small
market towns with a population of between 600 and 1,500 inhabitants from the mere villages. Tiny though they were by today's
standards, they had a local importance out of all proportion to
their size.

Some case studies

Let us look at a few Elizabethan towns in more detail, starting
with York, the secular and ecclesiastical capital of Northern
England, a county town and large commercial centre. Its annual
fairs and three weekly markets brought sellers and purchasers
from miles around and goods from overseas were brought up the
river Ouse right into the heart of the city, York remained one of
the leading provincial centres, despite its decline to less than 8,000
people in the 1520s after the collapse of its cloth industry and the
decay of its overseas trade. By the end of Elizabeth's reign its
population had risen to 11,500, and though this was 2,500 less
than the total number of inhabitants 200 years earlier, York had
climbed back from sixth to third position amongst England's
provincial cities. The youthful immigrants who swelled the population were attracted not only from the Vale of York but from
far beyond. Lists of freemen of the city must be used with great
caution, for their coverage was far from complete, but they
indicate patterns of immigration amongst the 'middling' groups
of townsmen – the tradesmen, craftsmen and shopkeepers who
together accounted for at least half the adult male population.
Surviving lists for York name 358 men for various years between
1535 and 1566. In *Tudor York* (1979) Professor David Palliser has
shown that nearly all of the 102 freemen (28.5 per cent) who were
born in the city claimed their freedom through their father. Only
12 of the 268 men who became free through completing an
apprenticeship or by purchase were born in York. In other words,
the sons of non-freemen Yorkers had very little chance of
becoming freemen themselves. As for the incomers, about 108
freemen (47.2 per cent) were immigrants who came from within
a 20-mile radius, 75 (29.3 per cent) came from between 20 and 50
miles and 73 (28.5 per cent) came from further afield. York had a
stronger pull than smaller towns and attracted migrants over
much longer distances than most places. Seventy-two freemen

(20 per cent) came from outside Yorkshire, including 33 who came from Cumbria. The city also acted as a magnet for humbler folk, those single persons and young families who hoped to improve their fortunes by moving into York in search of work and a more comfortable home. Nearly half of these poorer people came from within a 20-mile radius, but some of the others came long distances. Very often they moved on again after a short stay, for they found that reality was harsher than their dreams.

The social hierarchy in English towns took the same shape as in the countryside, tapering from a broad base composed of those who lived on or below the poverty line to a few outstanding wealthy families. The hearth tax returns of Charles II's reign commonly record 40 per cent or more of the urban population as being exempt from payment of the tax on the grounds of their poverty. Most householders were probably employees rather than employers, men who worked as journeymen or casual labourers. Independent craftsmen and small tradesmen formed a middling group, and at the top of urban society were the merchants who were as rich as the rural gentry. The opportunities for social advance were there for all to grasp, but in practice most had to be content with their station in life.

William Hoskins was the first to analyse in depth the economic structure of a sixteenth-century town, in his essay 'An Elizabethan Provincial Town: Leicester', which was reprinted in his book, *Provincial England* (1964). Leicester had about 600 households at the beginning of Elizabeth's reign and was largely contained within its medieval walls, surrounded by open, arable fields. It was the focal point for one of the richest and most densely populated farming counties in England. As in most provincial towns of the time, the wealthiest families lived in the central area and the poorest people lived in the thickly-populated outskirts. In 1544 the top twenty-four familes owned one-third of the wealth. The occupational structure of the town can be deduced from the freemen's registers, for between 1559 and 1603 an average of about twenty men per annum, almost 900 in all, were admitted to the freedom of the city. Ten leading trades accounted for about half the total number of admissions. Leicester did not have a staple industry at this time and the high degree of dependence on the surrounding countryside is evident at once. Well over half the freemen were occupied in providing clothes, food and drink, household goods and buildings. If the distributive

Plate 2.8 Stamford in 1727 (detail)

Stamford had been one of England's finest medieval towns, full of churches and monastic buildings and prosperous because of its international wool trade. But during the Tudor and Stuart period it declined to the status of a local market town on the Great North Road. A new era of prosperity came in the eighteenth century as the volume of traffic increased and the markets expanded, so that from the mid 1720s onwards Stamford was rebuilt in the Georgian styles popularized in the pattern books of Batty Langley, William Halfpenny and William Salmon. The town was by-passed by the railway in the mid-nineteenth century and so entered into another period of stagnation, the happy result of which is that Stamford is now one of England's best preserved Georgian towns.

This view of Stamford from the south was engraved for Francis Peck's *Academia Tertia Anglicana*, published in 1727, just before the eighteenth-century rebuilding got under way. It therefore provides a fascinating glimpse of the town as it appeared during the reign of George I. As today, the skyline is dominated by the towers and spires of the lovely churches that survived from the era of medieval prosperity. The thirteenth-century tower and fourteenth-century broach spire of St. Mary's and the fifteenth-century towers of All Saints and St John the Baptist were built in grey limestone from local quarries at Barnack, Clipsham, Ketton and Weldon, names that are known to builders and students of

trades are included with the above, then three freemen out of every five provided for the customer. Smiths, wheelwrights, butchers, tanners, graziers and husbandmen had direct links with the rural hinterland. The lists also show that the Elizabethan era was a period of considerable economic change as the woolstaplers were replaced by the butchers and the tanners; cattle rather than sheep became the basis of local wealth, especially after 1541 when the disappearance of the Wyggestons removed a family which had dominated the town's economy for two or three generations. Even though sons followed their father's trade with a high degree of regularity, it was rare for a family busines to last in Leicester for more than 100 years. The Norrice family were exceptional in remaining tanners from 1493 to 1670, otherwise only the Newcombers (bell-founders), Herricks (ironmongers), Tatams (tanners) and Stanfords (butchers) stayed in the same business for a century or more.

In his study of *The City of Worcester in the Sixteenth Century* (1973) Dr Alan Dyer has shown that Worcester was far more reliant upon a single trade than most Elizabethan towns, certainly much more so than Leicester. At the time of the 1525 lay subsidy a comparatively small group of thirty individuals (6 per cent of those taxed), who were assessed on goods valued at more than £30, dominated the political, economic and social life of the community. A broad middle section of self-employed tradesmen formed the backbone of this urban society, but nearly 50 per cent of those who were taxed were dependent on their wages and were likely to be reduced to poverty in times of depression. Worcester's population doubled from 4,000 to 8,000 between the mid-sixteenth and the mid-seventeenth century, a rise that is explained equally by natural increase and by immigration. The dominant trade was the production and processing of woollen cloth, crafts that engaged well over half the adult male population at the end of the Elizabethan era. Apart from the all-important cloth trade,

---

architecture throughout the land. The consistent use of local materials, not just for public buildings but for houses, cottages and other structures, was entirely typical of England before the age of canals and railways. Because of this our provincial towns acquired a distinctive appearance, a special character that has often been lost in recent years through glass-and-concrete redevelopment. Stamford has retained its splendid individuality and in its architecture it speaks eloquently of former periods of prosperity and decline.

however, the city had the normal, diversified economic structure that one would expect to find in a major provincial market centre and head of diocesan administration. Between them, Worcester men in the first half of the seventeenth century had at least 100 different occupations. The three weekly markets and four annual fairs were a regular attraction for buyers and sellers within a 10 or 12 miles radius. Worcester was well-positioned to fulfil this role, for it was sited at the edge of an arable area to the south and east and a pastoral zone to the north and west. The city had a relatively 'open' society and was the goal of countless migrants, but, as at Leicester, it is difficult to find many examples of families which stayed for more than three generations. Sixteenth-century towns do not appear to have had a solid group of stable families in the same way as so many contemporary rural parishes. Tudor urban families often either died out or disappeared very quickly.

Chesterfield will serve as our example of a small town in this era. In 1563 it had no more than 1,000 to 1,200 inhabitants, but it was still the second most important town in Derbyshire. The population of its large parish, which included several rural outliers, stood at about 2,700. The lay-out of the town had been established back in the twelfth century when a new market place had replaced the old, congested commercial area alongside the church. When William Senior drew his map of *c.*1635 Chesterfield had still not expanded beyond its medieval limits. A regular pattern of narrow lanes gave a special character to the Shambles at the eastern edge of the market place, as indeed it does today, and narrow street frontages and long gardens and alleys preserved the medieval property divisions of the old burgage plots. But Chesterfield had no rich merchants to build fine town houses round the market place; the more prominent families were not conspicuously different from the rest. The characteristic townsmen worked at a craft to meet purely local demands. About 85 per cent of the 215 probate inventories which were appraised within the parish between 1521 and 1603 were valued at less than £50 and 68 per cent were priced under £30. Chesterfield wills and inventories show that the manufacture of woollen cloth – the most important industry in Tudor England – was basic to both the urban and the rural economy, for one in every three or four people in the parish had equipment such as spinning wheels, cards or looms or small quantities of wool. Second in importance came the leather trades. The Chesterfield tanneries were sited at the edge of the town by the small river Hipper, a sensible precaution that was followed by most towns to keep away the smell and the flies. The tanners' chief customers were the shoemakers, but of course quite a variety of goods, ranging from bottles to garments and from saddles to straps, were made out of leather. Thirdly, Chesterfield shared in the region's involvement in metal trades, though to a much lesser extent than its northerly neighbour, Sheffield; the parish had its cutlers, scythemakers, nailers, locksmiths and Ralph Hethcote, the bellfounder. Of course, Chesterfield's range of occupations was limited when compared with what was on offer in Worcester, Leicester or York, but the stalls and shops gathered in and around the market place provided goods and services that attracted rural families from miles around. At the end of the seventeenth century Celia Fiennes enthused that Chesterfield's Saturday market was 'like some little faire, a great deal of corne and all sorts of ware and fowles'.

During the later years of the seventeenth century and the opening decades of the eighteenth a few provincial towns began to grow rapidly. Spa towns led by Bath, ports headed by Bristol and Liverpool and including the new venture at Whitehaven, and manufacturing centres like Birmingham, Leeds, Manchester and Sheffield began to grow at a significant rate. This thriving group included some of the old provincial capitals such as Bristol, Newcastle and Norwich. During the seventeenth century Norwich's population rose from about 12,000 or 13,000 to around 30,000, an extraordinary rate of expansion in a century where growth was generally sluggish after the 1630s. Dr Penelope Corfield estimates that the net increase of newcomers into the city reached about 400 per annum during the 1670s and 1680s. They came mostly from Norfolk and Suffolk, but (like York) Norwich was able to attract people from distant places. For instance, during the 1680s between 100 and 200 Huguenots settled in the city. Surviving papers relating to the removal of 433 paupers and vagrants between 1740 and 1762 show that 40 per cent of these unfortunates had come from other parts of East Anglia, 15 per cent had travelled up to 100 miles, 6 per cent had started from London and Middlesex and 39 per cent originated elsewhere, including thirty-three people from Scotland and sixteen from Ireland. Beggars and vagrants, of course, may have been exceptionally mobile. The places of origin of 1,601 Norwich apprentices between 1710 and 1731 show a preponderance of short-distance migration. Only 6 per cent came from outside the county; 43 per cent came from Norwich itself, 22 per cent came from the rest of Norfolk and 29 per cent of places were unrecorded. Norwich's growth was not at the expense of its rural hinterland, however, for the surrounding villages grew as well.

When we turn to the registers of the freemen who comprised roughly half the adult male workforce of Norwich, the importance of the worsted industry is immediately apparent. In the years between the Restoration of Charles II and the middle of the eighteenth century, textile trades provided employment for almost 50 per cent of the freemen. From the 1670s and 1680s onwards the colourful and varied light-weight fabrics known as 'Norwich Stuffs' became fashionable and gave a new stimulus to an old industry. The other half of the local freemen worked at the food and drink trades (10.5 per cent), clothing (8.9), leather (7.9), building (5.8), the professions (5.4), the metal trades (3.2) or at a variety of miscellaneous tasks. The late-seventeenth century prosperity of Norwich owed much to the consumer trades. Grocers, confectioners and tobacconists imported exotic goods in bulk and haberdashers, apothecaries, ironmongers and booksellers catered for growing local demand. The Norfolk county gentry began to build fine houses in the town, and to cater for their needs and those of the affluent merchants a new group of professional men, notably attorneys, architects and physicians, set up trade and flourished, as did their fellow professionals in other provincial towns. The hub of all this activity was found in and around the market place and the Guildhall and down towards the Cathedral. No clear distinction could yet be made between the wholesale and retail trades that were carried on in the 'shops' in the historic centre of the city. Norwich continued its ancient role as a major marketing centre, but its expansion owed more to the spectacular growth of the worsted trades. Weavers from as far away as Taunton and Exeter were found in Norwich in 1674, and many others came in search of employment in this labour-intensive craft.

Northampton was another elegant county town and regional market centre and was known far and wide for its horse fairs. It was much smaller than Norwich, but its population doubled from *c*.3,500 in the 1560s to *c*.7,000 in the 1770s. During the same period the number of apprentices more than trebled from 80 to 250 as the town became a specialist craft centre offering a wide variety of trades. Like many another eighteenth century town, its economy was becoming more complex and sophisticated. Northampton has an excellent series of apprenticeship registers which list the name, trade, father's name, and place of birth of nearly 3,500 boys between 1562 and 1776. Professor Alan Everitt's analysis of these registers, in *Ways and Means in Local History* (1971), shows that forty-five different trades and crafts were recorded between 1562 and 1601 and that this figure rose to eighty-three between 1654 and 1705 and then to 114 between 1716 and 1776. His analysis of the occupations recorded in the Northampton militia list for 1777, which names men aged between eighteen and forty-five who were liable for militia duty if required, reveals that craftsmen formed about half of Northampton's adult male workforce. Shoemakers already formed the largest group and various types of woodworkers were also prominent. Intimate links with the countryside were maintained, for the craftsmen drew upon local resources for their raw materials and also serviced a wide area.

Other sources show that the wealthiest group in town – the professionals and the innkeepers – were under-represented in the militia returns. The later seventeenth century had seen a marked rise in the number of lawyers, scriveners, physicians, surgeons, apothecaries and schoolmasters, whose most prosperous members formed a type of urban gentry who were able to lead a leisured life without the support of a landed estate. They and the principal innkeepers occupied the aldermanic pews at the front of All Saints church, where the social hierarchy was as carefully formalized in the seating arrangements as in any rural parish. The leading inn-keepers ranked amongst the richest men in Northampton, just like their counterparts in other busy towns. Inns provided much more than accommodation, for they were the venues for feasts and banquets, cultural and social activities, business ventures and political affairs. Professor Everitt has written that innkeepers were among the most mobile elements in the community, but that only a minority established dynasties that lasted for three or four generations. In Northampton, the Pratts were innholders from the reign of Henry VIII to George I, the Lyons family lasted for four generations and in the mid-seventeenth century had three brothers who were prominent in the trade, and the Peaches eventually acquired quite a chain of inns. They all belonged to an influential group of related families at the very centre of urban life in seventeenth and eighteenth century Northampton.

Sheffield was a very different type of town, but like most other places that developed into great Victorian cities it had already had a long history as a market and craft centre. As it was not a corporate borough it has no freemen's registers, other than those of the Cutlers' Company, but for certain periods the parish registers give the occupations of recorded males. From 1 October 1698 onwards they are particularly informative and individuals can be located either within the town or within the rural parts of the parish. During a five-year period up to 30 September 1703 the occupations of 763 of the 902 recorded townsmen are given in the baptism and burial registers. As many as 450 (57.3 per cent) worked in the cutlery trades or other metalworking jobs, and another 203 men (26.6 per cent) were employed in other trades or crafts. Seventeen richer individuals who were described as gentlemen or by the name of their profession formed only 2.2 per cent of the sample. They were gathered in the High Street and around the market place, but could not compete with the standard of living of those at the upper end of the social scale in the county towns and old corporate boroughs. Sheffield already had that working-class character that was to be so marked during Victorian times. When Daniel Defoe came this way during the first quarter of the eighteenth century he observed that:

> This town of Sheffield is very populous and large, the streets narrow, and the houses dark and black, occasioned by the continued smoke of the forges, which are always at work . . . . The manufacture of hard ware, which has been so antient in this town, is not only continued, but much encreased . . . .

By forges Defoe meant cutlers' smithies; it appeared to him that Sheffield already had a pronounced industrial character, and though it was very small by later standards it struck him as being 'very populous and large'. By 1736 the population of the town of Sheffield stood at 10,121, which was about three and a half times higher than it had been a couple of generations earlier in 1672.

The absence of a prosperous merchant class meant that Sheffield had few fine houses or public buildings. However, many townsmen were reasonably well-off by the standards of the time and were able to rebuild their modest dwellings. A visitor in 1725 wrote:

> There has been a great part of the town, which was made up chiefly of wooden houses, rebuilt within these few years and now makes no mean figure in brick particularly towards the north side of it, where there are abundance of new erections upon new foundations by which the town has lately been considerably enlarged.

Plate 2.9 Sheffield saw-smiths
An undated photograph (used as a postcard) of a traditional Sheffield craft that goes back to the eighteenth century. Ten saw manufacturers were recorded in Gales and Martin's *Directory of Sheffield* in 1787, when the making of circular saws was already a local speciality.

Setting the teeth of the saws was the final stage of manufacture. Each alternate tooth was struck with a hammer so as to bend it a little, then the saw was turned over and the remaining teeth were treated in the same way.

One can see from this photograph why foremen became the butt of music hall jokes.

By that time the Sheffield cutlers were selling their goods all over Britain and large quantities of knives, scissors, saws and scythes were being exported to America. Within a few years the improved navigability of the River Don enabled them to compete even more successfully in distant markets. The population of the town soon began to expand at a phenomenal rate. By the nineteenth century a new hierarchy of provincial towns had been established, led by manufacturing settlements that were often not even dignified by the title of borough, let alone that of a city.

Fisher Row, Oxford

Urban historians who deal with comparatively large populations limit the scale of their enquiries to aggregative studies. The sheer bulk of the material makes it difficult for them to do otherwise. In 1982, however, Dr Mary Prior published the results of a different approach and showed just how revealing a detailed study of an urban occupational group over the centuries could be. In so doing she demonstrated the vital role of the family in early-modern towns. Her book, *Fisher Row: Fishermen, Bargemen and Canal Boatmen in Oxford, 1500–1900*, depicts 'a very tight-knit community of boat-people who were united both by occupation and kinship'. Fisher Row lay on the west bank of the Castle Mill stream, a small tributary of the Thames, in three sections known as Upper, Middle and Lower Fisher Row. Three groups of river-people lived here; firstly the fishermen, then the bargemen who plied their trade on the navigable river, and finally the boatmen who married into the older families after the opening of the Oxford Canal in 1790. At its most populous, between the 1790s and the 1840s, Fisher Row contained some 300–400 people.

The early history of the inhabitants of the Row can be pieced together in a limited fashion from leases and from entries in the freemen's registers. During the sixteenth and early seventeenth centuries all the fishermen and most of the bargemen were freemen of fairly high status; their homes were modest yet comfortable and they held their property on leases for years at a low annual rent but high entry fine. Fishing was rather like farming in that a river fishery was a limited resource that could support only a restricted number of people. Families were there-fore nuclear and patriarchal and only one son inherited the patri-mony. Other sons, however, often married the daughters of neigbouring fishermen or bargemen. The Row was a highly-traditional society where the skills of the trade were passed on from generation to generation.

Oxford's Elizabethan and Stuart fishermen were not poor but they never rose to prominence in the city, despite being well-connected on occasion. They provided the citizens with a wide variety of fresh fish for its fast days and during the close seasons they exploited all the resources of the riverside that they could utilize. By-employments such as basket-making, hemp-dressing and wild-fowling gave them additional security. Families such as the Hickses, who occupied the second and third tenements, remained in the Row for several generations. Right through from the mid sixteenth century to the end of the seventeenth one of these families was always recorded as Bonner alias Pitt, a continuity in the use of a double-barrelled surname that Dr Prior thinks suggests a certain family pride. The Fisher Row community had few surnames and they used the same Christian names over and over again. When they were amongst themselves they used nicknames, but as these rarely appear in official documents the historian has a difficult task to disentangle one member from another.

The first boatman to be accepted into the freedom of the city was admitted in 1583. The different nature of a boatman's work compared to that of a fisherman led to different forms of inheritance and to a contrasting family structure. Primogeniture was not the inheritance system used by the bargemen for the successful bargemaster could provide openings for all his sons. Having several sons in the trade worked to the general benefit of the family business which could thereby offer a wider range of services. The nature of their work brought bargemen together in a mutually-dependent way. Boat-haling demanded enormous co-operative effort and trips down the river to London could take anything from nearly two to eight weeks when drought, flood, frost or wind made the going difficult or impossible. The families along the river were closely related and inter-marriage had fused them into a larger unit.

Fisher Row was similar to some of the contemporary rural communities which have been studied in depth in that it had a stable core of local families which remained for generation after generation while another group which included carters, drovers and seasonal workers who found cheap lodgings in the parish were always on the move. Dr Prior makes the point that the mobility of the inhabitants of a parish does not depend on how many people leave the district but on who they are. A high turnover of newcomers does not have a serious effect on the community if a substantial group of native families remain rooted in the same spot, but if over the years it is the oldest families that are emigrating then the parish structure will be unstable. In St Thomas's, the riverside parish which contained Fisher Row, the older families stayed where they were; amongst the most stable groups were the bargemen and fishermen. A list of the heads of households in Upper and Middle Fisher Row in 1772 shows that the area was inhabited by a series of closely-related families. In Mary Prior's words, 'the area had become a sort of large household under many adjacent roof trees. It is perhaps a matter of definition whether such families are counted as extended families or not'.

The barging families were of two sorts; the rich and the powerful families such as the Tawneys and the Clarkes of Lower Fisher Row, and the numerous poorer ones like the Gardners and the Crawfords of Upper and Middle Fisher Row. The Tawneys (ancestors of the great historian R. H. Tawney) were one of the oldest and most successful families in the community, for they married into the brewers who dominated eighteenth-century Oxford. Families such as the Gardners, on the other hand, never made links with outside interests but confined their activities to the moving of boats along the river. They suffered from this limitation of enterprise in times of depression.

The lack of developed commercial institutions at this time meant that businesses such as barging were inevitably family-based. The world of Fisher Row – and no doubt of other occupational groups in early-modern times – was one that thought in terms of family duties and privileges, of family alliances and of inheritance through the family. All households in the Row were inter-married, but whereas the nuclear family prevailed amongst the fishermen, the extended family was the norm for the bargemen and also for their nineteenth-century successors, the canal boatmen. Different patterns of work made different demands on the family. In the canal carrying business the number of sons who could be involved was limitless and women and children could help to work the boats. While the canal boatmen were away without their families the women who remained were drawn together for mutual support. It was the women, in fact, who provided stability for this new type of community.

The canal boatmen who came to live in Fisher Row upon the opening of the Oxford Canal in 1790 were a colourful group with distinctive dress, customs and style of boat decoration which had been developed in the previous two decades upon the canals of the Midlands. Work on a canal was a very different experience from boat-haling. Strong groups of men were not needed on the artificial waterways; two people and a horse sufficed. Because of the length of a trip, canal boatmen began to live on their boats and by the 1820s their wives and children sometimes lived and worked alongside them. Dr Prior writes:

> The boatmen came and went, so that the boat-people's community ashore was largely one of women, often living together, helping and supporting each other in the absence of their husbands. These households were not necessarily based on a home ashore at all times. During the life-cycle of the family it was easier to maintain a

home ashore at some times than at others. A home ashore was always regarded as desirable, but it was not always economically possible. The age of the children, their number, the ability of the wife to earn a second income at home, whilst the elder children helped run the boat, the responsibility for dependent relatives, the possibility of sharing a house: such factors governed the decision to keep up a home on the land.

Focal points for the community were provided by the pubs and the chapel, which also reinforced the Row's sense of separateness from the rest of the parish. For a boatman whose home was on the river, the pub was not only a social centre but a base where goods could be left, messages collected and horses stabled. The families which ran the pubs were closely related to the rest of the community. By the time of the 1841 census the three sections of Fisher Row were inhabited by one large kin-group. At first sight these bonds are not obvious for the surnames were numerous. The crucial links were provided by the women. Because a boatman was always on the move, his wife remained in the Row when she married, staying amongst the relations and friends she had known since she was a child. The nature of the work dictated the shape of the family and the particular ethos of this riverside community. Fisher Row is a special case, but Dr Prior's fascinating study has much to teach us about other occupational groups within our urban societies.

CHAPTER THREE
Late-Georgian and Victorian England

BASIC RECORDS

The family historian's initial task of tracing his ancestors back
through the nineteenth century is relatively straightforward,
thanks to the information provided by civil registration certificates
and census returns and by standardized Church of England registers. However, Nonconformist ancestors can be rather elusive.

Census returns

In 1801, when the first national census was taken, the population
of England and Wales was recorded at 8.9 millions. It is generally
accepted that large numbers of people evaded the attention of the
enumerators on that occasion and that if allowance is made for
under-recording the total should be raised to about 9.2 millions.
Later census figures are more reliable. Substantial growth had
already taken place during the course of the eighteenth century,
but after 1801 the pace quickened so that by 1851 the population
of England and Wales stood at 17.9 millions. By 1911, shortly
before the First World War, it had reached 36.1 millions. It is
essential for the local and family historian to grasp this basic
demographic information and to understand its profound consequences for the nature of English society. In 1801 most English
people still lived in a rural environment; only one person in every
three lived in a town and most of those towns were small by
modern standards. Half a century later the 1851 census provided
clear evidence that an historic turning point had been reached; the
returns showed that for the first time more people lived in towns

than in the countryside. By 1881 two out of every three people were urban dwellers and by 1911 the transformation was complete with only one out of every five people still living in farmsteads, hamlets or villages.

A national census has been taken every decade since 1801, except for the year 1941 when Britain was at war. The first four counts are of limited use to the historian for they do not list individual households, but they do provide population figures on a township basis. These figures are printed in *A Comparative Account of the Population of Great Britain in the Years 1801, 1811, 1821 and 1831*, published as a parliamentary paper in 1831. Later census figures were published as they became available. It is usually easier, however, to turn to an early volume of *The Victoria County History of England* (in counties which have been covered by that enterprise), where all the nineteenth-century data are listed in tabular form. From 1841 onwards much more information is available in the form of census enumerators' books. At the time of writing, the 1881 census is the latest to have been made available for public consultation because of the restriction imposed by the 100 years rule. The enumerators' returns can be consulted on microfilm at the Portugal Street annexe of the Public Record Office, just off Chancery Lane, and microfilm copies for local areas are often available at county record offices and major libraries.

The census taken in June 1841 is of less value than those taken in later years. The exact place of birth is not recorded; all that was required was a tick in the Yes or No column in answer to the question of whether or not a person was born in the county of his or her present residence. A further problem for the genealogist was caused by the decision to round down ages over fifteen to the nearest five. Thus, anyone listed as aged fifty-five could have been any age between fifty-five and fifty-nine. Nevertheless, the 1841 census is a useful source, close in date to the start of civil registration. The returns may explain a family relationship, they record each person's occupation, and at the very least they demonstrate that an ancestor was still alive at that date. From 1851 onwards the recorded ages were supposed to be accurate and the precise places of birth were noted. Armed with this information, the genealogist should be able to track down the relevant baptism entry in a parish or nonconformist register in the years before civil registration began.

Locating a census return for a household in a rural area is a relatively straightforward task, but those historians who are investigating a large Victorian town may at first be overwhelmed by the sheer bulk of the material. For the 1851 census, for example, Sheffield was divided into 139 enumerators' districts, whose boundaries sometimes ran down the middle of a street. A lot of time might be spent fruitlessly before the entry that one wants is found. But then one often comes across other entries to amuse one on the way, such as the record of an enumerator's problems in compiling part of the 1871 census for Sheffield shown in Table 2.

The enumerators were amateurs who made mistakes and sometimes misunderstood their instructions, and human errors occurred when the original schedules were copied onto the printed forms. Nor were the Attercliffe gypsies the only people who misled the enumerators through fear, ignorance or simple forgetfulness. Nevertheless, census returns are amongst the most reliable records that a local and family historian is likely to use. They were centrally organized, compiled on a uniform and universal basis, and backed by sanctions when co-operation was not forthcoming.

John Beckett and Trevor Foulds have recently used a computer to analyse the 1851 and 1861 census returns for the Nottinghamshire open field village of Laxton. In 'Beyond the Micro: Laxton, The Computer and Social Change Over Time', published in *The Local Historian*, volume 16, no. 8 (1985), pp. 451–6, they remark on the contrast between a high turnover of individuals in the village and an underlying stability of households. Laxton's population fell from 534 in 1851 to 500 a decade later. Only 247 individuals appeared in both returns; the local parish register records the burial of 61 people in the intervening period, but another 226 individuals disappeared from the local scene. Of the 500 inhabitants recorded in 1861, 247 had been there for at least ten years, 125 were children born since the previous census, and 128 (65 males and 63 females) were newcomers, mostly from neighbouring parishes. But Laxton was a much more stable community than these figures might lead us to suppose. No fewer than 75 of the 99 households recorded in 1861 had been there ten years earlier. During that decade only 1 in 7 farms had changed hands and only 1 in 4 cottages. Even 2 out of every 3 farm labouring families stayed put and overall 3 out of every 4 households remained virtually the same. Half the personnel of the village had changed, but in terms of household structure Laxton

Table 2 An entry from the 1871 census for Sheffield

Place	Name		Relation	Age	Occupation	Where born
Gypsey tent, Attercliffe	Henry (alias Francis Brown)	Stapleton	Head	51	Gypsey clothes peg maker	Not Known
River Street, Attercliffe	Black Bud	Stapleton	Son	12	Gypsey clothes peg maker	Not Known
	Cox	Stapleton	Son	10	Gypsey clothes peg maker	Not Known
	Granney alias Nuity	Stapleton	Unmarried Mistress	45		Not Known
	Eaney	Stapleton	Daughter	6		Not Known
	Frightful	Stapleton	Son	5		Not Known
	Black Sandy	Stapleton	Son	3		Not Known
	Nipper Harriet	Stapleton	Daughter	2 months		Attercliffe

(The only information the enumerator could get. Probably the informant has his own reasons for suppressing particulars.)

was a stable community. Moreover, movement into the village was predominantly of people born within a few miles of its borders. As in earlier times, people moved frequently within a wider neighbourhood than the parish, but usually they did not travel very far.

Civil registration

The civil registration of all births, marriages and deaths in England and Wales began on 1 July 1837 and continues to the present day. Indexes of all these events can be consulted free of charge at St Catherine's House, Aldwych, London, and upon payment of a fee a copy of a certificate may be obtained. Local registry offices will also supply copies of certificates if the event was recorded in their district, but they do not provide facilities for consulting indexes and so the genealogist has to have fairly precise information before a successful search for a certificate can be made. At St Catherine's House, however, one has access to indexes covering events in every part of the country. Providing one is fit enough to lift heavy indexes from the shelves and aggressive enough to elbow aside other searchers the task is relatively straightforward.

Registration districts usually cover very different areas from the administrative units that the local historian is more familiar with. They are much larger than parishes or townships. Even if one knows that an ancestor was buried in a certain parish, finding the appropriate registration district in the indexes can be problematic. The Heys who were born, married and died in Thurlstone township within Penistone parish, were indexed under Wortley registration district, which was named after a small village 6 miles away. A little elementary knowledge of the geography of the area that one is searching is usually sufficient to solve the problem of correct identification. In this connection it is worth bearing in mind that a hospital birth will be recorded in the registration district in which the hospital stands and not in the district which contains the parents' home. The Institute of Heraldic and Genealogical Studies, Northgate, Canterbury, have published two maps showing the registration and census districts as they were between 1837 and 1851 and between 1852 and 1946, though they do not mark exact boundaries.

The registration procedure is as prone to human error as any other system of recording. Names may be mis-spelt on the orig-

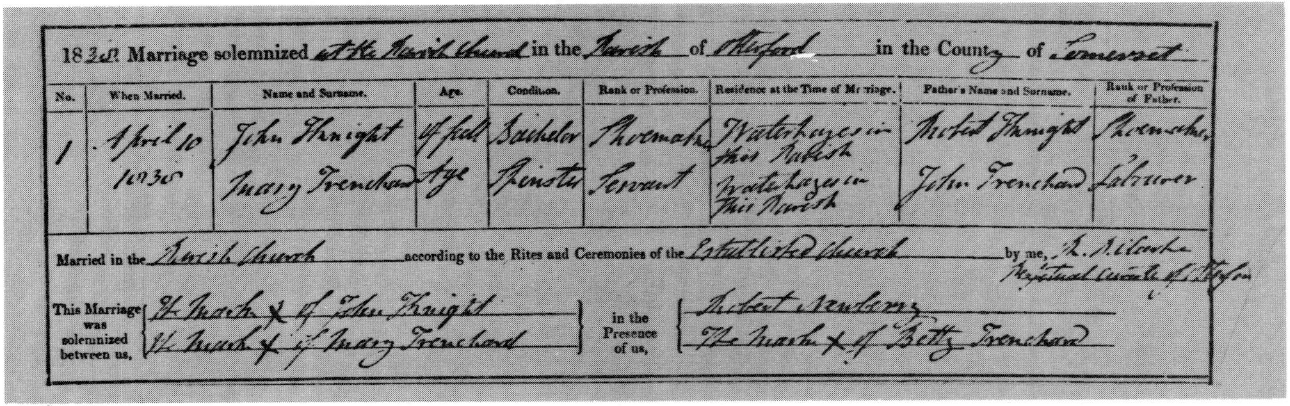

Plate 3.1 The marriage certificate of John Knight and Mary Trenchard, 10 April 1838

The certificate, which was found through a search of the indexes at St Catherine's House, records the marriage of two of my great-great-grandparents at the parish church of Otterford in Somerset. John Knight, the son of Robert Knight, shoemaker, followed his father's occupation at Waterhayes, an old stone and thatch farm on the side of a combe a mile to the east of St Leonard's church. Mary Trenchard, the daughter of John Trenchard, labourer, was working as a servant at Waterhayes at the time of her marriage. Unfortunately, the ages of the married couple are not given, for they were merely noted as being of full age, a common method of recording. John and Mary both signed with a mark, as did Betty Trenchard, one of the witnesses.

inal certificate, in the index or by the transcriber if a modern copy has been made. When I obtained the death certificate of Thomas Batty (1882), I read that he had lived at Mastington; I eventually discovered that this was a copyist's error for Markington. Such mistakes are easily made; the point is that one should not treat any historical document as gospel. Ages recorded on death certificates (and to a lesser extent on marriage certificates) were not always accurate because the informant did not know for sure. Sooner or later the searcher will fail to find a registration that he is looking for. This may be explained by misspellings or misreadings. (Hey recorded as Key, for instance) or by the choice of alternative Christian names (e.g. the second one used in preference to the first) or by evasion of the system before penalties were introduced in 1875. It has been estimated that in the early years of civil registration in some parts of England up to 15 per cent of births were not registered. Apparently, the counties of Surrey, Sussex, Middlesex, Essex and Shropshire were the worst recorded up to about 1860, after which time they were as efficient as anywhere else in the country.

Birth, marriage and death certificates each contain information that enables the researcher to take another step further back in time. Thus, although the age at death is not recorded in the indexes before 1866, it does appear on the actual certificates right from the beginning of the system in 1837. Marriage certificates, unfortunately, often enter 'Of full age' in the column marked 'Age', but where precise information is given it is an easy step to go on to discover the birth certificates of the married couple. The information provided by the certificate of the marriage of two of my wife's ancestors, solemnized at the church of St Andrew, Newtown Kinson in the county of Dorset, is shown in Table 3.

It was a simple task to find Moses Downer's birth registered twenty-one years earlier under the registration district of Fordingbridge, not many miles away just across the Hampshire county boundary. Even in Victorian times there were relatively few people named Moses. His birth certificate, however, casts doubts on the marriage certificate's claim that a Charles Downer was his father. This can be seen in the abstract of the details of the certificate shown in Table 4. There was a time, not long ago, when families would do all they could to suppress such information. An illegitimate birth in the degrading surroundings of the workhouse was about the deepest stigma that anyone could bear at the start

Table 3 Abstract of the marriage certificate of Moses Downer and Mary Sandey

When married	Name and surname	Age	Condition	Rank or profession	Residence at the time of marriage	Father's name and surname	Rank or profession of father
30 June 1888	Moses Downer	21	Bachelor	Labourer	Newton Kinson	Charles Downer	Deceased
	Mary Jane Sandey	19	Spinster	—	Newton Kinson	Charles Sandey	Labourer

Table 4 Abstract of the birth certificate of Moses Downer

When and where born	Name	Sex	Name and surname of father	Name, surname and maiden surname of mother	Occupation of father	Signature, description and residence of informant
2 January 1867 Union Workhouse Fordingbridge	Moses	Boy	—	Elizabeth Downer	—	X The mark of Elizabeth Downer, Mother. Union Workhouse, Fordingbridge

of life. Thomas Hardy's story of the death of poor little Fanny Robin and her new-born child in *Far From the Madding Crowd* is etched on the memory of all who have read it. Hardy was describing in fiction the real and very harsh position that unmarried mothers from the poorer sections of society found themselves in. Fordingbridge was within the Wessex region where Hardy set his tales, and Elizabeth Downer gave birth to her son in the workhouse just seven years before his book was published. Now that the workhouses have gone, the family historian is able to take a more detached view, to reflect on hardships endured and disabilities overcome, to ponder on the changing fortunes of families through the generations, and to feel a deep sympathy for those unfortunates whose lives were marred by remorseless poverty. The study of family history in its wider setting soon dispels the myth of 'the good old days'.

Nonconformity

The genealogist who has traced his family tree as far back as is possible through the use of the civil registration records kept at St Catherine's House, London, and local registry offices then turns naturally to the baptism, marriage and burial registers of the Church of England for the preceding generations. He may find, however, that during the decades immediately before the commencement of civil registration in 1837 the answers to his queries are to be found not in the records of the Established Church but in the registers of one or more of the various Nonconformist sects. Every local and family historian needs to acquire at least a working knowledge of the history of religious dissent in his selected region and a familiarity with the national background. In particular he must be aware that Nonconformity flourished in certain types of local communities and that the social composition of the various denominations was often markedly different from sect to sect. For a start he should read Alan Everitt's essay, *The Pattern of Rural Dissent: the Nineteenth Century* (1972), which makes many points of general interest through an analysis of the differing experiences of the counties of Leicestershire, Northamptonshire, Kent and that part of Lincolnshire known as Lindsey.

Professor Everitt emphasizes that general comments on differences between each county carry less weight than observations based on local variations in parish type. 'The significant fact', he writes, 'is that in each county Dissent tended to be associated chiefly with certain forms of local society, while it was largely absent from others'. One must, of course, always stress the human factor and beware the danger of geographical determinism; nevertheless, it is revealing to find that 86 per cent of estate villages in Kent had no Dissenting chapel, but that such places of worship were common in the scattered settlements of former forest or wood-pasture zones. 'Open' villages where landowner-ship was 'much divided' were receptive to Dissent and so were large parishes where population growth in the outlying parts had made nonsense of the old ecclesiastical arrangements. Market towns, industrial villages and boundary settlements were all likely to have their Nonconformists. Sometimes certain families adhered to the same religious beliefs for several generations. The continuity in the Dissenting tradition in such places is often remarkable.

On Sunday 29 March 1851 a census was taken of the attendance at all religious services held that day. This was the only occasion that the state made such a count. The results were profoundly disturbing for the Church of England. In the first place it was clear that well over half the population of England and Wales did not attend any form of religious service at all on that particular day. In the great Victorian cities of Birmingham, Liverpool, Manchester, Newcastle and Sheffield fewer than one in ten of the population went to church or chapel; the industrial working classes mostly stayed at home. Secondly, about half of those who did attend for worship chose to go to a Nonconformist chapel. In some parts of the country, e.g. Cornwall and the North-east, the proportion of Nonconformists was even higher. Throughout the country Dissenters normally formed at least one-third of all worshippers. The situation had been transformed radically since the mid eighteenth century when Nonconformist groups were relatively small and few in number. Even further back, in Charles II's reign, the Compton ecclesiastical census of 1676 had suggested that Dissenters then formed only 4 per cent of the nation at large, though in some communities Dissent had taken a much stronger hold. The Compton census figures probably understate the strength of Nonconformity, but it is clear that the number of adherents did not rise dramatically until the Evangelical Revival of the later-eighteenth and nineteenth centuries. Victorian Nonconformity was altogether different in tone and scale from the Old Dissent of 1660–1760.

The Old Dissenting sects consisted of the Presbyterians, Independents (also known as Congregationalists), Baptists, Unitarians and Quakers. Some congregations changed their allegiance over time. Moreover, the names were sometimes used loosely, so that for instance 'Presbyterian' congregations might in fact have been Independent or Unitarian. The family historian who wishes to use early Dissenting records should consult D. J. Steel, *Sources for Nonconformist Genealogy and Family History* (1972), but he should bear in mind that seventeenth and early-eighteenth century Nonconformists often used the baptism, marriage and burial services of the Established Church and that these events will be recorded in the Church of England registers.

Old Dissent gained a foothold where the Church of England was weakest, especially in isolated communities scattered throughout those large rural parishes that stretched over the moors, the marshlands and old wood-pasture areas and also in certain types of towns. Thus in 1676 an estimated 300 of the 3,000 or so communicants in the industrial parish of Sheffield were said to be Dissenters. The town and its surrounding rural communities already had a long tradition of Dissent, but just over 20 miles to the east the situation in Doncaster was very different. Here only eight of the 3,000 communicants were Nonconformists. In an address to Charles II in 1681 the mayor proclaimed that 'We can truly say without boasting that we have neither in our town nor corporation one dissenter from the present government in church and state'. Not until the Methodists came did Doncaster turn to Nonconformity.

The way in which an older pattern of Dissent was replaced by a newer one as a result of the Evangelical Revival is examined in my article, 'The Pattern of Nonconformity in South Yorkshire, 1660–1851', *Northern History*, VIII (1973), pp. 86–118. A few points of general interest might usefully be restated here. Lay support from the ranks of the rural gentry and the urban tradesmen had been vital in preserving Nonconformity during the years of repression after the Restoration. These determined sects emerged in the time of toleration as the early centres of Dissent. Often a rural gentry family dominated a chapel in the same way as an Anglican squire of an estate village imposed his authority upon the local congregation of the Established Church. If the family allegiance to a particular sect changed then the whole local membership might follow the same path. Thus, at Great Houghton near Barnsley Sir Edward Rhodes built a chapel *c.* 1650

Plate 3.2 High Flatts Meeting House, Yorkshire

In 1764 Archbishop Drummond was informed by the minister of St John the Baptist's church, Penistone, that about 100 people gathered for worship each Sunday in this Friends' Meeting House. The hamlet in which it stands was known locally as Quaker Bottom for all the house-holders were members. It stood close to the parish boundary and attracted people from many distant parts.

The building is eighteenth century in style but lacks decorative details and therefore cannot be dated closely. Meetings appear to have started here in the late seventeenth century and the Jackson family of Totties and Wooldale halls, prominent yeomen-clothiers, seem to have been the leaders. Not all the members were able to live up to the Friends' high standards. A minute book covering the period 1753 to 1768 refers to 'The bad Conduct of Geo. Cartwright In frequenting Alehouses over much' and to his subsequent contrition.

The congregation still numbered sixty-one in 1851, but by then much of the old force was spent and many Quaker meeting houses had closed.

in his own grounds and Dissenting forms of worship were used there well into the eighteenth century, but it was reported at an archbishop's visitation in 1743 that the family had returned to the Anglican fold and 'This Chapel is now united to the Church of England'. In the towns a rich and influential group of merchants, retailers, professional men and the like led their chapels in all the important decisions such as whether or not to move to a

Unitarian position. Dissenters normally formed only a minority of townsmen but they were often an influential one.

During the first half of the eighteenth century no other sect was as widely spread as the Quakers. George Fox's original appeal had been to the poor, but soon the Friends were led by the 'respectable classes' in the same manner as the other early denominations. All these groups lost in fervour what they gained in respectability and by the mid eighteenth century their force was largely spent. The Presbyterians drifted into Unitarianism whose rational approach attracted the ministers and the merchants but had little appeal to the poor; there was no 'enthusiasm' about it. The Old Dissenting sects failed as badly as the Established Church in meeting the challenge of population growth and the Industrial Revolution. Both were unfitted to meet the spiritual and emotional needs of the masses. Into this vacuum stepped Methodism.

Until late in the eighteenth century Methodism made only a limited advance. In the towns and industrial villages the early preachers often met with violent opposition and their reverses sometimes caused them to abandon their efforts. In 1764 the vicar of Ecclesfield told the Archbishop of York that the local Methodists would 'not be of any long continuance' and the vicar of High Hoyland wrote:

> Some Interlopers from Places infected with Methodism are endeavouring to propagate their Notions, but gain few Proselytes. There is no licensed or other Meeting House, except a few private Houses may be called so; where the Above Crazy Visionaries sometimes assemble.

The group of congregations known as the Sheffield circuit (which embraced north Derbyshire and most of South Yorkshire, including Doncaster) had only 910 members in 1773 and only 1,070 members nine years later. Methodism had clearly not yet achieved the success that was to come its way during the nineteenth century.

By 1851, however, Methodism had triumphed spectacularly. Its initial success came chiefly in the traditional Dissenting districts, but by the beginning of Victoria's reign it attracted people of all social backgrounds in almost every type of community except the estate village. Methodism had broken down the old geographical barriers so that now nearly all areas had their Nonconformists. The growing industrial towns and villages were particularly receptive to the new forms of Dissent; in 1837 the vicar of Leeds observed that in his town 'The *de facto* established religion is Methodism'. In all parts of the country Wesleyan Methodism had become the chief alternative to the Established Church and in purely agricultural regions religious differences often amounted to a choice between either the Church of England or Wesleyan and Primitive Methodism. In such areas as the industrial West Riding the combined members of the various Methodist sects now outnumbered the congregations of the Church of England. The few 'Crazy Visionaries' of 1764 had become the most powerful religious body of all.

The two chief alternatives to the Wesleyan form of Methodism were offered by the Primitives and the New Connexion. The appeal of the New Connexion was largely to the industrial poor; Primitive Methodism attracted humble folk not only in the towns but in the agricultural villages as well. They found a receptive audience among farm labourers, particularly in eastern England. By the 1870s the Primitives were strongly associated with agricultural trade unionism and the pulpit offered many an articulate labourer his first chance at public speaking. They were known amongst the respectable classes as the Ranters.

Two of the older sects – the Congregationalists (Independents) and the Baptists – responded enthusiastically to the Evangelical Revival and were able to increase their membership dramatically. During the 1770s and 1780s the Congregationalists built more chapels in south Yorkshire than did the Methodists, but significantly they erected no new buildings between 1836 and 1851, whereas at that time the various forms of Methodism were building chapels enthusiastically. Congregationalism appealed to the better-off sections of industrial society. At first their meeting places were simple, box-like structures but by the middle years of Victoria's reign pompous new buildings in the Gothic style favoured by the Church of England were being built instead. As the Wesleyan Methodists became increasingly respectable they too built grandiose chapels in the suburbs.

Meanwhile, the Established Church had made a substantial recovery. In the towns many new churches were erected with the financial provision of the 1818 'Million Act' and in the countryside squires and parishioners restored or substantially rebuilt thousands of medieval churches. The Roman Catholic Church also entered a period of renewed growth, particularly in Lancashire and other parts of the country where Irish people settled in large numbers. The Nonconformists continued to split into different sects – Particular Baptists and General Baptists, for instance – and to form intense new groups, often with peculiar local names. The 1851 returns record, for example, twenty-seven 'Israelites' who met in a room in Paradise Square, Sheffield and nineteen 'Brethren and Sisters United by the Blood of Christ' who assembled in the Garden School Room at Low Ackworth. At that time numerous Dissenting groups were meeting in private houses or cottages until the day when they had the resources to build their own little Zion or Bethel. A lot of them failed to reach that desirable goal.

By the middle years of the nineteenth century many an estate village remained impervious to Dissent, whereas the new settlements that had gathered round textile mills, collieries or canal-heads were markedly Nonconformist in character. Many of the old Dissenting centres now had thriving Evangelical congregations. In Penistone parish, for instance, the seventeenth-century Bullhouse Independents and the High Flatts Quakers were still active, but the subsidiary Quaker meeting-place at Lumb Royd had gone, and there were now three Wesleyan chapels, a New Connexion meeting-house, a Primitive Methodist chapel, a Congregational or Independent chapel of the Evangelical type, and a Baptist chapel, all products of the late-eighteenth and early-nineteenth century revival. This large parish now had two Anglican churches but Nonconformity was as pronounced as it had been in the seventeenth century.

The success of Nonconformity depended in large measure upon the types of community that were found throughout England. To recognize such forces is not to deny the human one. Each chapel has its own individual story, different from that of any other. But these histories are more intelligible when seen as part of a whole and when it is understood that the forces that encouraged or hindered their growth were deeply rooted in the local society of which they form so characteristic a part.

INDUSTRIAL TOWNS AND CITIES

At the beginning of the nineteenth century no provincial town had more than 100,000 inhabitants, though London was a colossus with a population of 865,000. Even when Victoria came to the throne in 1837 only five places in England and Wales contained more than 100,000 people. By 1891, however, twenty-three towns had reached that level of population. Their spectacular growth was partly due to natural increase but it was fuelled by immigration from the countryside, particularly after the railways had ushered in an era of cheap mass travel. By the mid 1850s England's major railway lines had nearly all been completed or were being constructed.

Victorian cities caused our ancestors to gape with awe, admiration or horror, for the world had never seen anything like them before. They must be seen by us not only as a new type of settlement but as places with individual characters and their own idiosyncracies. Their inhabitants were fiercely proud of the unique nature of, say, Bradford as opposed to Leeds, Birmingham contrasted with the neighbouring Black Country towns, and Manchester compared with anywhere else in the world. In his stimulating and pioneering book *Victorian Cities* (1963) Professor Asa Briggs shows how the new industrial settlements were very different from each other in terms of buildings and topography and their economic and social structures. Amongst the largest cities, despite the similarities in working-class housing and common problems of public health, the sharpest contrast was between the two giants, Manchester and Birmingham.

By the 1780s, when the population of Manchester township was about 40,000, observers were already commenting upon the growing gulf between a small group of self-made, wealthy factory owners and the mass of the labouring poor. In Lancashire the steam-powered cotton industry had created a form of society that was very different from anything that had gone before. The Revd. R. Parkinson thought that:

> There is no town in the world where the distance between the rich and the poor is so great, or the barrier between them so difficult to be crossed . . . The separation between the different classes, and the consequent ignorance of each other's habits and conditions, are far more complete in this place than in any country of the older nations of Europe, or the agricultural portions of our own kingdom.

The population of Manchester rose by an astonishing 45 per cent in the 1820s so that by 1831 it had reached 142,000.

Birmingham's industrial structure was very different. It was based on numerous small workshops rather than upon the large factories that characterized the Lancashire cotton industry. The parallels here are with Sheffield before huge new steel works were erected there during the second half of the nineteenth century. Industrial expansion in Birmingham and the Black Country meant the multiplication of existing types of unit. Birmingham had a far greater diversity of occupation than Manchester and indeed than most other Victorian cities. A large proportion of the workforce was skilled and relatively well-paid. Relations between masters and men were close and the opportunities for social mobility were considerable. The West Midlands area offers family and local historians the chance to pursue rewarding avenues of research in tracing and explaining the rise of numerous small businesses and in demonstrating the importance of the family network in transmitting traditional skills and providing financial backing.

Most Victorian cities had been urban centres since at least the Middle Ages, though of course they had been tiny in comparison with the size they attained in the nineteenth century. Newcastle upon Tyne had been an important medieval borough; other places had been small market centres whose burgesses had obtained some measure of independence from their manorial lords. Nearly all of them had a pronounced industrial character long before the Industrial Revolution. At the hearts of these industrial towns the old marketing and retailing functions remained of paramount importance. Many a town centre was like the Square in Arnold Bennett's description of 'Bursley' in *The Old Wives' Tale*, i.e. a self-conscious commercial area which scorned the staple manufacture in the streets beyond as 'something wholesale, vulgar, and assuredly filthy'.

But a few Victorian towns, notably Middlesborough, Crewe and Barrow-on-Furness, were entirely new creations, products of the railway age and decisions taken by entrepreneurs. Barrow grew from a single house into a fishing village of some 300 people by the 1840s and into a town of 40,000 people a generation later. In 1801 a mere twenty-five people lived in the four houses that comprised the settlement of Middlesborough and thirty years later the population stood at only 154. Then in the 1830s thousands of immigrants arrived to seek homes and work in the new town that had been laid out by Joseph Pease, the Quaker industrialist who had extended the famous Stockton to Darlington railway so as to export coal from his Teeside wharves. Later immigrants included Henry Bolckow and John Vaughan, ironmasters who exploited Cleveland's mineral resources and who more than anyone else were responsible for the town's replanning and rapid expansion. Workers flocked to Middlesborough from all over the place; according to the 1871 census nearly half the town's population were born outside Yorkshire. A Roman Catholic cathedral and a Jewish synagogue were prominent amongst its places of worship. This was a frankly proletarian town, laid out in regular rows of plain brick houses. Even a local guide written in 1899 had to admit that:

> At first sight Middlesborough is not calculated to create a particularly favourable impression upon the visitor. Its utilitarian aspect is somewhat too pronounced.

The local historian must therefore search for the peculiar identity of his own town by getting to know the place thoroughly on the ground and from maps, old photographs and prints, together with newspapers, directories, census returns and whatever other documents come to light during the course of his enquiries. He will also have to learn something about the administrative structure of his chosen place and how it has changed over time. A borough might not have covered the same area as a township, and a parish might have been something completely different. Ancient cities such as York or Norwich or Exeter were divided into numerous small parishes, whereas the burgeoning

industrial towns that straddled the foothills of the Pennines covered only a small part of huge parishes that contained villages, hamlets and scattered farmsteads within their bounds. Leeds parish had eleven townships and Manchester had as many as thirty; Bradford parish covered about 40,000 acres and Halifax parish – the largest in England – was twice that size. To take just one more example, the central urban township of Sheffield accounted for only one-twentieth of the 22,370-acre parish which stretched from the industrial villages of Attercliffe and Darnall in the east to isolated farms in the west. It is obviously essential for the local historian to know, when dealing with population figures and other matters, whether his information relates to the urban area only or whether it encompasses the surrounding rural parts of the parish as well. One can merely draw attention to the problem here, for local arrangements were complex and varied.

Family structure

Each Victorian town conjures up a distinctive image in one's

Plate 3.3   Aerial view of Hanley, Stoke on Trent (taken in the 1930s)
The Potteries followed a different way from most on the road to industrialization. Once a collection of villages that nestled close to the town of Newcastle under Lyme, during the late-eighteenth and nineteenth centuries these small settlements grew into a conurbation that eventually overshadowed its historic neighbour and became the city of Stoke on Trent. Overshadowed is an appropriate metaphor, for as Arnold Bennett wrote in *The Death of Simon Fuge*:

It was squalid ugliness, but it was squalid ugliness on a scale so vast and overpowering that it became sublime. Great furnaces gleamed red in the twilight, and their fires were reflected in horrible black canals; processions of heavy vapour drifted in all directions across the sky, over acres of mean and miserable brown architecture.

Burslem, the largest of the old villages (with forty-three of the district's fifty-two pottery kilns in the reign of Queen Anne), acquired a fine Georgian centre, but in Victorian times squalid rows of houses transformed the town's character. By the beginning of the nineteenth century Longton, Hanley and Stoke were becoming urban and Tunstall and Fenton soon reached a similar stage of development. Pot-making had once been a part-time occupation, with kilns erected in farm yards and claypits dug out from the roadsides in order to save land, but by 1832 there were 534 'bottle-kilns' in the district and a century later the number had risen to about 2,000. The master potters and businessmen lived in prosperous 'villas', but the masses were crowded into insanitary courts and terraces assembled around the smoking pot-banks.

mind, an overall impression that blurs the differences that existed within a town between one quarter or district and another. In Leeds, for example, the middle class suburbs to the north of the city had little in common with Hunslet and Holbeck, the working class townships to the south, where families were packed into rows of back-to-back houses or into cramped folds close to the mills, foundries, railway sidings and other places of work. But in *The Uses of Literacy* (1957) Richard Hoggart showed that even in these dismal surroundings people could find all they wanted in terms of home, work, friends and relations, food, drink, clothing and suchlike provisions, churches, schools and facilities for leisure and entertainment. A few terraced streets alongside a mill evoked as much community loyalty as did an ancient village. It was not until the end of the Victorian period, when electric trams provided cheap public transport, that new working class suburbs could be built out of town and away from the vicinity of the workplace.

In *Family Structure in Nineteenth Century Lancashire* (1971) Michael Anderson has shown that far from weakening kinship ties the Industrial Revolution may well have strengthened them. The Lancashire cotton industry grew so spectacularly after 1770 that by 1803 cotton had replaced wool as Britain's leading export, a pre-eminent position that it was to hold until 1938. By the middle of the nineteenth century Lancashire was the most urbanized county in England, with over half its population living in the fourteen towns which contained more than 10,000 inhabitants each. Most of these thriving places had been old market centres; only Oldham had grown from a few scattered moorland hamlets. The cotton industry also flourished in industrial villages and small company towns so that by 1851 almost 17 per cent of Lancashire men over the age of twenty and 15 per cent of women worked at the manufacture of cotton. Long hours of toil were nothing new, but the mills brought a discipline that at best was irksome and in many places was harsh. Recent legislation had improved matters, however; the 1833 Factory Act prohibited the employment of young children and the 1847 Ten Hours Act had at last given working people some time for recreation.

Preston's experience was in many ways typical of the other old market towns that had been overwhelmed by the cotton industry. In 1795 John Aikin could still describe Preston as 'a handsome, well-built town . . . rendered gay by assemblies and other places of amusement, suited to the genteel style of the inhabitants'. By 1851 its population had soared to 69,542 and the cotton trade provided work for 32 per cent of adult males and 28 per cent of the women. Preston had become a shoddy place to live, dominated by smoky factory chimneys and characterized by blackened rows of brick, terraced houses or crowded, insanitary courts and, worst of all, dark, damp cellars. Disgusting privvies, inadequate sewers, atmospheric pollution and the lack of piped water each contributed to Preston's unprecedented public health problems. Accommodation inside the houses was very cramped.

Anderson's analysis of Preston's immigration patterns, as revealed by the mid-nineteenth century census returns, shows that 70 per cent of the population were born outside the town. In a sample area 3,345 migrants were identified and shown to have been born in about 425 different places. Over 40 per cent of Preston's immigrants came from within a 10-mile radius and only about 30 per cent had come in from more than 30 miles away. The pattern was thus similar to those of earlier times. A major group of long-distance migrants came from Ireland. The Irish had first come to Lancashire in significant numbers in the middle years of the eighteenth century, and their ranks began to swell considerably after the 1846 potato famine. In 1841 Lancashire had about 106,000 Irish-born residents, and in 1851 about 192,000; in Preston the Irish formed 3.3 per cent of the population in 1841 and 7.4 per cent ten years later.

In almost all large towns in 1851 the immigrants outnumbered the native born. Many immigrants were young, had only recently arrived when the census was taken, and were ready to move again soon. Anderson's study of Preston has also emphasized the amount of movement that took place within the town. In the area of closest scrutiny only 14 per cent of males (45/311) and 19 per cent of females (75/390) aged over ten at the time of the 1861 census were living in the same house as the one they had inhabited in 1851; but many of them had moved only a short distance. Factory wages enabled young men and women to become economically independent of their families and some of them broke away completely, but most town dwellers maintained their family connections and were careful to preserve links not only with their immediate relatives but with a wider range of kin. Neighbours often helped in times of need, but people more readily turned to their kin in critical life situations such as sickness, unemployment, homelessness, old age and death. The family structure was a crucial source of aid in communities with a rapid turnover of personnel, poor health, uncertain employment prospects and deep poverty. Charles Booth found that 31 per cent of London's population in the 1880s lived in primary or secondary poverty and a decade later Seebohm Rowntree claimed that 28 per cent of the people of York lived in equal hardship.

The great industrial changes of the eighteenth and nineteenth centuries did not alter the traditional family structure of previous generations, but they did provide economic opportunities for earlier marriages and thus for more children. Wrigley and Schofield have shown that between 1650–99 and 1800–49 the age at first marriage for women fell by 3.1 years; most of the fall occurred during the second half of the eighteenth century and it was most apparent in industrial communities. Collectively, over five or six generations these small variations led to considerable population growth. The incidence of bridal pregnancy and bastardy rose significantly at the same time. Between 1680 and 1800 the proportion of brides who were pregnant at the time of their wedding grew from 15 to 35 per cent and the illegitimacy ratio rose from 1.5 to 5 per cent. Local studies have established a direct connection between rising prices and annual illegitimacy ratios, suggesting that frustrated wedding plans rather than promiscuity were responsible for the increased number of bastards. By the nineteenth century dearth and plague were tribulations of the past, but tuberculosis, typhus, typhoid and dysentery were major killers and the great cholera epidemics drew horrified attention to the need for urgent action to improve public health in the towns. It was not until the 1870s, however, that the number of deaths from tuberculosis and typhoid fell dramatically and cholera and typhus almost disappeared.

Everton and the Mould family

As the Victorian cities burst their ancient bounds many a rural village was engulfed and its character transformed. Thus Everton, a modest sized village since at least the time of Domesday Book, lost its separate identity during the middle decades of the nineteenth century and became a working-class quarter of Liverpool. In 1801 the rural township of Everton contained only 499 people; eighty years later the same area accommodated 109,812 inhabitants. At the beginning of the century an enthusiast described Everton as:

> A pretty village with a view which embraces town, village, plain, pasture, river and ocean. At sun-set the windows of the houses of Everton Brow flash back the glowing radiance, showing that nothing impedes the wide prospect westwards.

Thirty years later another observer wrote:

> Everton now abounds with handsomely walled pleasure grounds and well-enclosed fields, and is conveniently intersected with admirable roads, most of them well-paved, and many of the parapets are flagged for two-thirds of their breadth with admirable, well-laid strong flags.

However, the first working-class terraced houses were already being built on Everton Road, a street that was to be described in 1875 as 'a dense thoroughfare of a somewhat shabby and second rate character'. Poor immigrants from Ireland, Wales and adjoining parts of Lancashire and Cheshire had moved in and the old wealthy elite that had previously enjoyed Everton's rural isolation had left for more secluded homes beyond the township bounds.

The focal point for the exclusive society that was Everton in the first half of the nineteenth century was St George's church, which was built in 1814 to the designs of Thomas Rickman; it was the first church in the world to use cast iron extensively. In his account of *The Iron Church* (1977) Dr Richard F. Mould has interwoven the history of his own family with that of the Everton community in a way that enriches both subjects. Subtitled 'A short history of Everton, its Mother Church, and one of its mid-Victorian Churchwardens, including notes on how to start tracing a Family Tree', it highlights the fortunes of the Mould family and by so doing it provides insights into the character of a place that was overwhelmed by its powerful neighbour's rapid expansion.

Richard Andrews Mould was born at Whitchurch, north Shropshire, in 1807 and became a successful wine and sherry merchant with extensive vaults in the Exchange Chambers, Liverpool. He made annual visits to Spain and Portugal in connection with his business and he normally lived several months a year in London. In 1843 he moved from central Liverpool to Percy Villa in Northumberland Terrace, Everton, and during the hey-day of St George's church he was one of the most active parishioners. He served as a churchwarden from 1856 to 1863 and as a county magistrate. His estate was valued at £45,000 upon his death, and his status in local society was marked by the presence of the Lord Mayor of Liverpool at his funeral and the flying of the Town Hall flags at half mast.

R. A. Mould was a self-made man. His ancestors had been much more humble people, mostly tailors. His father, Thomas Mould (1781–1858), was a tailor, draper and hatter in Whitchurch and previous generations had lived nearby in Bronington, Welshampton, Hindford and ⌀Myddle. The earliest recorded member of the family was John Mould who had enclosed an 8-acre tenement out of Myddlewood during the reign of Henry VIII. Nearly all the Moulds, Molds, Mouldes and other variants of the name which appear in Shropshire parish registers can be placed on a single family tree. The Moulds left Myddle shortly after the Civil War and their leisurely progress northwards along what is now the A 495 can be followed in local parish registers until they arrived at Whitchurch early in the nineteenth century. Branches of the family then spread into Cheshire and Lancashire and two brothers emigrated to New Zealand. One of these brothers, George Mould (1843–1908), was born in Whitchurch and worked as a railway clerk before he went in search of a new life on the other side of the world. He left Gravesend on 22 January 1865 aboard the 'Greyhound' and arrived at Lyttelton on 7 May, fifteen weeks later. The following month he and a partner bought some land nearby in Akaroa, Banks Peninsula, where some of his descendants still reside. His granddaughter, Jessie Mould, has been keenly interested in the movements of her family over the generations and after she had discovered that her seventeenth-century ancestors were mentioned in Richard Gough's *History of Myddle* (1701–2) she published *More Tales of Banks Peninsula* and wrote in her foreword:

> To read how my own ancestors lived in the time of the Tudors and the Stuarts and to even learn that they occupied the 10th pew adjoining the South Wall in the Myddle Church has been the inspiration to write down some reminiscences of my own childhood and of the stories related to me, in the hope that they will be of interest, not only to the present generation, but maybe, also to that 500 years hence!

The story of the progress of the Mould family over nearly five centuries – apart from the exceptional career of R. A. Mould –

is in many ways a typical one. During the sixteenth, seventeenth and eighteenth centuries the Mould family moved home frequently but their mobility was on a small scale and most members earned their living as tailors or smallholders or a combination of the two occupations. Then in the nineteenth century some of the more adventurous men seized the new opportunities to make wealth in an urban environment or to tear themselves away from their ancestral roots to start life anew thousands of miles away. But even in New Zealand they never forgot those roots and today they rejoice in the knowledge of their family history. One day we shall have many more family sagas to set aside that of the Moulds and we will be able to speak with more confidence about general trends. In particular, we need to know far more about those numerous families which moved from the countryside but which experienced only a hum-drum life in the towns or at best only a modest prosperity.

Suburbs

During the 1860s the rapid growth of suburbs became a noticeable feature of England's largest towns and cities; from the 1880s onwards it became a marked phenomenon. Suburban life away from the noise and bustle of the work place was made possible by improved transport facilities in the form of horse-drawn omnibuses, suburban railways and eventually the electric trams. London expanded at a remarkable rate. It had already overshadowed all other places in 1801 when its population had reached 865,000, but a century later its inhabitants numbered over $4\frac{1}{2}$ millions, i.e. more than one-sixth of the entire population of England. The number of people in the capital's suburbs grew by about 50 per cent during each decade between 1861 and 1891 and by 45 per cent during the last ten years of the century. 'Greater London', as those parts that lay beyond the ring of the old county boundary became known, grew from about 414,000 inhabitants in 1861 to 1,405,000 in 1891 and to 2,045,000 at the turn of the century. During these amazing years of unprecedented expansion Greater London grew at a much faster rate than the national population as a whole and faster than the suburbs of any provincial city. Between 1881 and 1891 the most rapid population growth in England occurred in four London suburbs: Leyton (133.3 per cent), Willesden (121.9 per cent), Tottenham (95.1 per cent) and

Plate 3.4 Electric trams, Attercliffe Road, Sheffield, *c.* 1903
Electric trams provided cheap transport for the masses. The old, crowded
courts near the city centres could now be pulled down and new rows of
terraced houses could be built to accommodate the working classes in
suburbs alongside the tram routes. Trams hastened the process by which
city centres became shopping and entertainment areas instead of places
where people lived.

The first electric trams in Sheffield began operations in 1899. For a
few years the upper decks were left open to the elements, but from 1903
onwards they were covered. Drivers had no protection from the weather
until the fronts were encased in 1907. Sheffield's last tram ran on 8
October 1960.

West Ham (58.9 per cent). By the end of the nineteenth century
London's population was rising by an extra 100,000 inhabitants
per annum.

In *Labour and Life of the People* (1889–93), his two-volume
study of Londoners, Charles Booth wrote:

146

In many districts the people are always on the move; they shift from one part of it to another like 'fish in a river' . . . On the whole, however, the people usually do not go far, and often cling from generation to generation to one vicinity, almost as if the set of streets which lie there were an isolated country village.

The census returns show that when people left London they usually moved only short distances but that migrants into London came from all over the place. Compared with the rest of the country London's population was relatively youthful. Differences between the various districts within the capital were, however, marked. The development of one south London suburb has been examined in detail by Professor H. J. Dyos in his classic work, *Victorian Suburb: A Study of the Growth of Camberwell* (1961). In pre-Victorian times Camberwell was a middle-class suburb covering the 4,450 acres of the ancient parish of St Giles, which lay about 1½ miles south of London Bridge; its population in 1841 already stood at 39,868. Sixty years later Camberwell was a metropolitan borough whose population had multiplied more than six fold to 259,339. Other Victorian London suburbs could tell a similiar story.

Professor Dyos calculated that of the 75,000 people by which Camberwell grew during the 1870s, about 52,000 represented the balance of migration into and out of the district and 23,000 were the result of natural increase. After this decade of maximum development the stream of migrants dwindled until by the end of the Victorian era it had more-or-less dried up. Net immigration during the 1880s accounted for only about 17,000 of the total increase of about 49,000, and during the last decade of the century all the net gain of about 24,000 people was accounted for by natural growth. As the mass of the inhabitants of Camberwell could not afford to move further out to the wealthier suburbs, most families stayed put.

During the course of Victoria's eventful reign a rising proportion of London's immigrants headed south of the river. They came from all parts of the kingdom and abroad. In the 1840s only a quarter of London's newcomers ended up south of the Thames, but during the following three decades the proportion grew to a third. Two or three out of every ten who came to live in south London were north Londoners who had merely crossed the river, but of course they themselves may have been second generation immigrants to the capital. Professor Dyos estimated that newcomers never amounted to more than between 12 to 16 per cent of the total population of south London districts in any single decade, but that this rate of immigration was sufficient to create communities in which less than half the inhabitants had been born within that part of Greater London which lay south of the Thames. Such statistics aid our understanding of population movements but they mask the bewildering complexity that was the reality of the situation. The census returns show that the majority of Camberwell's population at any one time had been born in London – 65 per cent in 1861; 76 per cent in 1911 – but many families had moved frequently from district to district and from street to street. Only the family historian can charter some of these kaleidoscopic patterns of mobility and reduce them to an understandable human scale.

Camberwell did not have a major industry that distinguished it from other London districts, but it offered sufficient variety of employment to engage a majority of the workforce; other bread-winners did not have to go far to reach central London. Its former middle-class character was rapidly eroded as thousands of small houses were built on every available plot of land by speculative builders. An intricate street pattern arose from the divided ownership of the land and numerous tiny variations in house types appeared because so many different builders were at work. Between 1878 and 1880, at the height of Camberwell's feverish building activity, some 416 firms or individual builders erected a total of 5,670 houses. Most of these businesses were on such a small scale that over a half of them built no more than six houses during these three years and nearly three-quarters built no more than twelve; the bankruptcy rate was high. Altogether, these small builders were responsible for little more than a quarter of the houses. At the opposite end of the scale, about 1,800 houses, or nearly a third of the total, were constructed by the fifteen largest firms, each of which was responsible for between seventy-five and 230 buildings.

In the London suburbs the general tendency was for practically every district to eventually deteriorate in status as the better-off families moved out and poorer ones moved in. Otherwise, Professor Dyos concluded, the variety of human condition and physical environment to be found in Victorian Camberwell warns against the temptation to generalize further. Each of London's districts possessed its own distinctive character, an individuality that marked it off from its neighbours either by topographical features and architectural appearance or by social and occupational structure. The Central Area pulled all these parts together, as it were, and made them interdependent portions of the whole.

Hampstead was transformed from a small, eighteenth-century satellite town separated from the metropolis by steeply-sloping open fields into a high-class residential suburb very different from Camberwell. In *Hampstead: Building a Borough, 1650–1964* (1974) Professor F. M. L. Thompson has shown how the old settlement preserved its isolated character well into the nineteenth century because it lay off the main lines of communication out of the capital. Its population grew twenty times between 1801 and 1901 from 4,343 to 82,329 and the number of inhabited houses rose from 691 to 11,359. But even this spectacular rate of growth did not match that of many London suburbs. Hampstead's monastic past had led to the concentration of land in five compact estates, whose owners influenced the type of development permitted. The Heath was preserved as an open space and by 1900 the country villas of prosperous businessmen and professional families made Hampstead 'one of the largest and most prosperous of the well-to-do residential suburbs of London'.

Hampstead's genteel surroundings were a world apart from the East End of London, which comprised Stepney, Poplar, Bethnal Green and parts of Hackney, districts that attracted thousands of unskilled labourers to the docks, the street markets and sweated trades. Charles Booth described how each district had its own peculiar flavour because of its distinctive occupational structure, a flavour that could be detected in the streets from observing the faces of the people who lived there and noticing what they carried:

> Thus it will be seen that Whitechapel is the dwelling place of the Jews – tailors, bootmakers and tobacco-workers – and the centre of trading both small and large; Stepney and St George's the district of ordinary labour; Shoreditch and Bethnal Green of the artizan; in Poplar sub-officials reach their maximum proportion, while Mile End, with a little of everything, very closely represents the average of the whole district.

The Irish and the Jews formed two particularly conspicuous groups in their own quarters. In 1851 at least 5 per cent of London's population were of Irish origin. The Jews came from Central and Eastern Europe to evade persecution in 1848–50, 1863 and the 1880s, until national legislation was passed in 1905 to restrict the scale of immigration. Charles Booth's reports and the

Plate 3.5 James Joseph Wilkinson (1848–1934)
At least five generations of my wife's family lived in north London. Her
great-grandfather (seen here) was born on 29 June 1848 at 1 Hope Street,
Holloway, in the Islington registration district, the son of James John
Wilkinson, hatter, and Sarah Wilkinson, formerly Gostick. I worked back
through the indexes at St Catherine's House and found that his parents
were married on 27 February 1842 at St John's church, Islington. Both
partners lived in Holloway. James John's father was noted on the

need for bodies like the Salvation Army and Dr Barnardo's Homes show the other side of the coin to life in the Hampstead villas.

INDUSTRIAL VILLAGES

The Industrial Revolution was by no means merely an urban phenomenon. During the eighteenth and nineteenth centuries many villages were industrialized in the sense that the majority of their inhabitants worked as nailmakers or weavers, for example, or at some other ancient hand-craft or were employed in the new mills, ironworks, quarries and coalmines which had transformed so many parts of the English countryside. Rural crafts and industries had long provided extra income for small-holders and cottagers, but by Victorian times population and economic growth had created a large, landless labour force whose members had to earn their entire living from a single craft or a manual occupation. Craft villages were very different in character

---

marriage certificate as James Wilkinson, hatter, and Sarah's father was recorded as Joseph Gostick, clerk.

So far so good, but when I turned to the census returns I ran into difficulties. In 1851 Joseph Gostick, a sixty-four-year-old clerk born in Bedford, was living with his wife Jane at 52 Georges Grove in the parish of St James, Holloway, but a seven-hour search failed to find the Wilk-insons in the borough of Islington. I then searched the 1841 census returns for Islington and found Joseph and Jane Gostick and their three children living at Albany Place, Holloway. Sarah's age was rounded down to fifteen. Living with them as a lodger was James [John] Wilk-inson, hat maker, whose age was rounded down to twenty and who was said to have been born in the county of Middlesex. His parents were not living nearby. If I had found James Wilkinson, senior, in the 1851 census I would have discovered his age and place of birth, which would have led me to the relevant parish register for his baptism entry, thus enabling me to trace the line further.

Fortunately, the Mormon International Genealogical Index microfiche has suggested a new line of enquiry, for it notes the baptism of a James John Wilkinson, son of James and Mary Wilkinson, on 30 June 1816 at St Andrew's church, Holborn. This James John would have been just under twenty-five at the time of the 1841 census and so his age would have been rounded down to twenty. A search of the 1851 census returns for Holborn is now called for.

from their predecessors of a century or two before, and the new settlements which were dominated by a single workplace and where even the houses and public buildings were owned by the ironmaster, millowner or colliery company had no antecedents in an earlier age.

Industrialized villages were naturally most numerous in the North and parts of the Midlands, but even in the South some nineteenth-century rural communities were sustained to a large extent by wages earned at a particular craft. Far away from the great Victorian industrial districts, untouched even by the Midlands framework knitting industry, Northamptonshire conjures up an image of rural stability, great landed estates and 'close' villages. Two out of every three parishes were dominated by a squire or a small group of rich farmers. But even in this tranquil part of England many of the 'open' villages had a variety of local crafts, distributive trades and small industries, whose origins go back well into the eighteenth century. This is evident from the series of Northamptonshire militia lists dating between 1762 and 1786 which record the occupations of men aged between eighteen and forty-five who were liable for military service. Even the most purely agricultural villages had a handful of craftsmen and in a few parishes, notably Spratton, Moulton and Hardingstone, between 40 and 60 per cent of those liable for duty were employed in non-agricultural pursuits for the major part of their time. Most of these rural craftsmen were still part-time farmers or cottagers with a few acres of land and rights on the commons and wastes.

The boot and shoe trade, which had become firmly established in the county town of Northampton during the Civil War, spread to Wellingborough before 1760 and soon afterwards to Earls Barton, Higham Ferrers, Irthlingborough, Raunds, Rushden and Wollaston. The 1777 militia returns show how the two towns dominated the trade, for Northampton had 142 recorded shoemakers and Wellingborough 113, but Irthlingborough had only 17, Raunds 16, Earls Barton 11 and Hardingstone 7. The rural industry developed in response to a growing national demand for boots and shoes, together with the need for military and naval footwear during the French Revolutionary and Napoleonic wars; the construction of canals and later the railways opened up distant markets.

At first the boot and shoemaking industry was organized on an outwork basis from the towns. By the middle years of the nineteenth century a high proportion of the male workforce were without land and were working full time at the craft; women and girls also found employment in large numbers. Hardingstone had 22 male and no female shoemakers in 1841 but twenty years later 83 males and 43 females were occupied in this way. Long Buckby had 131 men and boys working at the shoemaking craft in 1841 and no females; ten years later numbers had risen to 273 males and 50 women and girls. The same trend is evident in the towns. In Wellingborough the number of male boot and shoe makers rose from 613 in 1841 to 814 in 1851 and to 861 in 1861; female numbers rose from a mere 37 in 1841 to 473 in 1851 and to 744 a decade later. The statistics for these and other places are gathered together in V. A. Hatley and J. Rajczonek, *Shoemakers in Northamptonshire, 1762–1911*, published as the Northampton Historical Series no.6 in 1971. Between 1841 and 1861 the number of male shoemakers in the county aged twenty or more almost doubled as both the urban and the rural population searched for employment.

Earls Barton is a good example of the way that an open agricultural village grew into a flourishing footwear centre from small beginnings in the third quarter of the eighteenth century. Its population rose from 729 in 1801 to 2,602 in 1891. By 1841, when 1,079 people lived in the village, 107 men and boys and just 3 females worked at the trade. Twenty years later the population had risen by 478 but the proportion of the workforce employed in footwear had grown more dramatically, so that not only were 301 men and boys working at the trade but also 123 women and 118 girls. A declining number of people contined to sew shoes by hand in their cottages or little workshops right until the end of the nineteenth century. Even today some Victorian houses in Earls Barton have a former 'shop' behind the kitchen or in a backyard; other cottagers worked in their living rooms. The first local man who can be described as a manufacturer was Thomas Dunkley, who was born in 1802 and who began his working life as a shoemaker; in 1851 William Dunkley was employing fifty men and twenty women and concentrating on a range of cheaper shoes. But factories never dominated the Northamptonshire villages and for most people the making of footwear remained a small-scale craft.

The opening of the Midland Railway in 1857 stimulated the boot and shoe trade in places that had a main line station. Kettering's population rose from 5,198 in 1851 to 29,972 sixty years later and the villages of Burton Latimer and Desborough grew spectacularly. Northamptonshire's rural footwear centres were very different in character from the county's estate villages but they were unlike the new Victorian settlements that had grown alongside coal mines, iron foundries and quarries. Their inhabitants were not totally dependent on the boot and shoe trade, nor were they so uncompromisingly working class. England had many such villages that do not fit into neat categories. Such settlements were profoundly characteristic of the Victorian age.

The census returns from the middle decades of the nineteenth century record an extraordinary wide range of rural occupations before mechanization and mass production destroyed so many of the traditional hand crafts. In the South Midlands and a few other areas where farm labourers could earn only a pittance crafts that employed mothers and daughters provided welcome extra income. Localized trades sometimes offered alternative employment, but the major crafts for women and girls were lace-making, straw-plaiting, glove-making and knitting. The centres of pillow lace-making were to be found in the South Midlands and some districts in Devon, where the craft had been established as one of the many new projects of the sixteenth and seventeenth centuries. It did not expand in a big way until the late eighteenth century when population growth and parliamentary enclosure depressed the standard of living of the poorest sections of rural society. The skills that were needed to make intricate patterns by manipulating bobbins and pins at speed were learned at an early age. Young children went to lace-schools from the age of five upwards and after they had reached twelve they were expected to earn their keep. Dr Pamela Horn has estimated that about a fifth of the Buckinghamshire and Bedfordshire lacemakers who were recorded in the 1851 census were under the age of fifteen. Though the Workshops Regulation Act of 1867 forbade the employment of children under eight in any handicraft and stated that those aged between eight and thirteen must attend school for at least ten hours a week, it was difficult to enforce these provisions and they were widely evaded.

The hand-made lace industry was destroyed by machine competition during the second half of the nineteenth century. In Buckinghamshire the number of lace workers fell from a peak of 10,487 in 1851 to only 789 in 1901; in Bedfordshire the number declined less spectacularly from 5,734 to 1,144 during the same period. Some females were able to switch to the plaiting of straw hats, bonnets and mats. The most suitable straw for this purpose was grown in Buckinghamshire, Bedfordshire, Hertfordshire and Essex, and Luton and Dunstable were the great centres of the trade. Straw plaiters started work at an early age and the occupation was a common one in the South Midland counties; for instance, in 1871 about a third of all Bedfordshire girls aged between ten and fifteen were recorded in the census returns as plaiters. The introduction of cheap plaits from China and Japan during the last quarter of the nineteenth century hit the industry hard just as fashion started to favour smaller hats and ones made from other materials. Bedfordshire female plaiters declined in numbers from 20,701 in 1871 to as few as 485 thirty years later as wages tumbled from ten shillings a week to as little as one or two shillings. By the end of the Victorian era female cottage industries no longer made much of a contribution to the family income of the labouring classes.

Framework knitting

The family historian who has traced his ancestors back to nineteenth-century Leicestershire, Nottinghamshire or south Derbyshire will have seen parish registers that time after time give a man's occupation as FWK. It means of course framework knitter. Not only men, but women and children too knitted stockings, socks, shirts, gloves, cravats and other fabrics on a frame in their cottage and continued to do so long after steam power had been applied to their craft during the middle years of the nineteenth century. William Lee of the Nottinghamshire parish of Calverton had invented the basic frame in 1589 but the craft first took hold in London and did not really spread to the Midlands until after the restoration of Charles II. By 1669 London had about 400 frames, Nottinghamshire 100 and Leicestershire 50. Apprenticeship indentures amongst the Inland Revenue records in the Public Record Office show, however, that by the second decade of the eighteenth century the geographical distribution of the craft in the Midlands had been largely determined; shortly afterwards Daniel Defoe observed, 'One would scarce think it possible so small an article of trade could employ such multitudes of people as it does, for the whole country seems to be employ'd in it'. At least 118 Leicestershire villages and hamlets had framework knitters amongst their inhabitants by 1800. Only the 'close' villages in the east of the county were immune. Felkin's enquiry in 1844

155

Plate 3.6 A Northamptonshire lacemaker, 1889

This photograph of an unidentified Northamptonshire couple was taken late in the nineteenth century when the hand-made lace industry was declining rapidly in face of competition from machines. The lacemaker's pillow is set on a traditional three-legged stool. She had probably learned the craft as a young girl and over the years would have earned much needed income to supplement her husband's labouring wages. She appears well-padded against the cold weather.

Old photographs such as this need to be treated with the same caution as documentary sources. Supporting evidence explaining why and when they were taken is often not available. It has been well said that the

reported the following number of frames: Leicester 4,140, Hinckley 1,750, Shepshed 1,209, Loughborough 906, Earl Shilton 650, Wigston 550, Sileby 500, Burbage 450, Whitwick 423, Thurmaston 400, Barwell 367, Oadby 350, Enderby 350, Blaby 322, Whetstone 297, Syston 280, Cosby 250, Sapcote 220, Countesthorpe 214, Barrow 210, Stoke Golding 206, Belgrave 200, Stanton 200, and so on in ever decreasing numbers.

Let us look at two or three of these framework knitting villages in more detail, starting with Countesthorpe to the south of Leicester. The parish register from 1 January 1813 to 31 December 1817 records the occupations of 74 men, of whom 51 (that is nearly 70 per cent) were framework knitters; the rest comprised 12 labourers, 2 woolcombers, 2 blacksmiths, a framesmith, a farmer and grazier, a publican, a gardener, a tailor, a brick mason and a soldier. Between 1833 and 1837 (inclusive) 61 per cent were framework knitters, but by 1867–71 the proportion had declined to 49 per cent. None of these figures takes account of the women and children who worked at the craft, but the broad trends are clear. A youth aged twelve–fourteen could work a frame with three months experience and could become proficient within six months. In the neighbouring parish of Cosby the 1851 census returns show that both William and Mary Burbage, a couple in their forties, were working at frames, that the four eldest of their ten children were framework knitters, and that three more children worked at seaming; the youngest worker was Elizabeth, aged six. These cottagers worked for middlemen known as baghosiers who were linked with the largest employers in town or with small rural factories nearby. Workshops housing up to a dozen frames had been introduced into the villages by the beginning of the reign of Queen Victoria, but the craft remained essentially a cottage industry for most of the nineteenth century. John Haines of Cosby told a parliamentary commissioner in 1845 that:

> I work for Mr Greenwell, who is a bagman and a grocer. His shop and warehouse are in the same building. My net wages after deductions should be 5s.10¾d. but Mr Greenwell always pays in

---

camera does not lie, but the photographer does. Photographers were attracted by unusual activities and rare survivals of old crafts, pastimes and costumes rather than by typical everyday concerns. The activity shown here had become sufficiently unusual by 1889 to catch the photographer's attention.

sugar, tea, candles, needles, fat, soap and bread – sometimes in flour. He has forty or fifty frames in Cosby working for him – we do not know which hosier in Leicester he supplies. My house rent is 1s.4½d. a week.

William Sheen of nearby Littlethorpe said:

I work at home on girls' hose and my daughter of 23 and my sons of 21 and 16 are also working their own frames. I earn 6s.1d. a week after paying frame-rent and charges for seaming and taking the work into Leicester. Even when trade is slack or when there are holidays I must pay half-rent for the frame. I used to own it myself but I had to sell it and then rent it back again. All the prices for hose have fallen by half in the last thirty-odd years. Most of the knitters in Littlethorpe have small gardens or rent an allotment. An old hosier in Narborough gives the children a little schooling. We run a sick club and pay in 1s.2d. a month; the benefit is 6s. a week.

Thurmaston, just to the north of Leicester, was another village that had become dependent upon framework knitting by the beginning of the nineteenth century. The parish register records 91 men between 1813 and 1817 (inclusive), of whom 60, that is 2 out of every 3, were framework knitters. The rest comprised a hosier, 15 labourers, 3 farmers, 2 victualers, a gentleman, a carpenter, a blacksmith, a shoemaker, a publican, a butcher, a grocer, a bricklayer, a soldier and an alehouse keeper. The occupational structure of the village was very different from what it had been just before the Civil War when the parish register entries had briefly given men's occupations; between 1636 and 1639 Thurmaston's register noted 8 labourers, 5 shepherds, 3 husbandmen, 2 innkeepers, 2 masons, 2 male servants, a carpenter, a miller, 1 curate, a weaver, a tailor, a shearman, a spinner and a mole catcher. By the nineteenth century the range of occupations had not increased; the expanding population had simply turned to framework knitting. Thurmaston had been a typical Leicestershire village with all its farmhouses and cottages clustered together and surrounded by its huge open fields until the enclosure award of 1763. By 1801 the population had risen to 706 and by 1851 to 1,251. A craft which had once been profitably combined with farming became a miserable cottage industry dependent upon the towns and the bag-hosiers. Trade cycles rather than the state of the harvest were now the chief determinant of the well-being of the community. A count of the 237 heads of households in the 1851 census returns reveals that 143 (that is 60 per cent) were framework knitters. This figure does not include the large numbers of younger men, children and females who were employed as knitters and seamers. In 1845 Thomas Hartshorne had told a parliamentary enquiry that Thurmaston had about 400 frames, which specialized in the production of children's socks and a few gloves. Frame rents were high and the six masters used the truck system of payment, whereby some of the wages were paid in goods. Twenty years previously only Thurmaston and neighbouring Belgrave made socks, but now the craft had spread to eighteen villages. Many women and children were employed. Both Thurmaston and Countesthorpe had become industrial villages in the sense that the majority of the population were employed at a single craft.

Some of the Midland villages with a large number of framework knitters had a more diverse occupational structure than the examples we have just discussed; they were not as completely dependent upon a single trade. Thurmaston's northerly neighbour, Syston, had 54 framework knitters, 5 framesmiths and 3 woolcombers recorded in the parish register between 1813 and 1817 (inclusive), but these craftsmen formed less than half of the 128 entries. Whereas contemporary Thurmaston had 15 different occupations recorded, Syston had 32. Syston's population rose from 1,124 in 1801 to 1,669 in 1851 and 2,930 in 1901, but this growth was not sustained by the hosiery trade. By 1863–67 Syston's register shows that the proportion of framework knitters had declined to 25 per cent. The village had always been larger than Thurmaston and had a healthy variety of crafts and trades. The 1863–67 register records 30 framework knitters, 2 framesmiths and 21 labourers; 9 men worked on the railways, 1 was a coal merchant, 1 a gas house keeper and another a gas fitter; the other craftsmen comprised 4 bricklayers and a brickmaker, 3 blacksmiths, 2 tailors, 2 shoemakers, 2 potters, 2 carpenters, a wheelwright, a cooper, a plumber and glazier, and a painter; the rest included 2 gentlemen, a clerk in holy orders, a surgeon, 3 farmers, 2 general dealers, 2 grocers, a draper, 2 cattle dealers, 7 butchers, a tripe dresser, a pig jobber, a fellmonger, 2 gardeners, 2 grooms, a coachman and 2 commercial travellers.

West Riding textiles

When we turn our attention to the West Riding of Yorkshire, another ancient textile district, we find similar patterns of development. About the year 1800, or just afterwards, my great-great-grandfather, John Hey, moved from Shelley in the parish of Kirkburton, where his ancestors had been settled for centuries, to the village of Thurlstone. His new home was only about 5 miles away from Shelley, but in terms of family history his decision to move was momentous. For the first time in at least three centuries my branch of the Hey family had set up home beyond the Kirkburton parish boundary. The senior members remained in Shelley and Kirkburton but a new branch was now established further south. Some of John Hey's descendants are still living in Thurlstone and others can be found nearby. On 15 December 1806 John was married at the ancient parish church of St John the Baptist at Penistone, about a mile away from his new home, to a local girl named Mary Woodcock. A few months previously his name had been included in a list of men aged between eighteen and forty-five who were liable for militia duty if the awful day ever dawned when Napoleon landed on the south coast. He was described in this militia list as a weaver, the same trade that his ancestors had pursued over the generations. In later records, notably the census returns of 1841 and 1851, he was said more specifically to follow the trade of fancy weaver, that is the manufacture of waistcoats and other garments with decorative patterns. His death certificate, which is dated 3 February 1855, gives his age as seventy three, his occupation as fancy weaver and the cause of his death as 'decay of nature'. He had finally petered out after a lifetime's toil at the loom.

What sort of place was Thurlstone, this dour Pennine village where John Hey had come to live and work? It must have been reassuringly familiar to him for it had many of the characteristics of the stone-built villages of the West Riding. Even today the older houses have gables and mullioned windows which show that they were built in the seventeenth century and some of the later cottages that were erected in rows or clustered in folds during John Hey's lifetime retain their long ranges of upstairs windows which allowed the maximum amount of light to fall on the looms. Thurlstone was described in 1837 in John Holland's *Tour of the Don* as 'a somewhat poor looking and scattered village, or rather hamlet, consisting of stone houses built, for the most part, on the left bank of the Don'. The village had been recorded in Domesday Book and had taken its name from the Old Danish personal name Thurulf and the earlier Anglo-Saxon suffix *tun*. Thurlstone township was a sub-division of the large parish of

Penistone and comprised not just the village but several scattered hamlets and numerous isolated farms on the edge of the Pennine moors. The open arable fields of the village had been enclosed by the agreement of the twenty-three owners of the strips in 1696, but 7,740 acres of common pastures and rough moorland wastes remained undivided until the enclosure award of 1816 created the rectangular fields and straight lanes that are now such a prominent feature of the landscape. The farmers concentrated upon dairy cattle and sheep and were dependent upon weaving as a second source of income. Some of the old farmhouses still have a range of windows that indicate the former position of a weaving chamber. To have a dual occupation was an ancient way of life that lingered on in this area well into the Victorian period.

The Thurlstone militia returns of 1806 name 129 men, of whom forty-one were weavers and twenty-one were clothiers, each of them humble men who worked at a loom in their own home. The recent growth of population meant that a smaller proportion of the workforce than before could also farm a smallholding in the manner of their ancestors; many of them were now occupied full-time at their craft and both their cottage and their loom were rented from the manufacturers. The returns also list two cloth-dressers, a dyer, a yarn-maker and a slubber (who prepared the yarn for spinning). No spinners were recorded because that task was performed by women. Children assisted in the preparatory stages of combing and carding the wool, for in Thurlstone and many other parts of the West Riding the woollen industry was still largely at the domestic stage of manufacture. Only four men aged between eighteen and forty-five were described in the returns as farmers. No doubt there were also older men who were farming in the township, but most farms were smallholdings and their occupants were usually described by their craft names. In 1806 Thurlstone also had 17 labourers, 3 millers, a millwright, 4 paper makers and an oil-presser. By that time six water-powered mills had been erected along a two-mile stretch of the River Don. They comprised the Bullhouse corn mill, a fulling mill (later a wire mill) which had given its name to a new settlement at Millhouse Green, the Ecklands bridge paper mill (later an umbrella works), the Plumpton cloth mill, the Thurlstone corn mill and another cloth mill which had been erected in 1740 as an oil mill for crushing rape and linseed. It is very common to find that mills were adapted to a variety of different purposes during the nineteenth century. Holland

Plate 3.7   Tenter Hill, Thurlstone

Long after water-powered scribbling and spinning mills had been built in the valley bottoms and had attracted new settlements around them, weaving remained at the domestic stage of manufacture. Weavers rented looms which were installed in the chambers of their cottages, buildings that are distinguished by an upper range of windows which are extended all along the front to catch the maximum amount of light.

This row of cottages known as Tenter Hill was probably built early in the nineteenth century. First edition 6–inch ordnance survey maps show that in the 1850s West Riding buildings such as these normally had crofts at the rear with tenter-frames for stretching woven pieces of cloth after their return from the fulling mill. This seems to be why the name was attached to this particular row.

The cottages are built of local sandstone with slate roofs; ashlar stone was used for lintels, quoins and mullions. They are three storeys high and one room deep, and originally the whole of the top floor was made accessible by internal doors.

reported in 1837 that Thurlstone village had three or four mills for grinding corn and for other uses. He observed that:

> In former years, before canal and railway facilities had so quickened the pace of competition in all kinds of business, considerable quantities of flour were made here. The miller attended the market at Wakefield to purchase grain, which he carried home, ground it into flour, and then distributed it to various customers who were scattered, somewhat extensively, about the moors.

In 1806 Thurlstone township had 6 masons and 3 colliers, for good stone quarries and the thin ganister seam of coal were at hand. The rest of the men aged between eighteen and forty-five who were liable for militia duty comprised a merchant, 2 book keepers, 4 blacksmiths, 3 shoemakers, 3 tailors, 2 chandlers, and a cooper, a joiner, a carpenter, a roper, a gardener and a preacher. As Thurlstone lay within the medieval parish of Penistone it did not have its own Anglican church until St Saviour's was built in 1904–5. Rather than travel a mile or more to the medieval church, many Thurlstoners turned to Nonconformity. The Independent chapel at Bullhouse had been erected by Elkanah Rich of Bullhouse Hall in 1692 in the early years of religious toleration and in 1786 another Independent chapel had been established 2 miles away at Netherfield, where the services were much more evangelical in tone. Further chapels were built in Thurlstone township by the Wesleyan Methodists (1795), Particular Baptists (1828) and Primitive Methodists (much later in 1914). The family historian in search of ancestors in this type of community has therefore several registers to consult. One of my great-grandmothers, Clementina Roebuck, was born on 17 February 1817 and the event was entered in the Thurlstone Particular Baptist register. At that time the Particular Baptists were meeting in a private house and it may have been that fact rather than family disagreements on doctrinal issues which led to her being baptized at Netherfield Independent chapel on 6 August 1817. Her younger sisters, Elizabeth and Hannah, had their births recorded not only at Thurlstone but at Lockwood Particular Baptist chapel, a dozen or so miles further north, near Huddersfield. The Roebuck family had probably been staunch Nonconformists for some time. Clementina's father was Enoch Roebuck (1794–1865), who was described in the census returns as clothier (1841), woollen clothier (1851) and wool handloom weaver (1861). Ebenezer and Hezekiah Roebuck, two woollen weavers in the same village, were probably his brothers; their Old Testament names give witness to their parents' religious beliefs.

In 1851 Enoch and Martha Roebuck and their unmarried children, Amos (27), Ruth (16) and Enoch (14), were described as woollen weavers. Enoch also had an apprentice, George Watson (20), who came from Wentworth several miles to the east. Ten years later the elder Enoch, Ruth (26), Henry (21) and a grandson, Enoch Roebuck Coldwell (15), were each earning their living as wool handloom weavers. Meanwhile, on 17 September 1838

Clementina had married George Hey, the third of the four sons of John Hey, the fancy weaver, and the only one not to follow his father's occupation. He became instead a boot and shoe maker. Perhaps he served an apprenticeship with a neighbour but there is no obvious family connection with any of the three shoemakers named in the 1806 militia returns. George was described as boot and shoe maker, born in Thurlstone, in the 1841 and 1851 census returns, but in 1861 was recorded as cordwainer, born in Penistone. This is just the sort of problem the family historian has to be aware of. Both descriptions were correct, for cordwainer was a somewhat old-fashioned term for a shoemaker and Thurlstone township lay within the parish of Penistone. It sounds as if an officious enumerator was at work in 1861; he insisted on the full name Clementina rather than the pet form Clemmey, which had sufficed ten years earlier. In later life George was able to combine his craft with farming work. In 1871 he was described as farmer of 20 acres and ten years later he had 28 acres. His death certificate shows that he was found on the floor of his cow house on Christmas Eve 1887, a day before his 71st birthday, having died from a heart attack.

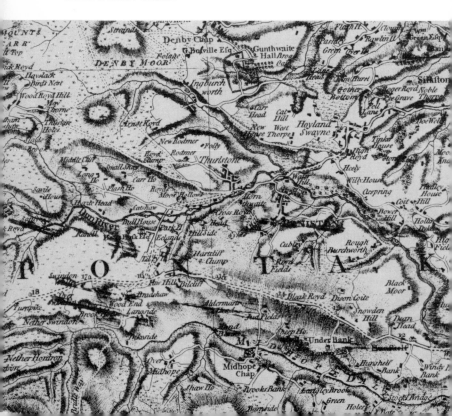

Villages as well as towns expanded rapidly during the first half of the nineteenth century. The population of Thurlstone township was 1,096 in 1801 and 2,018 in 1851. The scribbling and spinning mills which were erected in the river valleys soon attracted workers' houses alongside them. Such communities acquired their own distinctive character and many welcomed the Evangelical Revival with enthusiasm. A few miles north of Thurlstone the new textile settlement at Clayton West had chapels for the Wesleyans, Independents, Particular Baptists, Methodist New Connection and Primitive Methodists, and the new Wesleyan Reform movement met in Aaron Peace's warehouse, but those who preferred the services of the established church had to climb the steep hill to the ancient parochial centre at High Hoyland. Though the yarn was prepared and spun in the new water-powered mills in the valleys, weaving long remained a domestic craft that was practised in the older settlements on the hillsides. Some hamlets were dominated by a single manufacturer whose influence was as great as that of a squire in an estate village, but most villages had several warehouses belonging to small manufacturers. Independent clothiers of the old type who farmed a little land in addition to their work at the loom became outnumbered by a growing body of men who had no land to provide extra income but were simply wage-earners. When the weaving stage of manufacture was finally adapted to steam power, mills were erected in the hillside villages alongside the homes of the workforce.

The extent to which some villages were involved in the woollen industry by the beginning of the nineteenth century is demonstrated by the 1806 militia returns which survive for the collection of West Riding townships which lay within Staincross wapentake. Clayton West had 43 weavers, 7 dressers, 6 clothiers,

---

Plate 3.8 Thurlstone, *c.* 1772
Thomas Jefferys's map shows Thurlstone as a compact hill village before rows of new houses were built along the roads near the mills in the valley bottom. The settlement at Millhouse Green was not then in existence. Jefferys marked all the mill sites with a circular symbol.

Thurlstone township covered the western part of Penistone parish and included many scattered farms. These had been carved from the wastes –mostly, during the early Middle Ages – and some of their names had been adopted as surnames. Bilcliff farm, for instance, was recorded early in the thirteenth century and the surname (in a variety of spellings) is still a local one.

a woolcomber, a cropper and 10 tradesmen alongside 32 other men. Cumberworth township had 89 weavers, 6 clothiers, 3 cutters and 11 tradesmen, and only 31 men who were not involved in the manufacture of cloth. Cumberworth township ranked fourth in terms of size of population within the wapentake but only fifteenth in range of occupation. Even in this type of community, however, men did not always stay at the same job all their lives. John Hey's eldest son, Melling (1808–65), was described as a fancy weaver when his elder children were baptised between 1836 and 1842, but when his last child was baptised in 1846 he was working as a labourer and in the 1851 census returns his occupation was given as groom. The changeover from the domestic system of manufacture to that of the textile mill was completed during the next generation. In 1851 Melling's son George (aged fifteen) was a 'feeder in a woollen mill' and eleven-year-old Benjamin Smith Hey was a 'piecer in a woollen mill'. Ten years later, George had become a woollen cloth dresser but Smith (as he was normally known) walked 3 miles each day to Samuel Fox's new steelworks at Stocksbridge to work as a steel temperer. Upon his marriage he settled in Stocksbridge. This movement into factories and steelworks was not all one way, however. My grandfather, George Hey (1854–1916), worked in a Thurlstone cloth mill as a dresser or finisher when he was a young man, but on the occasion of his second marriage in 1900 he gave his occupation as waggoner. He had moved a mile or so up the valley to live at Bullhouse Lodge and work at the nearby corn mill. The lodge was an old farmhouse that had seen better days. Like many a similiar building it had declined in status but in recent years it has been handsomely restored to its former glory. The family historian who visits such a place would find it hard to believe that it was once the home of a mere waggoner if he had not seen old photographs that show its condition before the First World War. Many old farmhouses were, of course, sometimes divided into two or three cottages once their gentry or yeomen owners had vacated them.

In districts where industrial crafts such as weaving or metal-working had been long established many families had a history of involvement in one or more of the local trades over several generations. In 1851 the Ridge family monopolised the manufacture of brace bits and gimlets in the south Yorkshire village of Ecclesfield, with nine separate households working at the craft. A Ridge had been recorded in a list of nailers in the village back in Queen Anne's reign and the family's connection with metal hand crafts was not broken until 1970 when John Henry Ridge retired (at the age of ninety-one) from his part-time occupation of making gimlets in the last of Ecclesfield's little smithies. But the dramatic, large-scale industrial developments of the nineteenth century produced a markedly different form of society where the majority of workers were often recent immigrants from all corners of the land.

Coal-mining

Until well into the nineteenth century the nation's coalminers were not regarded as a race apart, living and working in closely-knit communities dominated by the colliery's winding gear and huge, ugly muck stacks, but merely as one of a number of groups of village craftsmen and labourers. In earlier times many miners had worked only a part of their time digging coal; the rest of their income came from labouring jobs or from a smallholding. Geographical isolation and the hereditary nature of their job made the collier-farmers of the Forest of Dean a distinctive, inward-looking group, but they were a special case. The North-east coalfield developed early because of access to sea routes to the capital; the other landlocked coalfields catered only for regional markets before canals and navigable rivers enabled them to lower their prices and until the railways opened up national markets. Such was the rapid rate of expansion that ensued that the workforce in Britain's mines rose from a mere 50,000 at the beginning of the nineteenth century to over 1 million on the eve of the First World War.

Where did all these miners come from? No two coalfields were the same, but if a general pattern can be discerned from the variety of experience it is that during the first half of the nineteenth century each region largely generated its own workforce from the natural increase of its population, but that the spectacular later developments drew not only upon local men who left the farms or rural crafts and industries in large numbers but also upon the surplus population of counties from all over the British Isles. In *Pit-Men, Preachers and Politics* (1974) Professor Robert Moore has noted that in the Deerness Valley east of Durham City many old mining families recall the time when their ancestors had rural occupations. Between 1851 and 1901 the agricultural labour force

167

in County Durham dropped from 10,004 to 5,049, and during the same period many others were thrown out of work when the lead mines closed. Deerness Valley colliers with distinctive Weardale and Teesdale surnames such as Nattress, Vipond and Hewitson probably came from lead-mining stock. When drift mines were first sunk in this valley during the 1850s the workforce walked in each day from the surrounding villages and hamlets, but from the 1860s onwards the coalmasters had to provide new accommodation; Pease and Partners, for example, had built 151 houses at Waterhouses by 1874. The families that came to live in these new terraced rows came from far afield, including some from Ireland.

A similar pattern can be traced in the Yorkshire coalfield. Until the 1860s or 1870s the natural increase in the local population was sufficient to fill the vacancies in the pits, but then the sinking of deep mines to work the Silkstone and Barnsley seams on a vast new scale increased the demand for labour to such an extent that immigrants poured in from Staffordshire, Lancashire, Cheshire, other parts of Yorkshire and elsewhere. When Denaby Main colliery was sunk on the eastern edge of the old coalfield in 1868 hardly any of the workforce had local origins; of the 166 colliers recorded in the 1871 census for the new pit village only ten were born in Yorkshire. Some pit villages were old agricultural communities which had been transformed by an influx of miners; others, such as Denaby Main and Fitzwilliam, were new creations founded at the edge of parishes and away from the older settlements. They had little in common with neighbouring villages whose squires kept the collieries and colliers out of sight.

Dronfield

The small Derbyshire town of Dronfield provides a vivid illustration of the way that an old market centre hardly bigger than a village could be gradually changed by industrial development and then transformed in character when the decision was made to build a new steel works there. A Thursday market had been established in 1662 and during the seventeenth and eighteenth centuries many local families had prospered through their involvement not only in farming but in the lead smelting and millstone trades. The fine stone houses that line the High Street reflect the change in architectural fashion from the gabled halls lit by mullioned windows to the more symmetrical tastes of the Queen Anne period. Then in the 1730s the vicar and the usher of the grammar school chose to build in brick; the usher's home was named the Red House because this material was so unusual in those parts at the time. Several more substantial gentry houses can still be found in the rural parts of Dronfield's large parish. In the *Universal British Directory* of 1792 the place was described as:

> a small neat market town . . . pleasantly situated in a valley, surrounded, except on the western side, with verdant eminences crowned with trees, of various hues, and beautifully interlaid with golden plots of shining cornland. The finest springwater in the Kingdom issues abundantly from the rocks, and winds, in serpentine directions, almost through every part. Here too is plenty of coal at a very reasonable rate; every necessary article of life is attainable on moderate terms; house rent is low; and land, in general, proportionally so. This place has long been celebrated for an uncommon salubrity of air, which at present encourages the residence of several respectable families, and undoubtedly has given rise to the numerous pretty buildings that salute the eye in almost every quarter.

The coal that is referred to in this eulogy was mined in pits that did not have to be sunk far to reach the Silkstone seam. These collieries were largely responsible for Dronfield's early industrial development, for when the 1861 census was taken 383 men, or 48 per cent of the workforce, were employed in local mines. Metalworking was the other growth area, especially after Edward Lucas & Son Ltd had established an iron foundry in the valley below the church in 1790. By 1861 the edge tool and other metal trades employed 253 men, or 32 per cent of the workforce. The population of Dronfield township had grown steadily from 1,182 in 1801 to 2,998 in 1861. Ten years later it stood at 3,253, then over the next decade it shot up to 5,169.

Mrs K. Battye's local history class have mapped the information recorded in the 1881 census returns and have related much of it to existing buildings. 711 people formed 149 households in the central area of the town. The older and more substantial houses were occupied by the professional and commercial classes. Dr Thomas Brereton lived at The Grange, Dr Samuel Rooth at Grange House, Samuel Lucas, iron founder, resided at the Hall, the Manor House was divided between a farmer/cattle dealer and a farmer/coal owner, and at The Rookery Mr W. H. Rangeley was looked after by his 'devoted begum' who was born in

Tobago. Behind the major properties were a number of cottages huddled together in yards or strung out along the lanes. Farwater Lane and Goodwin's Yard provided accommodation for 190 people in 34 households, including 24 miners, 10 labourers, 10 metal workers, a grocer, a farmer, a carter, a shoemaker, a musician and many others. Some are more easy for the genealogist to pick out than the rest. A seventy-two-year-old boot and shoe maker living with his daughter's family in Outram's Yard had the splendid name of Euclid Shufflebottom.

The central core of the town was mostly occupied by those families which had lived in Dronfield before the momentous decision was taken in 1873 by the new company of Wilson Cammell to found a large steelworks specializing in the manufacture of rails made from Bessemer steel. The chosen site was on Callywhite Lane and Mill Lane opposite the Dronfield Silkstone Colliery and close to the Midland Railway, whose nearby station had been opened in 1870. The country's railway network was expanding rapidly and the manufacture of steel rails was a lucrative business for Sheffield firms.

In *Steel Town: Dronfield and Wilson Cammell, 1873–1883* (1983) J. Austin and M. Ford have described the way that the town was changed by the coming of the steel works. The heads of various departments, foremen and other key workers were recruited from just across the county boundary in Sheffield and south Yorkshire; the rest of the labour force came from many parts of Britain and Ireland. In 1881, when the works employed some 500–600 men, the census returns noted that 19 per cent of the workforce came from the Dronfield area, 12 per cent from elsewhere in Derbyshire, 12 per cent from the Sheffield area and 57 per cent from further afield, especially from Staffordshire, Cambridgeshire, Lincolnshire, Nottinghamshire and Yorkshire. These newcomers were mostly housed in new areas on the fringes of the town, especially between Green Lane and Snape Hill to the north of the river valley. Here 'The Dronfield Freehold Land Society' built both cottages and middle-class houses on a 19-acre site divided into 180 allotments; the streets were named after local landowners and after Princess Alexandra, the wife of the Prince of Wales. A group of fifty company houses known as Cammells Row were built close to the works on Chesterfield Road.

For nearly ten years the company flourished and Dronfield thrived, but when the home market for steel rails was saturated and firms had to look overseas for customers the land-locked

Plate 3.9   A family of basket weavers
An undated photograph of members of the Richardson family, who lived and worked at Green Lane, Dronfield. They applied the traditional skills of their craft to the manufacture of baskets for the local coke industry. Another family of basket weavers worked at the hamlet of Summerley, near some coke ovens.

position of the Sheffield area became a decided disadvantage. On 'Black Friday', 2 April 1883 the last rails were cast at Callywhite Lane and Wilson Cammell moved their entire business to the Cumbrian coastal town of Workington. By 11 April 221 houses were unoccupied; shops were closed and property values collapsed. About a third of the town's population moved out, many of them following the company to Workington. A Cumbrian newspaper observed that, 'Never before had an almost complete community been transplanted into West Cumberland'. The 'Dronnies', as the migrants were known, helped to swell

Workington's population from 14,400 in 1881 to 25,200 in 1891. During the same decade Dronfield's population fell from 5,169 to 4,166. It took forty years for Dronfield to recover to its 1881 level.

MARKET TOWNS

Victorian market towns tend to be regarded – if they are thought of at all – as slumbering relics of the past, places of little account that had been relegated to minor status by the new industrial cities. Guide books and handbooks for travellers often dismissed them as being of little interest. Thus in his guide to the East Riding (1906) Joseph Morris described Market Weighton as 'a dull little town' and Howden as 'a dull and depressing little town'. No doubt some of them were rather on the dreary side but that is not the full story by any means. Though towns such as Thirsk which had been by-passed by the railways had lost some of their former vitality, others continued to expand, to rebuild and to prosper during the Victorian era. Many if not most of them had doubled in size during the first half of the nineteenth century. Characteristically, they ranged in size from about 1,000 to 4,000 people in the early years of Victoria's reign, but the ones that were administrative, legal or ecclesiastical centres as well as market towns were sometimes larger than that. Most were of local importance only, serving a limited rural hinterland in the way they had always done since the Middle Ages. Their leading families were professional people – clergy, solicitors, doctors, teachers, bankers, surveyors and so on – and also wealthy tradesmen such as millers, maltsters, tanners, ironmongers and innkeepers, but the characteristic figure in all these small towns was the craftsman. Often, as many as half the inhabitants of a Victorian market town were craftsmen who both lived and worked on premises which were sited as near to the market place as possible. They offered a wide range of services to the surrounding rural families. For much of the time these small market towns may well have appeared sleepy to travellers who were familiar with the hustle and bustle of the big cities, but every week on market day and more especially at the time of the annual fairs they were transformed by an influx of visitors. The Victorian age was not simply one of progress, measured in terms of population growth and economic activity.

Life in the countryside remained firmly rooted in the past. The ancient rhythms still mattered; continuity was not destroyed by the unprecedented changes, but was the most obvious characteristic of rural areas.

No better picture of a mid-nineteenth century market town can be found than the portrait of Dorchester in Thomas Hardy's *The Mayor of Casterbridge*. The 'antiquated borough' of Casterbridge 'was the complement of the rural life around; not its urban opposite'. It 'lived by agriculture at one remove further from the fountain-head than the adjoining villages – no more'.

> The agricultural and personal character of the people upon whom the town depended for its existence was shown by the class of objects displayed in the shop windows. Scythes, reap-hooks, sheep-shears, bill-hooks, spades, mattocks, and hoes at the ironmonger's; bee-hives, butter-firkins, churns, milking stools and pails, hay rakes, field-flagons, and seed-lips at the cooper's; cart-ropes and plough-harness at the saddler's; carts, wheel-barrows, and mill-gear at the wheelwright's and machinist's; horse-embracations at the chemist's; at the glover's and leather-cutter's, hedging-gloves, thatchers' knee-caps, ploughmen's leggings, villagers' pattens and clogs.

When the church struck eight:

> a bell began to toll with a peremptory clang. The curfew was still rung in Casterbridge, and it was utilized by the inhabitants as a signal for shutting their shops. No sooner did the deep notes of the bell throb between the house-fronts than a clatter of shutters arose through the whole length of the High Street. In a few minutes business at Casterbridge was ended for the day.

Dorchester had a population of about 6,500 in 1851, half of whom resided in the parish of Fordington. The Fordington end of town was notorious locally for its slums and rough characters. Dorchester was at its busiest on market day but it was far from silent at other times. In addition to the usual inns and shops, professional residences and a few town houses belonging to the local nobility and gentry, it contained two barracks, county courts, a prison, a workhouse, a hospital and a museum. When Thomas Hardy was given the freedom of the borough in 1910 he made a comment of particular interest to family historians: he said that 'of the shops as I first recollect them [he was born in 1840] not a single owner remains; only in two or three instances does even the name remain . . . Nothing is permanent but change'. Is this quick turnover of names typical of the experience of Victorian market towns? We do not know, for this is an under-researched topic and nineteenth-century market towns have not yet attracted much serious attention. The family and local historian can make a significant contribution here.

One exemplary study is *Early Victorian Country Town: A Portrait of Ashbourne in the Mid Nineteenth Century* (1978), edited by Adrian Henstock. Under Henstock's guidance a group of local historians plotted information from the 1851 census enumerators' books on the near-contemporary tithe award map and filled out the picture from newspapers and other sources. They were able to show that a high proportion of the buildings that still front the main street leading from the church to the market place were retail shops, public houses and other commercial properties whose owners lived on the premises, usually above or behind the shop. The triangular market place was tightly packed with such properties and much of the original space had been filled with permanent buildings where once only stalls had been allowed. The market places of many an old town throughout the country have been encroached upon in similar ways.

The craftsmen and working classes who formed the bulk of Ashbourne's population lived in small terraced brick cottages along the minor streets or in small yards behind the major properties. These houses were rarely seen by travellers who passed through the town on their way from Derby to Manchester. The yards were reached either by a narrow alley or through a tunnel entrance; they took their name from the owner or sometimes from the occupant of the property that fronted the street. Yards were a typical feature not only of industrial cities but of many a small country town which had to accommodate a rising population. Ashbourne had about 25 yards, whose houses provided shelter for some 750 people, or nearly a quarter of the town's inhabitants. In addition to these yards terraced cottages that were similar in size and appearance were built to the north of Mutton Lane. These properties formed a marked contrast to the fine Georgian brick buildings in the main streets and to the recently-acquired, impressive collection of public buildings that gave a prosperous air to the face of the town. An analysis of the birthplaces of all the heads of households recorded in the 1851 census showed that 57 per cent were born outside Ashbourne. The largest group of immigrants came from within a 5-mile radius, but almost as many came from 5–10 miles and as many again from beyond 20 miles; only half this number came from between 10 and 20 miles. A more complicated pattern of movement was revealed by an analysis of the birthplace of children in those sixty-four families which had children under the age of twelve. This showed that many young families moved frequently; by 1851 the pattern for this group was fairly evenly distributed between the 5-, 10- and 20-mile radii and beyond.

Some Victorian market towns acquired a pronounced industrial character, especially after the railways had provided cheaper raw materials and had opened up distant markets. But such places retained their ancient functions and the market area kept its traditional character intact. At the other side of Derbyshire from Ashbourne, Chesterfield's population rose from 4,267 in 1801 to 7,101 in 1851, but most of the important industrial developments – especially the potteries, ironworks and collieries – took place beyond the borough boundary in the outlying parts of the parish, particularly in the township of Brampton. The old market town was surrounded but not transformed by these activities. The physical appearance of Chesterfield's market place was altered by the erection of a huge market hall in 1857, but even today the shape of the area is that determined upon back in the twelfth century when a decision was taken to found a new market at what was then the edge of the town. Stalls are still set out in the open air and the market place is hemmed in by shops, banks and public houses whose frontages still respect the ancient property boundaries.

Lincolnshire examples

The various trade and commercial directories that were published at regular intervals during the nineteenth century are a particularly useful source for the study of old market towns. They do not list all the inhabitants by any means, but as a large proportion of the workforce were employed in trades, crafts and services a good idea of the occupational structure of a town can be quickly gained from a scrutiny of the classified entries. Moreover, there is much of interest to be gleaned from the general remarks that are made about each place. William White's *History, Gazetteer and Directory of Lincolnshire* (1856) is a typical example of the genre. At that time, Lincolnshire was the second largest county in England but it was thirteenth in terms of population; it had only 208,557 people in 1801 and 407,222 fifty years later. Lincoln, Stamford, Boston, Grantham and Grimsby had reputations that had spread

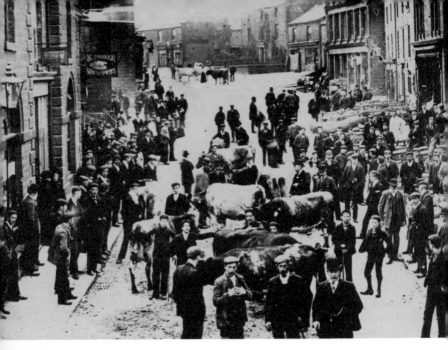

Plate 3.10 Market day at Penistone in Edwardian times
Market day seems to have been an all-masculine affair at Penistone early this century. The livestock market was held in the central streets until its removal to the present site in 1910. The view looks up Market Street towards High Street.

Penistone market was founded in 1699 and was originally for corn as well as for dairy cattle and the local breed of sheep. The building in the foreground on the left was erected in 1763 as a cloth hall in the middle of the old market square. Thursday was chosen as market day so as not to clash with the Wednesday market at Barnsley. Inns and shops were built in the central area when the market proved successful.

beyond the county boundaries, but otherwise Lincolnshire's market towns were just neighbourhood centres.

On perusing the pages of White's 1856 directory it is noticeable how many of these small market towns had been rebuilt and improved during the first half of the nineteenth century. We read, for instance, that Spalding 'has now a very neat and generally modern appearance, having more than doubled its population and buildings since 1811, and most of its ancient houses and public buildings have been rebuilt; many of them during the last twenty-five years'. Sleaford was described as a flourishing and important market town that had been 'much improved and beautified during the present century'; its population had risen from 1,483 to 3,372 between 1801 and 1851. And Bourne was said to be 'a well-built and pleasant market town, which has doubled its population during the last forty years'. The improved navigation schemes of the later eighteenth century had been beneficial in stimulating the local economy. Even the small river Slea had been made navigable for light craft and Sleaford had benefited from 'a cheap and easy transit for corn, coal, timber, stone, lime and other merchandise, to and from Boston, Lincoln and other places'.

Louth had prospered in this way after a canal had provided a direct link with the mouth of the Humber, 10 miles or so away. 'By means of it', the directory informs us, 'vessels trade regularly to London, Hull, and various parts of Yorkshire, carrying out corn and wool, and bringing in return timber, coals, groceries, etc'. Trading vessels went down the canal every week to Grimsby and Hull and every month to London. Land transport to all parts was provided by seventeen carriers operating from the inns and by the railway which had reached Louth in 1848. The directory told its readers that:

> The principal chartered market is held every Wednesday, and is well supplied with corn and cattle; but that held on Saturday is chiefly for meat, vegetables, butter, fruit, etc. Since 1802, a sheep market has been held every Friday during spring and autumn; and on every alternate Friday here is now a fat stock market. The annual fairs are held April 29th for sheep, and 30th for cattle and horses; on the Fridays before September 18th and October 28th, and on November 23rd, for cattle, etc. The latter is called the Michaelmas fair. The Market place occupies a large area and the broad avenues, leading to it, in the centre of the town, and is lined with neat buildings, well stocked shops, and several commodious inns; but the Cattle market is at Quarry hill, on the south side of the town, where there are convenient sheep pens. . . .
>
> The Corn Exchange, in the Corn Market, is a large and handsome building, in the Italian style, erected in 1853, on the site of the old Guildhall. . . .
>
> On the small river Lud here is a carpet and rug manufactory, and two corn and two bone mills. Here are also several extensive tanners, fellmongers, curriers, ropers, maltsters, brewers, lime burners, etc; as well as several iron foundries and agricultural machine works. The navigation wharfs are at Riverhead, at the east end of the town, where there are large granaries, and coal and timber yards.

On the other side of the Lincolnshire Wolds, 13 miles south of Louth, Horncastle was 'a thriving and well-built market town, distinguished for its extensive horse fairs'. Between 1801 and 1851 its population rose from 2,015 to 4,921. By then Horncastle had a handsome appearance and contained many well-stocked shops with elegant frontages: 'The erection of the Corn Exchange, the Butter Market, the Railway station, the County Court Office, the new Vicarage House, and the chaste little Chapel of Ease have greatly improved the appearance of the town'. The other places of worship comprised the ancient parish church and Wesleyan, Primitive Methodist, Independent and Baptist chapels. Eleven inns provided carrying services to other parts of Lincolnshire and vessels regularly left the wharf for Lincoln, Boston and Hull.

Our final example from this Lincolnshire directory is Gainsborough, 'an ancient market town and port, with a railway station, situated on the Trent'. Boatmen plied their trade down the Trent to Stockwith, Keadby and other river ports and up the Idle to Bawtry, while steam packets provided regular services to Hull, Newcastle, King's Lynn, and London, and intermediate places. In 1856 Gainsborough had 13 wharfingers and shipping agents, 6 marine store dealers, 10 ship and sloop owners, 4 ship and boat builders and a sailmaker. The 13 coal merchants and some of the 12 corn and seed merchants no doubt operated from the wharf. An extensive network of carrying services was also provided from the 19 inns in or near the market place. Gainsborough had:

> Two Fairs, or Marts, as they are commonly called, [which] are annually held here, under a charter from Charles II, one on Easter Tuesday, and the other on the Tuesday after the 20th of October, each continuing nine days (exclusive of Sunday) for the sale of cloth, pedlery and other merchandize; but horses, cattle, and swine are exposed for sale only on the Wednesday; and cheese on the first two days of each fair or mart . . . . The horse and cattle fair is held on Bridge hill; the cheese fair in the market place; and the mart for cloth, toys, etc. in the Mart yard. The Corn Exchange occupies part of the Old Hall [Gainsborough's medieval manor house]. The Butter and Poultry Market, built in 1852, is a neat building with a glass roof. The market, held every Tuesday, is well supplied with corn, cattle, and all sorts of provisions. A hiring for servants is held on November 5th, and is numerously attended.

As one reads the pages of classified entries the rich variety of professions, trades and crafts to be found in Victorian market towns is brought home in a vivid manner. Gainsborough had 44 hotels, inns and taverns, 9 beerhouses and 4 eating and boarding houses. Its professional people included 6 attorneys, 7 auctioneers, 6 surgeons, a physician and no less than 28 firms providing fire and life insurance. Amongst the familiar occupations were traders in more unusual commodities such as the 2 ginger beer makers, 7 guano, etc. merchants (artifical manures, etc.), 5 gypsum merchants and 2 tobacco manufacturers. The town provided a living for 15 bakers and flour dealers, 8 blacksmiths, 27 boot and shoe makers, 24 butchers, 11 confectioners, 21 grocers and tea dealers, 7 hatters, 10 hair dressers and perfumers, 18 joiners and builders, 9 drapers, 11 maltsters, 17 milliners, 24 tailors and drapers, 8 watch and clock makers and numerous others. It is hard to think of any useful commodity that was not on offer in this thriving market town. Gainsborough had 3 banks, several schools, and places of worship for Anglicans, Catholics and 6 different dissenting sects. Its population in 1851 had risen to 7,261.

Pocklington

Further north, in Yorkshire, Pocklington was amongst those scores of ancient market towns which continued to fulfill their traditional roles during the Victorian era. Its inhabitants liked to call it the Woldopolis and to regard it as the hub of life in that part of the East Riding. Markets had been held there from time immemorial, almost certainly from long before a royal grant was obtained in 1245 for an annual four-day fair. Domesday Book shows that way back in the eleventh century Pocklington was the centre of a large royal manor containing a church and three water mills and that its inhabitants included fifteen burgesses. Some sort of urban community was already there in embryonic form. The church served an enormous parish which covered 26,000 acres and included seventeen townships within its bounds. Pocklington was indeed the most important place for miles around. During the later Middle Ages All Saints church was rebuilt, largely through the profits of the wool trade, and in 1514 the lord of the manor founded a school which attracted the sons of the richest families in the neighbourhood. By the eighteenth century Pocklington society included a number of gentlemen, attorneys, apothecaries, merchants and those rural clergy who preferred to live in the town rather than in the cultural isolation of their rural parsonages. By then the market place accommodated seven annual fairs (three for horses and four for cattle, cheese, cloth and leather) in addition to the weekly Saturday market, and all about the central area the full variety of shops, inns, businesses and workshops that one associates with a market town were to be found. For further information we need to turn to David Neave's booklet, *Pocklington, 1660–1914: A Small East Riding Market Town* (1984).

Pocklington's population rose from 1,502 in 1801 to 2,546 in 1851 but two excellent plans of the town, drawn up by William Watson in 1844 and 1855, show how little the medieval lay-out had been altered over the years other than by encroachments onto the market place. Such plans are of great value to the local and family historian for they show all the buildings and properties in the town and give the names of every occupant. Most of Pocklington's streets had been called gates (a word that had been introduced into this country by the Vikings), but during the nineteenth century Hungate was re-named George Street, Southgate became Regent Street, St Peter's Gate was changed to Union Street and the colourful name of Pudding Gate was altered to Pavement. Only Chapmangate and St Helen's Gate retained their ancient forms. Many an old street name up and down the country was lost in this way during the course of the nineteenth century. A genuine improvement rather than the cosmetic change of re-naming took place in Pocklington during the century after 1780 when the old timber, mud and thatch buildings were gradually replaced by newer homes, shops and public buildings that were constructed of brick and roofed with pantiles or slates. Watson's 1844 plan shows at least twenty-eight thatched buildings, but eleven years later the town had only two. Many of the new buildings were the work of Thomas Grant (1823–1907), a local builder – architect who, according to his obituary, was responsible for 'the major part of the principal property in Pocklington'. By the mid-Victorian era the parish church had been restored and the Wesleyan, Primitive Methodist, Congregational and Roman Catholic chapels rebuilt, the town also had two National schools, Wesleyan and Roman Catholic schools and a revived grammar school, together with a library and a newspaper. The professional people and the wealthy tradesmen ran the place but the characteristic figures in the town were the shopkeepers and the craftsmen.

The Wesleyan Methodist chapel in Chapmangate was built in 1864 on the site of its predecessor of 1813. It was designed in the Grecian style by Edward Taylor, a York architect who used red brick for the body of the building and stone for the dressings. A large portico supported by six Doric pillars provided a suitably impressive entrance to the chapel, for by then the leading

Plate 3.11   William Watson's Plan of Pocklington, 1855 (detail)
William Watson made two careful and beautifully executed plans of the
East Riding market town of Pocklington in 1844 and 1855. These include
elevations of all the buildings and the names of each head of household,
sometimes with their occupation. They are of great value to the local and
family historian, especially when used in conjunction with the census
enumerators' returns.

The plan shows how the old market area had been partly infilled with
shops, inns and public buildings, many of which still survive. A wide
range of services were on offer.

Wesleyans in the town had become rich and respectable. Houses
for the circuit ministers were built on either side of the chapel in
1864 and 1869. They are a useful visual reminder that the chapel
attracted worshippers from the surrounding countryside.
Amongst the rural members of the congregation that filled the
chapel in its early days were my great-grandparents from Allerthorpe, a mile or so away. They were married here on 15 July
1871. George Webster was a twenty-four-year-old saddler, the
son of John Webster, an Allerthorpe groom. His bride, Mary
Kell, was the twenty-six-year-old daughter of Thomas Kell, an
Allerthorpe farm labourer. George was probably already working

181

in Pocklington, walking into work each day, for a saddler would not have had much employment in the small village where he lived. Earlier that year on census night George was residing with his parents in Allerthorpe. His elder brother, Richard, lived nearby with his wife and young daughter, and like his father worked as a groom, possibly at nearby Waplington Hall, a large, gabled house that had been built some thirty years earlier. Ten years later Richard was farming 12 acres in Allerthorpe and his family had grown to seven children; his parents were now living alone on another smallholding of 14 acres.

The 1871 census entry for their neighbours the Kells is summarized in Table 5. When I started my enquiries into our family history I was told that Mary Kell was two years older than George Webster and that she had previously been engaged to his elder brother who had died before they could marry. The presence of an illegitimate child to that elder brother had been kept a dark secret. He was listed as Edwin Kell, boarder, aged fifteen in the 1881 Pocklington census, but when the family moved from the East Riding to Easingwold about 1888 he was passed off as George and Mary's eldest son.

George and Mary Webster eventually had another twelve children and found it difficult to make ends meet. In my grandmother's oft-repeated phrase, 'Pocklington was riddled with saddlers'. Upon their marriage they had moved from Allerthorpe to the market town and in 1881 were living and working in the Market Place, next door to Henry King the ratcatcher and close to two other saddlers. The competition made them decide to move to Easingwold, some 22 miles away as the crow flies and nearer 28 miles along the winding roads. I always regret that as a youth it never occurred to me to ask why they chose Easingwold and how they knew of a vacancy for someone who could combine the saddlery trade with being the landlord of the *Jolly Farmers* pub. Nor did it occur to me then to enquire how it was possible in those days for a keen Wesleyan Methodist to become a publican. I shall never know the answers now, for these things are passed on only by word of mouth and are not written down. The move and the dual occupation are confirmed by a documentary source, however, for the entry under Easingwold in the pages of Bulmer's *Directory of the North Riding of Yorkshire* (1890) notes: 'Jolly Farmer, Spring Street: George Webster' and 'Saddlers and Harness Makers: George Webster, Spring Street'. Easingwold was described by Joseph Morris as 'a quiet old town, with a number

Table 5 The 1871 census entry for the Kell family

Thomas Kell	head	widower	66	farm labourer	born: Holme on Spalding Moor
Mary Kell	daughter	unmarried	26	dress maker	born: Allerthorpe
Edwin Webster Kell	grandson		6	scholar	born: Allerthorpe
Elizabeth Wright	servant	unmarried	62	servant	born: Holme on Spalding Moor

of respectable houses'. Its population had risen slowly from 1,467 in 1801 to 2,240 in 1851, but then it had declined steadily to 1,932 in 1891.

My grandfather remembered his father-in-law as a smallish man with black hair and dark brown eyes, a good singer who sang in choir festivals in York Minster. He always insisted on saying grace before meals, but he was a very bad tempered man, a 'clever sort' who drank himself to death. He collected the left-overs in his customers' beer mugs and afterwards re-sold them as a special brew. It was perhaps no wonder that his 'quiet, nice' wife had hair that had gone white by the time she was thirty. Nevertheless, the move to Easingwold, a small market town that was similar in many ways to Pocklington but with fewer saddlers, was a beneficial one, for the family certainly did better once they were there. George died in 1906 at the age of fifty-nine and Mary lived to be eighty-four. The *Jolly Farmers* has been demolished, but I remember it as a brick and pantile structure at the top end of the town. And I remember the family story of how on the eve of my grandmother's wedding day her elder brother Ted had been locked out by her father and had broken a window to get in. Now that I know that George was not his father I can better understand why they always clashed.

FARMING FAMILIES

The 1851 census for England and Wales recorded about a quarter of a million farmers and graziers, of whom more than 23,000 were women. After 1851 the number of agricultural labourers fell steadily, but the number of farming families remained about the same for the rest of the century. Most of these families had deep roots in the countryside as we have seen and their ancestry can be traced back several centuries. This long attachment to local places is not always apparent at the level of an individual parish but it can be observed time and time again if one studies a wider neighbourhood. The stability of some farming families was as marked in Victorian England as it had been in the past. Moreover, these ancient local dynasties had inter-married several times and had created a network of connections throughout the countryside. In this way the bonds between people and place were cemented; farming families had links with parishes further afield but they were conscious of a well-defined neighbourhood that was peculiarly their own.

When the Faversham Farmers' Club in east Kent celebrated its 200th anniversary on 21 June 1927 its claim to be the oldest of its type in the country went unchallenged. The father of the club, Prideaux George Selby, marked the occasion by publishing a history of the club and its members, a history that included 131 short biographies of all the members since the club's inception, thus covering most of the old yeomen families that farmed near the town. Selby observed that for the first 100 years members mostly lived and died near their original homes or at the most within 20 miles of them and that five-sixths of the members had been connected by blood or marriage with previous members; they almost always married into the families of their near neighbours. Families such as the Cobbs and the Hiltons could be traced back several generations in the same neighbourhood. The Neames (who provided the largest number of club members) were an old east Kent family whom Selby could trace back to the fifteenth century. They had come into the Faversham area when Thomas Neame (1746–1817) moved to Selling Court and married a Cobb. Later Neames married into such other local families as Abbot, Bayden, Beale, Chapman, Dell, Stunt, Tassell, Wightwick and Wildash and only one ventured as far afield as Sussex in search of a bride. Such a story as this can be repeated many times amongst the farming families in other parts of the country, particularly those which shared Kent's topographical features and scattered settlement patterns.

In his essay, *Transformation and Tradition: Aspects of the Victorian Countryside* (University of East Anglia, 1984), Professor Alan Everitt has written:

> If you had belonged to one of the farming clans of Kent in the 1860s and 70s you would have found yourself part of a vast local

Plate 3.12 A pony and trap
The life-style of a well-to-do Victorian farming family is captured in this photograph of a couple in their horse-drawn carriage. They are probably Mr and Mrs Milnes of Oughtibridge Hall in south-west Yorkshire, for the photograph is taken from the Milnes family album of 1892–95.

cousinage, often with fifteen or twenty other branches in the county, sometimes many more, and with few or no branches as yet elsewhere. Like the gentry of the seventeenth century from whom many of them were descended, they were also closely connected with one another by inter-marriage as well as by ancestry.

Professor Everitt has used Kelly's 1870 *Directory of Kent* to reconstruct the 221 most important farming dynasties in the county, dynasties that had 4,450 separately-established branches. These families were remarkably insular; in numerous cases their surnames were derived from minor Kentish settlement names such as Blaxland, Greenstreet and Chittenden, and they had rarely spread beyond the county boundary. Thus the 23 Hambrooks, 21 Homewoods, 16 Kingsnorths and 13 Groombridges were found in limited groups of parishes and the forty branches of the Deane family were entirely confined to Kent. They and many others were 'intensely localized in outlook and connexion'. The 4,450 branches recorded in the directory can be classified as 1,143 families headed by farmers, 2,453 families of craftsmen, tradesmen, innkeepers, manufacturers in the market towns, etc. and 854 families of professional people or minor gentry. Even the latter group had rarely moved far, restricting their movement to the nearby villages and market towns. Kent was an old-enclosed county of dispersed farmsteads, many of whose sites had been occupied since medieval or pre-conquest times. The property had been anciently divided into small family farms, so it was difficult for outsiders to stake a claim and for the grasping to build up a great estate. The Kentish pattern may well be repeated in other parts of the country with a similar agrarian structure, particularly in the pastoral areas of the West and the North, but in the great Midland Plain where the large arable fields of communal husbandry prevented villages spreading beyond their ancient confines perhaps the continuity and inter-linking of dynasties was not such a marked phenomenon. We need many more histories of farming families from all the regions of England before we can be sure. Even then, the picture that emerges will probably be full of small details, constantly changing from whichever angle one looks at it, rather than a clear statement produced by broad strokes of the brush. Let us therefore look in more detail at one particular family whose history I myself have researched.

The Battys: a case-study of a Yorkshire family in the eighteenth and nineteenth centuries

The low Howardian Hills on the southern fringe of the North York Moors roll gently down into the flat, fertile lands of the northern Vale of York. To the east, the river Derwent acted as the ancient boundary between the North and East Ridings. From the west, the river Ouse and its tributaries the Swale, the Ure and the Nidd flow in from the Pennines. All the main lines of communication head south for the city of York. In this neighbourhood in Victorian times lived many inter-related farming dynasties, including that of my mother's ancestors, the Battys. Their gravestones are to be found at the foot of the fine octagonal tower of St Michael's church, Coxwold and grouped together in a corner of St Nicholas's churchyard a couple of miles away at Husthwaite.

For 150 years or so they had gradually built up their estates, so that by the mid-Victorian period they had established several successful branches and had acquired 1,000 acres of land between them. But when the age of Victorian High Farming came to an end so did their prosperity; the Great Agricultural Depression brought their ruin and now there are no Battys left in the area.

The family established roots in Coxwold during the first half of the eighteenth century when the names of Richard and John Batty were first entered in the local parish register. John was living in the parish of Coxwold, when he married in 1736; his descendants can be located more precisely at Thornton on the Hill, 2 or 3 miles south of the church. Meanwhile, Richard had established the senior branch of the family at Coxwold Park, a farmstead that still seems to distance itself from the village and which can be reached only along rough tracks and paths. Richard was buried at Coxwold on 28 May 1789, having died of dropsy at the good old age of eighty-eight. His widow, Frances, died of palsy 2 years later at the age of eighty-two. Between 1736 and 1755 they had baptised seven boys and two girls, whose names are faithfully recorded in the parish register.

A family historian will of necessity as well as of devotion spend hours and hours on every minor detail of his family tree. The people whose names he has seen written in many and varied archives are his own flesh and blood and therefore worthy of such attention; painstaking, detailed work is absolutely necessary if he is to disentangle the many threads of the story. But his reader or listener cannot be expected to share his pleasure to the full. Suffice it to say, therefore, that two of the children of Richard and Frances Batty established branches that spread to many parts of the northern Vale of York during the later-eighteenth and nineteenth centuries. James (1750–1815) inherited Park Farm at Coxwold and Richard (1755–1833) set up a new home at Woolpots 2 miles to the south.

Succeeding generations of the Batty family followed the same practice whereby the junior members moved from the parental home upon marriage to a nearby farm which had conveniently become vacant. In this way they gradually spread over a wide neighbourhood. This process can be illustrated from the personal histories of the children of James and Ann Batty of Coxwold Park. James and Anne had four boys and two girls, but as both the eldest boy and the eldest girl died in childhood the next children were given the same names; they were named Richard and Frances after their grandparents. Frances and her youngest brother James died in their early twenties, but the family line was continued by the remaining two boys, Richard and Thomas.

Plate 3.13 St Michael's Church, Coxwold

St Michael's church occupies a hill-top site, appropriate for such a dedication. It succeeded a monastery that had been founded by the mid-eighth century and it served a wide parish in the Middle Ages. The building was designed in a fifteenth-century Perpendicular Gothic style with attractive openwork battlements that are similar to those at Thirsk, St Martin le Grand at York and the Greyfriars tower at Richmond. The unusual octagonal tower is crowned with an openwork parapet similar in style to other Yorkshire examples at Skirlaugh, Tickhill and All Saints Pavement, York. The chancel, which was rebuilt in 1774, contains several memorials of the Bellasis family of Newburgh Priory.

Their life histories are worth considering because in their movement from farm to farm in order to better themselves they were typical of many other English farming families.

Richard Batty (1799–1878) was earning his living as a butcher in the parish of Coxwold when in 1820 he married Rosamond (or Rosy) Dixon, a Husthwaite girl. They set up home at Scackleton Grange, a farmstead 8 miles east of Coxwold in the parish of Hovingham, not far from the great house at Castle Howard. Here their children, Robert and Frances, were born in 1821 and 1825. Their movements can be traced with the help of the census returns which record the places of birth and the ages of their children. By 1828 or 1829 they had made the major decision to move right across the Vale of York to Wallerthwaite, a farmstead along the lane from Markington within the parish of Ripon. Wallerthwaite is 23 miles as the crow flies from Scackleton and considerably longer by the winding roads. The reason for this move would have remained obscure had not the Coxwold parish register recorded the marriage on 29 March 1821 of Anne Batty, widow, and Richard Darnbrough, a widower of the parish of Ripon. Anne was Richard Batty's widowed mother. Richard's youngest brother, James (1810–34), came with him; a Coxwold gravestone records James's death at Wallerthwaite at the age of twenty-four. I learnt later the Battys had earlier connections with the Markington area.

In the 1841 election for two West Riding MPs Richard Batty of Wallerthwaite voted for the Tory candidates, Wortley and Denison, against the Whigs, Milton and Morpeth. It is not clear how long Richard and Rosy stayed at Wallerthwaite, but when the 1851 census was taken they were living at Tollerton, 14 miles due east and 8 miles from their ancestral home at Coxwold when plotted on a straight line on the map. Richard was by then a prosperous farmer who employed nine labourers to work his 300 acres of land. He continued to do well at Tollerton; by 1873, according to the *Return of Owners of Land* (1875), he was farming 413 acres of fertile land whose annual rental value amounted to £662, and his son Robert farmed another 73 acres valued at £124. Richard Batty died at Tollerton in 1878 and was buried amongst his ancestors in Coxwold churchyard next to his wife, Rosy, who had died twenty-four years earlier. It is interesting to note that the bodies of other members of the Batty family were returned to Coxwold or Husthwaite to be buried even though they had lived outside the parish for most of their lives. One wonders how

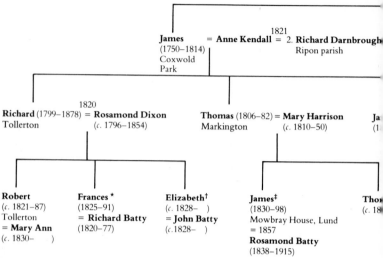

(Note: *, † and ‡ indicate cousins who married each other.)

Richard
(*c.* **1701–**
Coxwolc

		1821	
James	= **Anne Kendall**	=	2. **Richard Darnbrough**
(1750–1814)			Ripon parish
Coxwold			
Park			

	1820		
Richard (1799–1878) = **Rosamond Dixon**		**Thomas** (1806–82) = **Mary Harrison**	Ja
Tollerton (*c.* 1796–1854)		Markington (*c.* 1810–50)	(1

Robert	**Frances** *	**Elizabeth**†	**James**‡	**Tho**
(*c.* 1821–87)	(1825–91)	(*c.* 1828–)	(1830–98)	(*c.* 18
Tollerton			Mowbray House, Lund	
= **Mary Ann**	= **Richard Batty**	= **John Batty**	= 1857	
(*c.* 1830–)	(1820–77)	(*c.* 1828–)	**Rosamond Batty**	
			(1838–1915)	

Table 6   The Batty family tree

far this was typical of other farming families of Victoria's reign.

Meanwhile, Richard's younger brother Thomas Batty (1806–82) had married Mary Harrison and they too had moved from farm to farm as the opportunity presented itself. The brothers' marriages show that the Battys had been accepted by the leading farming dynasties of the area. On different occasions during the nineteenth century both the Dixons and the Harrisons were described in directories as not only principal landowners but lords of the manor of Husthwaite. The Dixons lived at Throstle Nest and the Harrisons at Acaster Hill, two farmsteads not far from Woolpots. Later generations of the Battys were to use both surnames as Christian names for their children.

Upon his marriage to Mary Harrison Thomas took over his elder brother's previous residence at Scackleton Grange. Their eldest son James was born there and was baptised at Hovingham church on 7 May 1830. Between 1832 and 1845 their next six children were born in the neighbouring parish of Dalby, but in 1851 the census enumerator listed the family at Wallerthwaite and noted that their three-year-old son Robert had been born there. It looks as if Thomas and his family moved to Wallerthwaite when his elder brother Richard left that farm for Tollerton. By

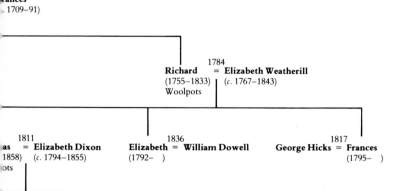

rances
, 1709–91)

1784
Richard = Elizabeth Weatherill
(1755–1833) | (c. 1767–1843)
Woolpots

1811
as = Elizabeth Dixon
1858) (c. 1794–1855)
ots

1836
Elizabeth = William Dowell
(1792–)

1817
George Hicks = Frances
(1795–)

rd *
77)
ces Batty
91)
on Swale

Robert Dixon
(1823–87)
= Mary Barker
(1837–1907)

Elizabeth
= ? Flawith

Frances
= ? Cass

Thomas
(1826–87)
Lund

John[†]
(1828–)
= Elizabeth
Batty
Woolpots

Rosamond[‡]
(1838–1915)
= 1857
James Batty

1851 Thomas was a widower and his household arrangements were supervised by his mother-in-law, seventy-three-year-old Rachel Harrison; his 200 acres were worked by six agricultural labourers. He was still there ten years later, but by 1871 he had moved to Aldwark in the parish of Alne, not far from his elder brother at Tollerton. Information about desirable vacancies was no doubt spread by the family network. Despite being a widower for over thirty years Thomas never remarried. Towards the end of his life he returned to Markington to live at Morcar with his daughter, Frances, and his son-in-law, George Knowles. He died at Morcar in 1882.

It is now necessary to retrace our steps a little before embarking upon the pursuit of another branch of the Batty family. The second Richard Batty whom we have been concerned with – the one who lived from 1755 to 1833 and who moved from Coxwold to Woolpots – had a son, Thomas, who was baptised in 1785 at Husthwaite. This Thomas was subsequently described as 'of Baxby, gentleman'. Baxby manor house stands in a secluded position in the valley to the west of Husthwaite village, nearly a mile to the north of Woolpots, but the township of Baxby extended much further south. The Rachel Harrison whom we mentioned earlier was born in Baxby township in 1778. Prior to setting up home in this township, however, Thomas and his wife, Elizabeth (Dixon), had lived for a time at Youlton, not far from Aldwark and Tollerton; their son Richard was born at Youlton in 1820. This Richard inherited the Youlton farm and married his cousin Frances, the daughter of Richard and Rosy Batty. At this point the family historian's head starts to spin; there are so many Battys with the Christian names Richard, Thomas, James and Frances and now they are marrying their relations! This particular Richard and Frances farmed 200 acres at Youlton in 1851, but later they moved 4 or 5 miles north-east to Myton on Swale. Richard died at Myton Old Hall in 1877 but his body was brought back to his native parish of Husthwaite for burial; his widow was buried by him in 1891.

Enough has been said to indicate the intricate web of family connections behind the ownership or tenancy of some of the principal farms in this part of the Vale of York. Properties changed hands in ways that bewilder the family historian, who has only a limited range of records to guide him. Many more details could be given but for our present purposes it is sufficient to note that at the time of the 1871 census returns, when Victorian farming was still at a peak of prosperity, the Battys occupied seven farms and the heads of two other branches were carpenters and butchers in Coxwold. Two years later these seven farms covered between them over 1,000 acres of land.

The first thirty-five years or so of Victoria's reign were a golden era for farmers, an age of continuous prosperity known to historians as the period of High Farming. Between 1830 and 1880 agricultural output rose by 60 per cent. It was a period that farming families looked back upon nostalgically at the end of the century. For farm labourers on the other hand it was time of great hardship when rising numbers caused the supply of labour to exceed demand, thus keeping wages low. Labouring families did not share the benefits of increased production. But farming families prospered if they had sufficient land and if they put their minds and hands to it. This prosperous era of High Farming came to an end in the mid 1870s when imported corn, particularly that from the American prairies, forced wheat prices down by a half and those of barley and oats by about a third. At the same time, Australian imports caused wool prices to fall sharply. Refrigerated meat did not have quite the same effect on the market for the quality of British beef and mutton remained superior, but this extra competition made things even more difficult for the home farmer. He was handicapped further by a series of wet summers between 1878 and 1882. The last quarter of the nineteenth century is referred to by historians as the Great Agricultural Depression, a time when many a farming family was driven to bankruptcy. Its effects were not equally severe, however. Those farmers who concentrated upon livestock, dairy products and fresh vegetables continued to do well and those who were adaptable enough and whose situation enabled them to change from cereals managed to survive. The corn-growing districts fared badly.

Those members of the Batty family who were my mother's immediate ancestors were amongst those who lost all. The James Batty who had been born at Scackleton Grange in 1830, the eldest child of Thomas Batty and Mary (Harrison), had married his cousin Rosamond Mary Batty, the daughter of Thomas and Elizabeth Batty of Woolpots. According to my grandmother, Mary Webster (who had married into the family in the expectation that she was doing very well for herself and who felt bitter about their decline), the Battys chose cousins as their marriage partners to keep their wealth within the family but this tendency weakened the stock and was the cause of their undoing, together with another Batty characteristic, their 'bone idleness'. In fact the story is more complicated than she allowed, or possibly knew. According to the 1871 census returns, James and Rosamond had a daughter, Elizabeth, and three sons, James Thomas, Harrison and William. What was not revealed until a blanket search was made of the Husthwaite parish register was that they had two more children who had died young. One of these was Mary, who was baptised at Husthwaite on 17 May 1857, only four months after her parents' wedding. That was why Rosamond had married her cousin at the age of eighteen at St Michael's Church, Coxwold.

James Batty was living at Wallerthwaite with his father at the time of his wedding. The newly-married couple set up home at Woolpots, where Elizabeth was born in 1858, but three years later the census enumerator recorded them at Mowbray Cottage (later called Mowbray House) near Stillington, where James farmed 173 acres of land. Living with them was Rosamond's elder brother, Thomas, whose occupation was given as 'Retired Farmer' even though he was only thirty-four years of age; he had been well-provided with a legacy of £1,800 when his father died in 1858. The 1871 census returns shown in Table 7 suggest that the family

Table 7 The 1871 census return for Mowbray House, Stillington

Stillington; Mowbray House

Name	Relation	Age	Status	Occupation	Birthplace
James Batty	head	40	married	Farmer	born Scackleton
Rosamond	wife	32	married	Farmer's Wife	born Youlton
Elizabeth	daughter	12		Scholar	born Woolpots
James T.	son	7		Scholar	born Stillington
Harrison	son	3			born Stillington
William	son	1			born Stillington
Thomas Batty	brother	45	unmarried	Annuitant	born Youlton
Sarah J. Robinson	servant	19	unmarried	Domestic Servant	born Easingwold
Annie E. Plowman	servant	14		Nurse Maid	born Tollerton
Anne Houland	servant	45	married	Servant	born Easingwold
George Palister	servant	16		Farm Servant	born Raskelf
John Knowles	servant	15		Farm Servant	born Tholthorpe

(The servants came from villages nearby.)

were prospering as the era of Victorian High Farming drew to a close.

I have a mug in my possession marked 'Thomas Batty, Stillington Lane, 1875'. Six years later, however, the family were living at a much smaller farm of 76 acres at the Lund, Easingwold and were employing just one farm boy and a young girl as a general domestic servant. They were on the downward slope as the Great Agricultural Depression began to bite. Thomas, the annuitant, seems to have come to their rescue for he spent £1,805 on purchasing 41 acres at the Lund; perhaps James had sufficient money left to buy the other 35 acres? Thomas died at the Lund in 1887 and James died there eleven years later. By then the family were clearly living beyond their means and soon they were to lose everything. My grandfather, Harrison Batty (1868–1954), would never talk about his early life. In his mid-thirties when three of his five children were already born, he had to leave the Lund to pay off his debts and went to work as a farm labourer. During the next few years he moved to Topcliffe and then south to Sherburn in Elmet and Shadwell; in 1912 he answered a newspaper advertisement and became pig-keeper at Peacock farm on the Earl of Derby's Knowsley estate, near Liverpool; then a year or two after the war he moved again, this time to a smallholding on the Yorkshire side of the Pennines and to a job in an engineering works. This family tale has a romantic ending, however, for at the age of sixty-six he was able to return with his son to the Lund, the farm he had left three decades earlier. He spent about six years there before moving back to south-west Yorkshire to spend his retirement in a cottage near his daughters. I remember him as a quiet, contented man who was well thought of by his neighbours. His family's story will be told in more detail in the next chapter when we consider how to use the varied sources that are available to the historian who is tracing the history of a farming dynasty.

THE LABOURING POOR

It is very common for family historians to find that they have agricultural labourers and farm servants amongst their eighteenth and nineteenth century ancestors, to discover that rural members of their family tree were frequently described in parish registers and census returns as 'ag. labs'. The classic Victorian division of rural society into three groups – landlords, tenant-farmers and landless labourers – had already been apparent in some arable areas before the great rise of the national population from the mid eighteenth century onwards, but it became more evident when population levels rose too high for all to have a share in the land. Demographic growth was a rural as well as an urban phenomenon. Even in those parts of the countryside that were largely untouched by industrialisation the number of inhabitants doubled or trebled between 1750 and 1900. Inevitably, the proportion of people who earned most of their living from working other people's land increased substantially. By 1851 the agricultural labour force had reached its absolute peak of 1.88 millions. Soon, however, these trends were to be reversed and the mid nineteenth century can now be seen as one of the great watersheds in the history of the countryside. By the end of Victoria's reign the agricultural workforce had been reduced by a third after labouring families had torn up their roots and migrated to the industrial regions or even overseas.

The term 'agricultural labourer' conceals the variety of skills that were necessary to perform the many tasks on the farm from hedging to mowing and from ditching to leading the plough horses. In general, labourers were married men who lived either in the tied cottages that went with the job or in rented accommodation away from the estate villages, whereas those described as farm servants were unmarried and lived on the farm where they worked. Labourers were employed either on a regular basis for a weekly wage or on a casual basis for piece-rates; servants were hired by the year for their board-and-lodging and wages that were given them at the end of their contract. But in practice the terms shade imperceptibly into each other. In Bedfordshire in the 1840s, for example, farm servants were given board wages to find their own accommodation and in Berkshire in the 1860s about a third of the farm labourers were hired by the year but paid by the week.

Those who were only casually employed were sometimes able to supplement their farm labouring wages with work at other tasks but the price of their independence was the scourge of under-employment and their being laid off in wet weather. We know very little about these alternative sources of work for they were not usually recorded, but a variety of odd jobs in the woods, quarries, sand, clay and gravel pits and elsewhere kept a labourer going in the winter months. The importance of the cottager's pig is emphasized in nineteenth-century rural literature and sometimes a wife was able to add to family earnings by dressmaking, taking in washing and so on. Conditions varied greatly from place to place and over time. The most fortunate labourers were those who lived in woodland areas, where perhaps fuel could still be gathered, a cow grazed on the heath and seasonal work obtained stripping bark, cutting ferns and performing other tasks. In the North and parts of the Midlands industrial earnings forced up wages on the farms, but Southern England had little industry and a labour surplus in the first half of the nineteenth century, so southern wages were kept low. The diet of a labourer's family in the South was meagre and monotonous, his accommodation was generally inferior, and in many places his inability to find fuel meant damp clothes, rheumatism and ill-health. Those regions which concentrated on growing cereals were the ones where the poor fared worst of all. 'Invariably have I observed', wrote William Cobbett, 'the more purely a corn country, the more miserable the labourers'.

'Open' and 'Close' parishes

The composition of rural villages depended not only on the variety of work that was available but upon whether or not land-ownership was concentrated in a few hands. Nineteenth century commentators, from the 1830s onwards, distinguished between 'open' and 'close' parishes and this is a useful distinction for the local historian to bear in mind even though numerous villages did not fit neatly into either category. A 'close' parish was one where a squire or a small group of farmers could limit the number of available cottages and restrict the immigration of landless labourers who might become a burden on the poor rates. An 'open' parish on the other hand had no such controls for the land was divided into many portions amongst smallholders and cottagers; 'open' villages were populous, sprawling, rather unruly and a magnet for migrants in search of work. Such a place was Juniper Hill on the Oxfordshire–Northamptonshire border, Flora Thompson's *Lark Rise*: 'the spot God made with the left overs when He'd finished creating the rest of the earth'. About 1820 Juniper Hill was just a hamlet of six dwellings on the open heath, but two generations later it 'consisted of about thirty cottages and an inn, not built in rows, but dotted anywhere within a more or less circular group. A deeply rutted cart track surrounded the

whole, and separate houses or groups of houses were connected by a network of pathways'. Open communities such as this were regarded with suspicion if not downright hostility by the respectable classes who considered them shabby, ill-disciplined, lawless, radical in politics and religion or worse still heathen.

But the squires and farmers of 'close' parishes had to rely upon nearby 'open' parishes for their workforce. In 1850 James Caird thought it commonplace that farm labourers 'lodged at such a distance from their regular place of employment that they have to walk an hour out in the morning and an hour home in the evening, or from forty to fifty miles a week'. At the same time, Gilbert à Beckett noted that in East Anglia:

> in almost every Union where the course of my inquiry has taken me, I have found some one or more densely populated parishes in the neighbourhood of others very thinly inhabited by labourers, and in some instances, having scarcely any cottages at all. In the former, the dwellings are for the most part wretched, damp, unwholesome, inconvenient, excessively high rented, and crowded with inmates, to such an extent as to render it impossible that health and comfort should be enjoyed.

In Oxfordshire an assistant commissioner enquiring into the employment of children in agriculture in the late 1860s said:

> I don't think I visited any open village in which there were not some very bad cottages.

Plate 3.14   Edensor, Derbyshire

'Everything tends to show his Grace's taste, good feeling, and liberal disposition towards those in humble circumstances' was the comment in Bagshaw's 1846 gazetteer on the recent rebuilding of this village on the Chatsworth estate.

Those parts of Edensor which could be seen from the great house were removed in the 1760s and 1770s when 'Capability' Brown landscaped Chatsworth Park, and James Paine designed a new village inn which was built at the north-western entrance to the park. Two generations later, the sixth Duke of Devonshire enlarged Chatsworth House, improved the gardens, and remodelled the remaining part of the village. Between 1838 and 1842 his gardener, Joseph Paxton, planned the new lay-out and together with John Robertson adapted designs from contemporary builders' pattern books to create a picturesque, though solidly-built village. Some of the inhabitants were re-housed in good accommodation nearby at Pilsley.

The medieval church of St Peter was rebuilt from 1867 onwards to the designs of Sir George Gilbert Scott, incorporating some of the ancient material.

In his article on ' "Open" and Close" Parishes in England in the Eighteenth and Nineteenth Centuries', published in the *Agricultural History Review*, vol. 20, part II (1972), pp. 126–39, Dr B. A. Holderness has shown that 'close' parishes remained a mid-Victorian scandal until the Union Chargeability Act of 1865 substituted a system of rate-assessment by poor-law unions for the old parish poor rate. In the worst areas the problem persisted until at least the 1880s. 'Close' parishes were particularly numerous in the light soil uplands of the East Riding, Lincolnshire, Nottinghamshire, east Leicestershire, north-west Norfolk and the Cotswolds, but they were also a feature of clay and alluvial soils where arable or mixed farming was practised, especially in the Midland Plain. On the other hand, the pastoral uplands and the old forest districts had few villages of the 'close' kind, for they were divided into small farms that were dependent only on family labour.

Seasonal demands for labour on the large arable farms of eastern England were met by the notorious gang system, whereby work was subcontracted to a gang-master who organized a labour force from the nearby 'open' villages and market towns. The system had its origins in Norfolk, where such large 'open' parishes as Castle Acre, Gayton, Great Massingham, Litcham, Middleton and Swaffham bordered numerous 'close' villages. By the middle of the nineteenth century nearly all these particular 'open' parishes had at least one public gang that did specific tasks such as weeding or picking potatoes when they were called upon. The system was widely used in Norfolk, Suffolk, Cambridgeshire, north Lincolnshire and parts of the East Riding between the mid 1820s and the late 1860s. Gangs included women and children, and some of them were large; March had 388, Spalding 380, Chatteris 260 and so on. *The Sixth Report of the Children's Employment Commission* (1866) brought the gang system to national attention and the following year legislation effectively stopped it.

Settlement records

A recent work that is essential reading for anyone concerned with the poorest sections of society is Dr Keith Snell's book *Annals of the Labouring Poor: Social Change and Agrarian England, 1660-1900* (1985). His analysis of applications for poor relief under the terms of the Settlement Act of 1662 clearly demonstrates the seasonal nature of unemployment and the worsening situation from about 1780 onwards. In corn-growing districts a labourer's chances of obtaining work declined once the harvest was gathered in, so that the winter months were often dismal ones for the poor; in pastoral areas employment opportunities dwindled after the annual spring calving. These two regular turning points coincided with the yearly hiring fairs, which in arable districts were held in the autumn around Michaelmas or Martinmas and in pastoral parts in spring about Old Lady Day or May Day. Hiring fairs survived longest in the pastoral districts of the North and the West where the tradition of farm servants 'living-in' continued throughout the Victorian period.

The evidence of the settlement records points to a significant decline in female agricultural work in the corn-growing parts of Southern and Eastern England from about the middle of the eighteenth century onwards. Before then women had helped the men in such tasks as reaping, loading, spreading dung, ploughing, threshing, sheep shearing and so on, but demographic pressure reduced the necessity for female labour so much that by the mid nineteenth century women's role in agriculture was an insignificant one. The parliamentary Poor Law Reports of 1834 and later, together with the Reports on the Employment of Women and Children in Agriculture of 1834 and the late 1860s, show that by then women and girls in the grain-producing areas helped with the spring weeding, stone picking, haymaking and gleaning but that 'in other months they are generally unemployed'. Buckinghamshire, Bedfordshire and some adjacent counties offered alternate employment in lacemaking and straw-plaiting, otherwise unmarried women had little choice other than to enter domestic service or poorly paid jobs such as dressmaking in the capital city. Women's role in agriculture was reduced further by the continued decline of family farms as smallholders were driven off the land.

Families at this social level were better off in pastoral districts where smallholdings had more chance to survive and where female wages remained buoyant. In areas which concentrated on livestock women still played an essential role, particularly on dairy farms and in the haymaking season. Moreover, male real wages did not fall until after the Napoleonic wars. Professor W. A. Armstrong has written that the abiding impression of the period 1750–1850 is of an extraordinary regional and even local variety of living standards and experiences; these standards varied not only from region to region but over time. The great rise in the national population was the principal cause of rural poverty in the early nineteenth century but there were contributory factors as well. The French wars brought soaring prices and great hardship in years of harvest failure, particularly in 1795, 1800–1 and 1812, and the end of the wars brought extreme depression in 1814–16 when falling prices forced farmers to reduce their staff. The Southern counties suffered the worst effects of surplus population, for few opportunities of industrial employment were available.

On the whole the old poor law was admininstered generously and humanely. Seventeenth and eighteenth century overseers' accounts mention a surprising variety of items and services for which relief was granted. Thus in the east Derbyshire parish of Ripley we can follow the ways in which Edward Sare was helped during his declining years:

1685: Payde for A paire of shoowes for Edward Sare, 4s.6d.
1685: Paid for a wascoat cloth frocke one sherte and makeinge them up for Edward Sare, 8s.1d.
Paid for washinge Edward Sare and for salveing his legg, 2s.8d.
1696: Payd to Sarah Anttony for washing Edward Sare, 1s.0d, paid for a pair of Britches for him, 2s.4d.
1697: Paid for washing Edward Sare, 6d. For a shirt for him, 2s.0½d, for linsey wolsey to make him cloths, 8d, for making the shirt aforesaid, 3½d, for a frocke cloth, 2s.1d, Thrid & lasse, 6½d, a pair of stockens, 4d, For mending his shoes, 1s.2d, Strongwater, 1d.
1698: Payd for Ale for Edward Sare & bread, 8d, For a powder for his mouth 4d, for cloth for britches, 3s.0d, a Lofe, 6d, Quicksilver, 2d, for Collering the briches, 4d, Oatmeale, 7d, 4 pieces of wood for his bed, 1s.0d, For him in cloth for the said britches, 7d, Salve, 1s.6d, For fetching Willm. Woollatt to him & laying the plaister on him, 6d, A Sheepskin 8d, Sope, 6d.
1700: Payd to Edward Sare when hee was badley before hee dyed, 2s.6d.

The strains only began to show after about 1780 when expenditure began to rise rapidly. It reached its peak in 1817 amidst the throes of the post-war depression. Mounting expenditure on poor relief caused such an outcry amongst the rate-paying classes that in 1834 the Poor Law Amendment Act abolished the old parish system and replaced it with a new administrative structure based on unions of parishes and run by guardians.

Dr Snell has shown how the poor treated proof of a settlement claim on a parish much as a family heirloom, a guarantee of relief during a period of poverty which compensated for any restriction on the freedom of movement. Family knowledge preserved details of old removal cases going back many years. It was essential for the poor to gain a settlement and the most straightforward way was to be hired as a servant for a year. Leaving home at the age of fourteen or so, a boy or girl moved from one yearly hiring to another, each period of service in a parish earning a settlement and replacing earlier ones. After 1780, however, as expenditure on the poor rose to unprecedented heights, some farmers – particularly in the arable areas of the South and East – became reluctant to hire servants for a full year in case they became a charge on the parish. At the same time, social pretension decreed that it was no longer fashionable for servants to live in the farm house and to share their meals with the farmer's family; social segregation became the order of the day and was much commented upon by contemporaries. The change was a gradual one, for even in the South large numbers of servants were still hired for the full year during the 1820s and 1830s and in the North and in pastoral areas generally living-in remained a flourishing tradition during Victoria's reign, but there is no doubt of the trend and its harmful consequences for the poor.

In the South one consequence of the difficulty of obtaining a settlement was that the poor were reluctant to move far from 'their' parish in case they fell on hard times and needed relief. Southern agricultural districts no longer experienced the high degree of labour mobility which had characterized seventeenth and early-eighteenth century England. Thus it was that in the middle years of the nineteenth century Southern villages experienced greater family stability than at any time during the previous two hundred years. In the North, however, and in other areas where pastoral farming and industries offered better employment prospects the old patterns of mobility persisted.

Dr Snell's analysis of settlement records for the Southern half of the country shows that in the East the average age at which boys left home to become apprentices was 14.2 and to commence farm service 14.8; girls left on average eighteen months later. In the West, where girls found work as dairymaids, both sexes left home at the same age, a little earlier than in the East. By the age of nineteen most farm servants were earning an adult wage, though as with apprentices they were not considered to be adults until they were twenty-one. Settlement examinations suggest that the typical ages at marriage were twenty-six for men and twenty-four for women. Weddings commonly took place shortly after the completion of a yearly hiring, with peaks in May–June in Western parts and in October in the South-east. During the late eighteenth and early nineteenth centuries many brides were already pregnant upon the occasion of their marriage; 'No child, no bride' was a common saying. Labouring families with young children were particularly vulnerable in times of unemployment until these children were old enough to earn part of their living. Women had fewer opportunities to contribute to the family income but they were expected to manage the household finances. In Flora Thompson's hamlet the men handed their wages 'straight over to their wives, who gave them back a shilling for the next week's pocket-money. That was the custom of the countryside. The men worked for the money and the women had the spending of it'.

For many a labourer's family, life in an overcrowded cottage during the period 1780–1850 was a constant struggle. The New Poor Law, implemented after 1834, made things worse at a time when real wages in agricultural districts were falling, when the practice of farm service was declining, when 'close' parishes were keeping out the poor and parliamentary enclosure was forcing cottagers off their bit of land.

Enclosure

The family and local historian who is concerned with rural society during the late-eighteenth and early-nineteenth centuries will need to consider the effects of parliamentary enclosure if an award was made for his particular parish. Between 1750 and 1850 some 6 million acres of open arable fields, commons and wastes in England and Wales were enclosed by about 4,000 private acts of parliament. In other words, land which had previously been farmed in common was divided between all those who had had common rights over it and was henceforth farmed by separate owners. Many of the subsequent awards have been deposited in record offices and have been catalogued on a regional basis; the standard reference work for the country at large is the late Dr W. E. Tate's *Domesday of English Enclosure Acts*, edited by M. E. Turner (Reading University, 1978). Enclosure awards which

Plate 3.15   Naseby Village (Northants), 1855

This early photograph of a Northamptonshire village (known throughout the land because of the decisive Civil War battle fought nearby in 1645) shows that most of the houses and cottages were still built with mud walls and roofed with thatch.

In his *History and Antiquities of Naseby* (1792) the Revd John Mastin wrote of the village: 'If we except a few of the modern and best houses, it is built principally with a kind of kealy earth dug near it; excellent in its kind, and the best calculated for building I ever saw; walls built with this earth are exceedingly firm and strong, and, if kept dry, are said to be more durable than if built with soft stone or indifferent bricks. There are walls in some of the houses said to be two hundred years old built of this earth, and were they drawn over with lime-mortar, and marked or lined, to appear as stone work, which might be done at a moderate expence, their appearance would be respectable; but as the present occupiers are only tenants at will, improvements of this kind are hardly to be expected'. Instead, the new coat which the walls 'have once a year consists of cowdung spread upon them to dry for firing'.

Other houses in the village were cruck-framed. 'The oldest houses in Naseby are, as to the wood part, mostly oak, and some of them of the most antique architecture, called forked building, which forks are all of oak, very rough, strong, uncouth, and put together in a rude manner'.

As to the inhabitants, the minister observed: 'They speak a kind of provincial dialect, and in general vociferate very loudly; supposed to be principally owing to their being brought up in so elevated a situation; where the winds, storms and tempests, particularly in the winter season, prevail so far as to confound the language'.

205

cover the entire parish, i.e. which deal with open-fields and ancient enclosures as well as commons and wastes, provide a complete picture of land ownership at a particular date. These awards tend to date from the earlier phase, *c.* 1750–80, and to deal especially with the heavier soils of the Midland Plain, where much of the land was subsequently converted to pasture. However, in many parts of England – particularly in the Northern and Western pastoral zones – open arable fields had never formed more than a small proportion of the available land and had often been enclosed by agreement long before the eighteenth century. Many parishes therefore have awards that deal only with the commons and wastes; those that were totally enclosed in an earlier age have no award at all.

Obtaining a private act of parliament was an expensive last resort when farmers could not agree upon the desirability of enclosure. Parliamentary approval was given when the farmers of 75–80 per cent of the land (measured in terms not of acreage but of value) expressed their willingness to enclose; the wishes of the majority were then imposed upon the minority who disapproved. The commissioners appointed under the terms of the act allotted parcels of land in proportion to the size of a claimant's common rights. The biggest farmers got the largest share as the right to graze livestock on the commons had varied according to the size of farms and the ability to keep animals in hay over winter. Some recent immigrants had no common rights at all and local attitudes to squatters varied enormously from parish to parish and also over time. The practical consequences of enclosure favoured the rich and hurt the poor, but the variety of experience makes it difficult to generalize. Each parish has its own peculiar history; it is quite possible to find within a particular neighbourhood that one parish had enclosed all its land well before the eighteenth century, that another was owned mostly by absentees and that a third was still farmed in open fields by local men with just enough land to manage on. The local historian will need to determine whether in his own parish enclosure was responsible for great social changes or whether it was merely a manifestation of forces unleashed by the national population explosion.

The voice of the rural poor was rarely heard when enclosure took place. Many must have been of a similar opinion to Thomas Wood, who refused to sign the petition to enclose the Yorkshire parish of Ackworth in 1772 because:

it would hurt him that he kept a few Cows on the Common in Summer took land of Mr. Turton at 40s. per Acre for Hay in Winter, and if it was not for the Commons he could not pay Rent for his Land nor have Milk for his family.

Several of the richer inhabitants of Ackworth also refused to sign because enclosure 'would hurt the poor'. The labourers' voice was eloquently expressed by John Clare, who was sixteen years old when an act was passed to enclose his native Helpstone which lies half-way between Stamford and Peterborough. In his poem, *The Mores*, he was quite clear that families such as his own had been harmed by enclosure:

> Inclosure came and trampled on the grave
> Of labours rights and left the poor a slave . . .

Clare also lamented the visual effects of enclosure and the loss of access to the countryside:

> Fence now meets fence in owners little bounds
> Of field and meadow large as garden grounds
> In little parcels little minds to please . . .

> These paths are stopt – the rude philistines thrall
> Is laid upon them and destroyed them all.

Thomas Bewick was equally bitter about the enclosure in 1812 of his native Northumberland fell or common, which covered 1,852 acres:

> By this division, the poor man was rooted out and the various mechanics of the villages deprived of all benefit from it . . . The wisdom which dictated this change is questionable, but the selfish greediness of it quite apparent.

George Sturt, writing under the pen-name of George Bourne, saw how an 'ancient mode of life had been cut off at its roots' by enclosure. In *Change in the Village* (1912) he wrote:

> To the enclosure of the common more than to any other cause may be traced all the changes which have subsequently passed over the village. It was like knocking the keystone out of an arch.

The small allotment that the cottager received in lieu of his rights to graze a cow or two and to collect fuel from the common was inadequate for his purposes. Legal expenses and the cost of hedging often forced him to sell. Whereas before enclosure he could supplement his labouring wages by his own industry, now he was totally dependent upon his wages and was a mere hireling.

Without their own livestock the poor were helpless when times were bad. They became increasingly dependent upon parish relief. Many left the countryside for the towns; those who stayed behind found that life was a constant struggle.

We need to ask, though, what would have happened if the commons had not been enclosed? The astonishing growth of population, even in rural areas, was such that either an increasing number of families would have been barred from claiming common rights or else the commons would have been so over-stocked that the quality of the grazing would have been lowered drastically. The rich did well out of enclosure but at least the nation's agricultural productivity was improved.

The impact of parliamentary enclosure varied enormously. The local historian who is concerned with social and economic change at the time of the enclosure movement would do well to read Dr J. M. Martin's article on 'Village Traders and the Emergence of a Proletariat in South Warwickshire, 1750-1851' published in the *Agricultural History Review*, vol. 32 part II (1984), pp. 179-88. Martin argues that in the Feldon district prior to enclosure such open-field villages as Brailes, Tysoe and Priors Marston had large numbers of families who combined a local trade or craft with work on very small holdings. Not all village traders were cottagers, for they included some men of substance such as maltsters, but the characteristic figure was the craftsman-cottager with a small, but for him significant, stake in the land and grazing rights on the commons. For example, in the 1730s more than 100 of the 160 Atherstone cottagers kept up to two horses and two cows which were 'plentifully supplied with grass' in this way. However, many of these cottagers were unable to prove their claims before the enclosure commissioners and so they lost all rights under the award. The immediate consequences of enclosure were serious for these social groups. At Alcester in the 1770s many of the 280 cottagers with common rights were unable to meet their share of the cost of enclosure and were forced to sell up during the interval between the act and the award. The long-term consequences were pronounced; the 1851 census returns for the east Feldon district show that over 60 per cent of occupied males were landless labourers. Not only had they lost their land, the old village crafts and trades had withered away too. Before enclosure, the strips of the open arable fields 'had formed the lynch-pin of an age-old system of cottage farming on a minute scale'. A generation or two after enclosure rural society in this district consisted of two groups – a new class of tenant farmers and their labourers – who 'faced up to each other in mutual antipathy and low regard'.

Emigration

In 1851 nearly 1:4 of the national workforce was employed in agriculture; farming was easily the largest single source of employment, as it always had been. Thereafter numbers declined in both absolute and relative terms until by the eve of the First World War agricultural workers formed only 1:10 of those in work. Cheap fares on the railways provided opportunities for young men and women to leave the fields and seek higher wages in the towns and industrial villages, so that by 1861 or 1871 many an agricultural village had fewer inhabitants than it did at its mid-century peak. The exodus from the countryside had begun long before the Great Agricultural Depression turned betterment migration into sheer necessity. The depression forced farmers to reduce their labour force and to turn increasingly to pastoral farming, which required fewer hands. The decline of many of the traditional rural crafts made the situation worse. If men, women and children had not left the countryside in droves in the 1870s and 1880s rural districts would have suffered widespread unemployment. In fact, so many labourers left that the squires of some estate villages made determined efforts to improve the quality of their cottage accommodation in order to keep an adequate workforce. In such cases village populations rose again during the last quarter of the nineteenth century while those of their neighbours continued to decline.

Those who remained on the land saw their standard of living improve, for wages rose when labour was scarce. Even so, farm labourers were still the nation's poorest group of workers, especially those in the purely agricultural counties of the South. The families that stayed behind were the unadventurous ones. Low wages led to low productivity and to a slow, sullen rate of work. In *Lark Rise to Candleford*, her marvellous evocation of rural life on the poverty line in late-Victorian Oxfordshire, Flora Thompson wrote of the neighbouring labourers, 'They detested nothing as much as being hurried'.

Contemporary commentators recognized that the farm labourers who lived in the most wretched conditions were those from the South-western counties of Somerset, Devon, Dorset and Wiltshire. In his book on *The English Peasantry* (1874) F. G. Heath wrote:

> What would strike a stranger most forcibly on visiting Somersetshire during the spring or summer is the contrast afforded by the loveliness of the scenery and the wretchedness and squalor prevailing amidst the agricultural population of the villages.

He went on to say:

> It was really a pitiable sight to see the bedrooms of several of the Montacute cottages which I visited. An old table, and perhaps a broken chair in addition, would constitute in most cases the articles of what could scarcely be called furniture. Seldom a vestige of carpet on the floors. A few bedclothes, perhaps, huddled down in one corner. At night these had to be distributed amongst the several members of the family, who, lying about on different parts of the floor, could not possibly in cold weather get a reasonable amount of warmth . . . . In all the homes of the peasantry in Montacute there was, in fact, at the time of my visit a chilling air of misery and wretchedness. And yet this village was renowned for the prosperity of its farmers, the land in the district being some of the richest in the whole of the county.

In the fertile Vale of Taunton Deane the wages of agricultural labourers were on average 9 or 10 shillings a week, though in some places men received only 8 shillings. In addition all received a daily allowance of cider. Somerset labourers generally worked from 7 a.m. to 5.30 p.m. with half-an-hour 'forenoons' for lunch and an hour for dinner, but they often had to work later with no extra pay other than the traditional supper at harvest time. Carters and shepherds received 1 shilling a week more than labourers but were expected to work longer hours. Women were paid 7d. or 8d. a day for work in the fields, though elsewhere in the country female agricultural labour was becoming a thing of the past. With such pitiful rewards for their toil it is no wonder that many labouring families decided to seek a new life in the industrial districts or overseas. Somerset's population had risen from 274,000 in 1801 to 444,000 in 1851 but during the second half of the nineteenth century (at a time when the national population was still rising rapidly) it fell back to 433,000 in 1901. The small parish of Thurlbear near Taunton, which we shall be concerned with later, was typical of many others in this respect. Its population of 151 at the beginning of the nineteenth century had risen to a peak of 212 in 1851, but forty years later it was back to 151.

Emigration was organized by philanthropists and trade unions

Plate 3.16 Digging for coal during the 1912 strike

On 1 March 1912 one million coal miners withdrew their labour in the industry's first national strike. The Miners' Federation of Great Britain, founded in 1889, were trying to force the owners to accept the principle of a minimum wage of 5s.0d. per day for every man and 2s.0d. for every boy over the age of fourteen who worked underground. The strike lasted six weeks and was only partially successful.

During the strike it was common for colliers to dig for coal for their own use by outcropping shallow seams and to pick coal from the colliery muck stacks. This group is gathered round a pit that had been sunk through some rough land at the edge of one of Sheffield's working-class suburbs. Photographers recorded several such scenes for sale as postcards.

and was greatly facilitated by the train and the steamship. In 1839 the Great Western Railway opened their line from London to Bristol, three years later Taunton was connected to the capital, and in 1860 a line from London via Chard reached Exeter. When fares fell even the poorer members of society were able to travel long distances. Advertisements in local newspapers encouraged families to quit not just the region but the country, with offers of assisted passages across the seas. Many of these emigrants went from the ranks of the rural poor.

In 1815, at the close of the Napoleonic wars and the beginning of deep recession, the first official figures on the number of people leaving these shores to set up home abroad show that 1,889 went that year to North America. In 1852 the number of emigrants who crossed the Atlantic during those twelve months reached 277,134. Yet these figures do not tell the whole story, for others went elsewhere. According to official returns, 983,227 emigrants left the United Kingdom before 1840, and 58,449 of these went to Australia and New Zealand. An estimated 10 million people left the British Isles permanently during the course of the nineteenth century. They and other European immigrants were largely responsible for the astonishing growth of the population of the United States, which rose from about 4 millions in 1790 to 23 millions in 1850. The exodus from the Continent of Europe was without parallel in the history of the world.

Some emigrants were able to leave home because their fares were paid out of public or charitable funds. Thus, between 1835 and 1840 over 19,000 people were provided for in this way by Poor Law Guardians in the agricultural counties of the South and the East. But most passages were unassisted. The journey was usually a terrible one, though by 1850 big American sailing packets from Liverpool had replaced the old brigs, and soon the passage was made more tolerable by steamships. After the 1846 potato famine in Ireland emigration from the British Isles reached new levels, which were maintained until young men were attracted into the army or navy to fight in the Crimean War or to quell the Indian Mutiny. Government figures, which underestimate the extent of emigration, say that 2,740,000 left Great Britain and Ireland between 1846 and 1855; they mostly went across the Atlantic but about 430,000 went to Australia, New Zealand or South Africa. Whole families and groups of families went together, spurred on by the posters and advertisements which had long decorated their cottage walls. During the second half of the nineteenth century emigration continued apace; the decade from 1871 to 1881 saw a 140 per cent increase in the number of farm labourers, shepherds, gardeners and carters who moved abroad, and by 1910 nearly half a million people a year (including those Europeans who left via British ports) were leaving the British Isles for a new life overseas.

In his book, *The Cornish in America* (1969), Dr A L. Rowse has traced families with distinctive Cornish names to their present homes in the New World. He has estimated that in the United States there may well be seven or eight times as many people of Cornish name and descent than there are in Cornwall itself. Some had settled in America long before the nineteenth century. The

Chenoweths, for example, went to Virginia early and fanned out from there. Now, there are several thousand Chenoweths in the United States, many more than in Cornwall or indeed in the whole of Britain. But the Victorian era was the peak period for Cornish emigration, especially after the collapse of the copper mining industry in the late 1860s. Some miners went to work in Welsh and Yorkshire coal mines, some left for London, others for Spain, Australia and New Zealand, but most miners swelled the ranks of those who despaired of earning a decent living in the Old World and set out in search of a better existence in the New. Consciously or unconsciously, they were taking part in the most momentous migration the world had ever seen.

CHAPTER FOUR

Excursions into family and local history

The more the family historian becomes aware of national trends and regional characteristics the more absorbing he will find his ancestors' story. A broader range of knowledge will help to explain the environment in which they lived and the circumstances in which they found themselves. It will often provide a clue as to why they prospered at one particular period and fell upon hard times at another, why they decided to move home or why they stayed put for generation after generation. And at the same time the personal histories of one's ancestors will illuminate historical periods and episodes that have previously been dark to us, while contrasting fortunes will enable us to look upon the great issues of social history with a certain detachment, free from the prejudices of class and the blinkered outlook of those who seek from history merely the confirmation of their own attitudes. Family history often allows us to see both sides of the coin, especially if we adopt the broad approach of finding out who our sixteen great-great-grandparents were. My mother's father's family were prosperous farmers in the northern Vale of York; my father's mother's family were farm labourers from the border country where Somerset meets Devon and Dorset until they decided to tear up their roots and leave the wretched poverty of this beautiful but depressed part of England to go in search of work in the industrial North. Explaining how I traced these ancestors may help those readers who have not yet pursued their own lines of enquiry and will highlight some of the problems that we all have to face. It will also enable me to show how an interest in family history can be widened into the even more rewarding study of the local history of the places where one's ancestors lived.

214

THE GARLANDS

My grandmother, Mary Ann Hey (née Garland), died on 16 November 1948 at Mirefield, 2 or 3 miles west of Penistone on the edge of the Pennine moors. The inscription on her gravestone claims that she was eighty-three though actually she was only eighty-two; she was in her eighty-third year and tombstones will often express it in that way. We all knew that she was born in Somerset, for she said that she came from Chard. Family memory is an important starting point even if it is not a strictly accurate one. I found out later that she had lived at Chardstock, near Chard, as a girl but had been born further north near Taunton. By subtracting her age from her year of death I was able to get an approximate year of birth and it was not too troublesome to identify her in the indexes of the birth registers at St Catherine's House, London, under the registration district of Taunton and the sub-district of Pitminster. Her birth certificate told me that she was born on 15 May 1866 in the small parish of Thurlbear, $3\frac{1}{2}$ miles south-east of Taunton, and that her parents were Amos Garland, farm labourer, and Mary Garland (née Knight), who signed the certificate with a mark. This information led my mother to remember that Mary Knight had been a dressmaker, a useful occupation that provided much needed extra income for the family. Later, I was able to confirm some of these details from the Thurlbear parish register, which recorded my grandmother's baptism on 17 June 1866, just over a month after her birth.

My next step was to search the indexes at St Catherine's House for the marriage of Amos and Mary. This took place at Thurlbear parish church on 28 January 1864. Amos was a twenty-three-year-old labourer, the son of William Garland, labourer, and he too signed with a mark. Mary was twenty-four and was residing in the parish of St Mary Magdalene, Taunton, where perhaps she was working at the dressmaking trade. Her father was John Knight, another labourer. The information on the marriage certificate led me easily to the registration of Amos's birth. He was born at Thurlbear on 25 August 1839, the son of William Garland, labourer (who signed with a mark), and Ann Garland, née Webb. Mary's birth was a little more difficult to identify as more than one Mary Knight appeared in the St Catherine's House indexes; the St Mary Magdalene register at Taunton provided no help on this point. I turned therefore to the census returns, which

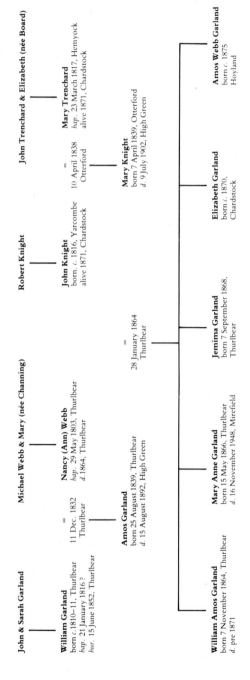

Table 8 The Garland family tree

from 1851 onwards name the place of birth (though not always accurately) of everyone who was listed.

The census room at the Public Record Office has all the census returns for England and Wales available for consultation on microfilm. The 1841 returns do not give the place of birth (except to say which county each person was born in) and the ages of everyone over fifteen are rounded down to the nearest five. Nevertheless, they are useful in listing all the members of a family who were living together on census night. At Thurlbear William and Ann Garland had four children – William (8), John (6), Hannah (4) and Amos (2) – and living with them was Ann's father, Michael Webb (65), an agricultural labourer. Ten years later the 1851 census returns for Thurlbear are more informative. They show that one of a group of farm labourers' cottages at Long Water was occupied as follows:

Name	Status	Age	Occupation	Birthplace
William Garland	head	40	Agricultural Labourer	Thorn Falcon
Ann Garland	wife	48		Thurlbear
Michael	son	24	Agricultural Labourer	Thurlbear
William	son	18		Thurlbear
John	son	16		Thurlbear
Hannah	daughter	13		Thurlbear
Amos	son	12		Thurlbear

A new name has appeared since 1841, that of an elder son, Michael. William Garland was eight years younger than his wife and would have been only sixteen when Michael was born. The 1861 census returns, however, suggest that he was not Michael's father. Michael Webb's surname reveals that he was Ann's illegitimate son born before she married William Garland. The returns recording the members of the Garland and Webb families still living at Long Water are shown overleaf.

By now the younger William, John and Hannah had left the family home, possibly when they had married. Michael Webb had married a girl from the next parish and had lived for a time in Taunton, where his daughter had been born, but he had moved back into his mother's cottage, probably after the other children had gone and the elder William Garland had died. A search of the

Name	Status	Age	Occupation	Birthplace
Ann Garland	head, widow	58		Thurlbear
Michael Webb	son, married	33	Railway labourer	Thurlbear
Amelia Webb	daughter-in-law	31		West Hatch
Ann Webb	grand-child	6	Scholar	Taunton
Amos Garland	son	21	Agricultural labourer	Thurlbear
John Wilkinson	lodger	42	Agricultural labourer, carter	Thurlbear

indexes at St Catherine's House, starting in 1851, resulted in the discovery that William Garland had died on 15 June 1852 after a heart attack at the age of forty-one. His widow, Ann, was present at his death in his Thurlbear cottage and she signed the certificate with a mark.

By 1871 the Garlands had left Thurlbear. I tried the census returns for Chard but they were not there either. Only when the 1881 census returns became available for study under the 100 years rule did I find them again, this time in south Yorkshire. A search of the parish registers of Thurlbear and adjacent places such as Thornfalcon was the obvious next step in order to fill in some of the gaps and to try to trace the Garlands, Knights and Webbs further back in time. These registers were deposited at the Somerset County Record Office at Taunton and I was fortunate when Dr J. H. Bettey of the University of Bristol's Department of Extramural Studies undertook a preliminary search for me. I was later able to follow certain lines of enquiry there myself.

The marriage of William Garland and Ann Webb was found to have taken place at Thurlbear parish church on 11 December 1832. This event, of course, did not appear in the marriage indexes of St Catherine's House as civil registration did not commence until July 1837. The baptisms of each of the children listed in the census returns are recorded in the Thurlbear register, together with that of another child, Mary Anne, who was baptised on Christmas Day 1836 but who presumably died before the 1841 census was taken. On each occasion William Garland was described as a Thurlbear labourer. His own baptism entry,

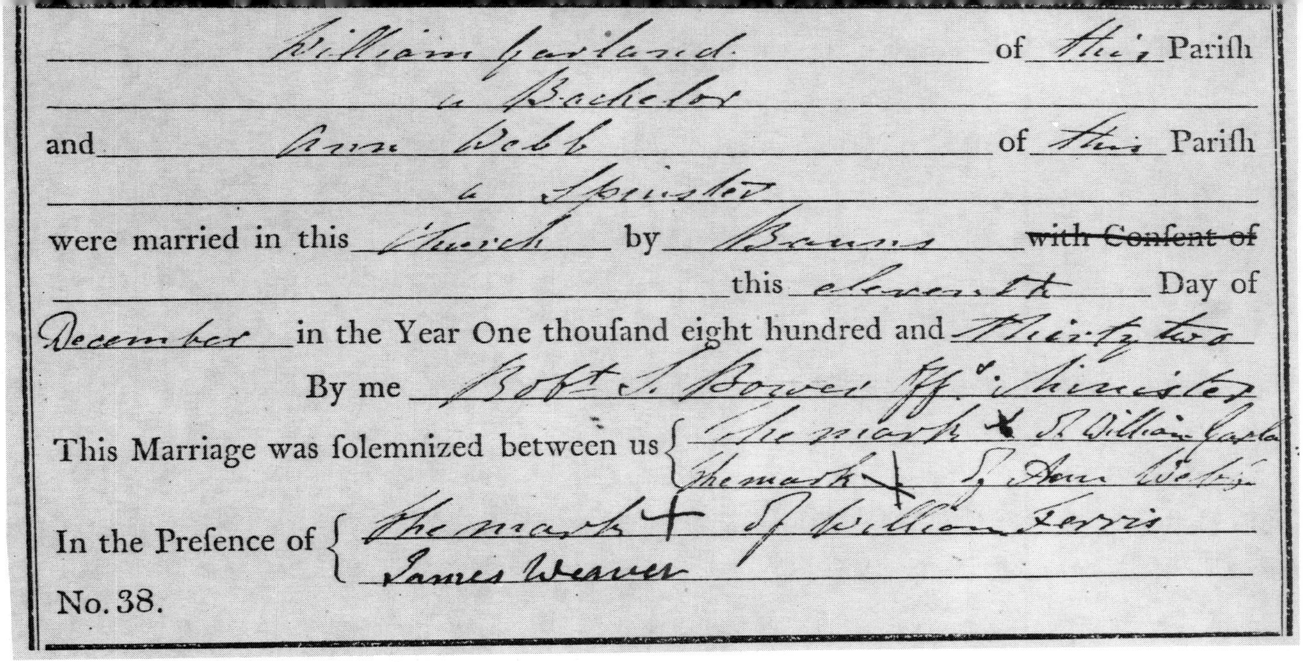

William Garland of this Parish
a Bachelor
and Ann Webb of this Parish
a Spinster
were married in this Church by Banns ~~with Consent of~~
this eleventh Day of
December in the Year One thousand eight hundred and Thirty two
By me Robt. S. Bower Offg. Minister
This Marriage was solemnized between us { The mark + of William Garland / The mark + of Ann Webb
In the Presence of { The mark + of William Ferris / James Weaver
No. 38.

Plate 4.1 A record of marriage
The entry in the Thurlbear parish register (Somerset County Record Office, D/P/thurl.2/1/4) of the marriage of William Garland and Ann Webb, 11 December 1832. Both parties signed with a mark, as did one of the witnesses. James Weaver appears regularly in the register as a witness who could sign his name. Only thirty-seven marriage ceremonies were performed in Thurlbear church between 1813 and 1837.

however, is rather puzzling. The information gleaned from his death certificate and the 1851 census had implied that he was born in Thornfalcon parish in 1810 or 1811. The Thornfalcon baptism register disappointingly does not confirm this assumption; the only William Garland who is recorded is the William, son of John and Sarah Garland, baptised on 21 January 1816. Could this possibly be our man, despite the discrepancy in dates? John and Sarah Garland, curiously enough, had baptised two other children, Sarah and Amos, only six and a half months earlier. The choice of the Christian name Amos certainly suggests a link with my family. On turning back the pages of the Thornfalcon register I found that John and Sarah Garland had baptised two other children together on 4 June 1809, namely John and Mary Ann. The possibility of twins can be ruled out because John was said to have been born on 30 October 1805; he was three and a half years old at the time of his baptism. It certainly seems possible that the William Garland baptised in 1816 was about four and a half years old at the time. If so, we can only surmise that illness had prevented his baptism with Sarah and Amos the previous summer. No other Garlands are recorded in the Thornfalcon register, and as we know that William was born there his parents' lax behaviour (proved on a previous occasion) seems the best explanation for his delayed baptism.

His wife's baptism entry presents another problem, but one that is easier to solve. The census returns had suggested that she was born at Thurlbear about 1803, the daughter of Michael Webb, an agricultural labourer. Her name is recorded consistently as Ann. There is no difficulty in identifying her parents' wedding. Michael Webb married Mary Channing on 17 December 1792 at Thurlbear parish church; they both lived in Thurlbear at the time and each signed the marriage entry with a cross. Nor is it difficult to note the baptisms of their seven children between 1793 and 1807. However, when we come to the sixth child, baptised on 29 May 1803 (the very year that Ann, the daughter of Michael Webb, was said to have been born) we find that the name which is recorded is Nancy. No Ann appears. Could the minister have misremembered the name when he recorded the baptism, or could Nancy be a diminutive form of Ann? This troubled me for some time until I discovered that Nancy was indeed a common pet form of Ann. The family historian has always to be on the lookout for this sort of thing. Some pet forms are not at all obvious; my grandmother, Mary Webster, was always known as

Polly (presumably derived via Molly), as were many other Victorian girls with the name of Mary.

The baptism of Michael Webb, Ann's illegitimate child, took place at Thurlbear on 24 June 1827. The letters 'B.C.' denote bastard child, but the father was not named. The Thurlbear registers also confirm the civil registration record of Amos Garland's marriage to Mary Knight on 28 January 1864. Their eldest child, William Amos, was born on 7 November that year and was baptised just over a month later but he died while still young. The register also records the births and baptisms of my grandmother, Mary Ann (1866), and her sister Jemima (1868), but after that the family disappeared from the local scene. I knew from family memory that when they came to Yorkshire they settled in or near the industrial village of High Green, a few miles north of Sheffield. With that in mind I turned to the microfilms of the 1881 census that are available at the South Yorkshire County Record Office. I found the Garlands living at the third of a group of four buildings known as Hillers Houses, Mortomley, just down the road from High Green. They were recorded as follows:

Name	Status	Age	Occupation	Birthplace
Amos Garland	head	41	Coke Drawer	Somerset, Taunton
Mary Garland	wife	41		Somerset, Taunton
Mary Ann	daughter	14	Scholar	Somerset, Taunton
Jemima	daughter	12	Scholar	Somerset, Taunton
Elizabeth	daughter	10	Scholar	Dorsetshire, Char[d]stock
Amos W.	son	6	Scholar	Yorkshire, Hoyland

The birthplaces of the first four people were not strictly accurate and this misinformation could have led to a fruitless search of parish registers had this been my first clue. The birth of young Amos in Hoyland shows that the family had moved north by 1875, but Elizabeth's birthplace reveals that before that the family had gone to live at Chardstock on the Dorset-Devon-Somerset border, a couple of miles or so from Chard. That explained why my grandmother had said that they had come from Chard.

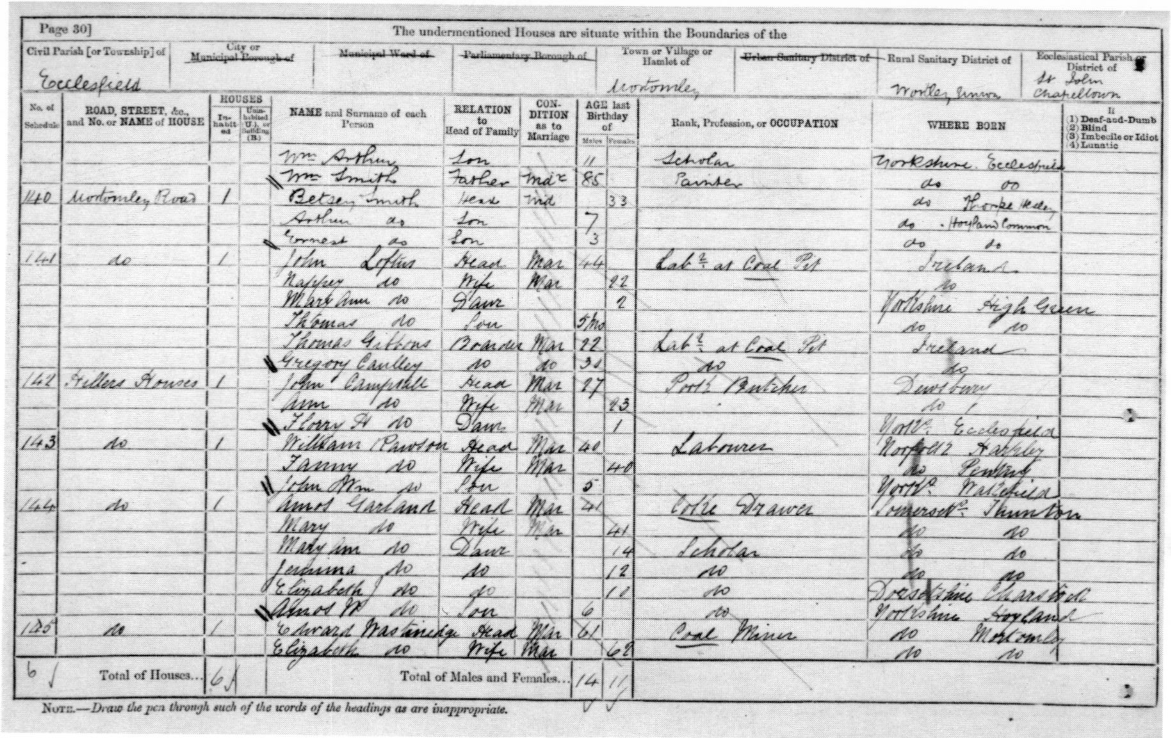

Page 30] The undermentioned Houses are situate within the Boundaries of the

Civil Parish [or Township] of Ecclesfield | ~~City or Municipal Borough of~~ | ~~Municipal Ward of~~ | ~~Parliamentary Borough of~~ | Town or Village or Hamlet of Mortomley | ~~Urban Sanitary District of~~ | Rural Sanitary District of Wortley Union | Ecclesiastical Parish or District of St John Chapeltown

No. of Schedule	ROAD, STREET, &c., and No. or NAME of HOUSE	HOUSES In-habited	HOUSES Un-inhabited (U.), or Building (B.)	NAME and Surname of each Person	RELATION to Head of Family	CON-DITION as to Marriage	AGE last Birthday of Males	AGE last Birthday of Females	Rank, Profession, or OCCUPATION	WHERE BORN	If (1) Deaf-and-Dumb (2) Blind (3) Imbecile or Idiot (4) Lunatic
				Wm Arthur	Son		11		Scholar	Yorkshire Ecclesfield	
				Wm Smith	Father	Widr	85		Painter	do do	
140	Mortomley Road	1		Betsey Smith	Head	Wid		33		do Thorpe Hesley	
				Arthur do	Son		7			do Hoyland Common	
				Ernest do	Son		3			do do	
141	do	1		John Loftus	Head	Mar	44		Labr at Coal Pit	Ireland	
				Nappey do	Wife	Mar		22		do	
				Mary Ann do	Daur			2		Yorkshire High Green	
				Thomas do	Son		5 Mo			do do	
				Thomas Gibbons	Boarder	Mar	22		Labr at Coal Pit	Ireland	
				Gregory Cawley	do	do	31		do	do	
142	Hillers Houses	1		John Campbell	Head	Mar	27		Pork Butcher	Dewsbury	
				Ann do	Wife	Mar		23		do	
				Florry A do	Daur			1		Yorks Ecclesfield	
143	do	1		William Rawson	Head	Mar	40		Labourer	Norfolk Hackley	
				Fanny do	Wife	Mar		40		do Penting	
				John Wm do	Son		5			Yorks Wakefield	
144	do	1		Amos Garland	Head	Mar	41		Coke Drawer	Somerset Taunton	
				Mary do	Wife	Mar		41		do do	
				Mary Ann do	Daur			14	Scholar	do do	
				Jemima do	do			12	do	do do	
				Elizabeth J do	do			10	do	Derbyshire Chesterfield	
				Amos W do	Son		6		do	Yorkshire Hoyland	
145	do	1		Edward Wastnidge	Head	Mar	61		Coal Miner	do Mortomley	
				Elizabeth do	Wife	Mar		62		do do	
6	Total of Houses...	6		Total of Males and Females...			14	11			

NOTE.—*Draw the pen through such of the words of the headings as are inappropriate.*

Plate 4.2 The 1881 census enumerator's return for Mortomley

This return shows the Garland family in the third of the dwellings known as Hillers Houses. Such returns provide a great deal of genealogical information and allow the local historian to study the occupational structure of his community and the places of origin of the inhabitants. Even from this single page we learn that families had come in search of work in

Elizabeth's recorded age suggested that it would be worth searching the 1871 census returns for Chardstock. The Garlands were found there, living with Mary's parents in that part of the parish known as Kitbridge, a secluded hamlet of four houses in the valley of the river Kit just south of the village.

Name	Status	Age	Occupation	Birthplace
John Knight	head	54	Farmer	Yarcombe, Devon
Mary Knight	wife	54		Hemeyock, Devon
Jemima Knight	daughter	14		Chard, Somerset
Amos Garland	son-in-law	32	Labourer	Taunton
Mary Garland	wife	32		Otterford, Devon
Mary Ann	daughter	5		Taunton
Jemima	daughter	3		Taunton
Elizabeth	daughter	1		Chardstock

This return provided the vital piece of information that Amos Garland's wife, Mary (née Knight), was born at Otterford, a parish which is actually just inside Somerset and within the civil registration sub-district of Pitminster. This cleared up the doubts as to which of the Mary Knights indexed at St Catherine's House was my ancestor. Her birth certificate shows that she was born on 7 April 1839 at Otterford, the daughter of John Knight, who at that time was a cordwainer (i.e. a shoemaker), and Mary Knight (née Trenchard). John Knight signed the certificate with a mark and gave his address in Otterford, almost unbelievably at first sight, as Nacker's Hole. This place can be readily found, however, on the 1:25,000 Ordnance Survey map (sheet ST 21/31) right at the southern limit of the parish, where Knacker's Hole Lane forms the county boundary between Somerset and Devon. A somewhat hazardous journey along narrow, twisting lanes sunk between high hedgerows, brought me to this lonely spot one sunny autumn afternoon, when the place appeared at its most romantic. The house was still there on the hillside overlooking the stream which flows deep in the hollow where horses had once been slaughtered for their meat, bones, hides and hair when their working life was over. Unfortunately, the present occupants were away from home, but the house seemed little altered (apart from

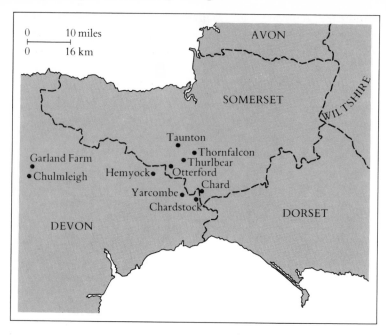

Fig. 4.1   The homes of the Garlands and Knights

some heavy repointing of the rubble stones that composed the walls) since the time that the Knights had lived there.

At various stages of his life John Knight was described as shoe-maker, labourer and farmer. Men sometimes changed their occu-pations over the years and smallholders such as John often earned their living from doing whatever job was at hand. He had been born in Yarcombe, the next parish to the south, where his father, Robert, had also worked as a shoemaker, and at the time of his marriage on 10 April 1838 he was living at Waterhayes, another isolated farmstead in the parish of Otterford. Mary, his bride, was a domestic servant at Waterhayes. She had been born a few miles further west in the Devonshire parish of Hemyock, the daughter of John Trenchard, labourer, and Elizabeth (née Board), who had married at Yarcombe church in 1788. John and Mary were married at the parish church of St Leonard, Otterford, where sheep now graze in the churchyard. Both she and John signed their marriage certificate with a cross. As we have seen, their eldest child, Mary, was born the following year at Knacker's Hole; eighteen years later their youngest child, Jemima, was born about 8 miles away at Chardstock. Their movement from one settlement to another within a few miles radius was entirely typical of the mobility patterns of English families down the centuries.

On my first visit to the district where my grandmother lived as a child I was naturally drawn to St Thomas's church at Thurlbear, the place where her parents had been married and where she had been baptised in the Norman font. The church was greatly restored in the 1860s, especially the chancel, but the Norman nave arcades survive and so does much of the fifteenth century Perpendicular work, particularly the tower and its peal of four bells. The church remains the focal point of this quiet little village; indeed, if it had no church it would hardly qualify for the description of village, for it consists merely of a few scattered farms and cottages. Thurlbear is now even smaller than it was in the nineteenth century. Most of the neighbouring settlements, including Thornfalcon, are no larger.

To the north of the church stands the village school, built in 1872 soon after the Garlands had left the parish. 'Train Up A Child In The Way He Should Go' proclaims the inscription, adding the information that, 'This School Was Built by Voluntary Subscription For the Parishes of Thurlbeare and Stoke St Mary AD 1872'. The Education Act of 1870 had authorized the building of Board Schools where no satisfactory school existed, but in many farming villages local squires hastily improved the educational provision so that they could retain control. Perhaps this is what had happened at Thurlbear? Prior to 1872, according to oral memory recorded in R. A. Sixsmith's short *History of Thurlbear* (Taunton, 1956), the children were taught to read and write for a few pence a day in the room over the stables, converted from an old barn; Kelly's 1861 *Directory* noted 'a school for boys and girls supported by voluntary subscription'. My grandmother was still an infant when she left Thurlbear, however, and she no doubt received her earliest education in the village school at Chardstock.

Thurlbear's name is derived from   ¹ English words meaning 'hill with a hollow', an etymology that fits the local topography. The old manor farm to the south of the church is now called Church Farm. From the sixteenth century onwards the manorial lords were the Portmans who had given their name to the neighbouring parish of Orchard Portman and who had risen in the world through practising law. In 1556 Sir William Portman, the

225

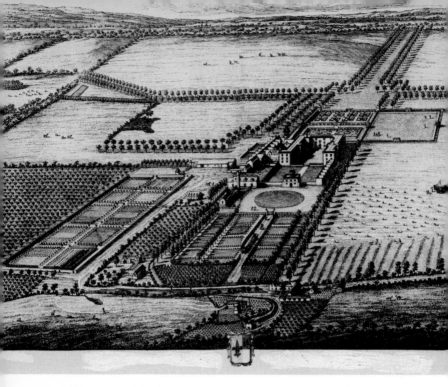

Plate 4.3 Orchard Portman House, Somerset
The house was drawn by Leonard Knyff and engraved by Jan Kip for inclusion in their *Brittania Illustrata*, published in 1707. It was built in the middle of the sixteenth century and given new windows, a pedimented door and a balustrade to bring it up to date about 150 years later. Formal gardens and long avenues of trees enhanced its setting, though pastures and meadows came close to the house. It was demolished during the second half of the nineteenth century, but it would have been a familiar sight to the Garlands, who lived a few hundred yards away and who worked as farm labourers on the estate.

Lord Chief Justice and himself the son of an Orchard lawyer, bought the manor of Thurlbear with his son, Henry. During the nineteenth century the Portmans owned about half the land in the parish, and from 1860 to 1885 a member of the family who rejoiced in the name of Fitzhardinge Berkeley Portman was rector of Staple Fitzpaine with Orchard Portman and Thurlbear. His duties in Thurlbear were performed by a resident curate, William Lance, who married Amos and Mary Garland in 1864 and baptised my grandmother.

The map accompanying the Tithe Award of 1837 shows that (apart from the glebe land belonging to the church) the other half of Thurlbear was owned by ten landowners. However, four of these owned less than 2 acres and another three owners had less than 4 acres. Most of the land was divided between large farms, for it was the Portman policy between 1837 and 1855 to increase the size of their holdings and to let them on long leases. In 1855 Moses Chorley of Badger Street had 390 acres, Richard Burrough of Greenway held 327 acres and Mr Bond had 60 acres, most of them in the Marshes; only one other tenant had more than 5 acres. Mr Sixsmith writes that this policy has been partially reversed in the twentieth century. In 1956 Thurlbear had six farms and four smallholdings and by then the Portman estate had been purchased by the Commissioners of Crown Lands and the sporting rights in the local woods let to a syndicate. In modern times no family has held a farm for more than a generation or two.

The Vale of Taunton Deane in which Thurlbear lies is a very rich and fertile area. Early in the seventeenth century John Norden called it 'the Paradise of England'. Excellent crops can be grown and herds of cattle reared for their beef and for their dairy products. And of course the apple orchards produce the famous cider. In 1633 Thomas Gerard, a local antiquary, wrote that Orchard Portman 'well brookes the name, for it is sceated in a very fertile soyle for fruit; and the whole Countrey thereabouts seems to be orchards, insomuch that all the hedgerows and pasture groundes are full frought with fruite trees of all sorts fitting to eat and make cider of'. For much of the nineteenth century the farmers maintained high standards and high prices made them prosperous. The labourers did not share in this prosperity.

In common with the rest of England, Somerset parishes saw expenditure on the poor rise steeply during the later eighteenth and early nineteenth centuries. The county applied the Speenhamland system whereby wage levels were supported from the poor rates. Seasonal unemployment remained an intractable problem at a time of population growth and enormous numbers of people were forced to seek relief. The notorious winters of 1794–95, 1829–30 and 1830–31 brought great hardship and a report in 1833 claimed that 'Men of all trades wander for employment . . . many hundred [are] on the tramp'. Even in times when work was available, the physical contrast between the comfortable farmhouses and the overcrowded cottages was an indictment of the humanity of a society which allowed such things to happen. The South-west was one of the loveliest parts of England, but its low wages and bad housing were a disgrace.

In Thurlbear the labourers were housed together in Marsh Bay near Longwater Bridge on the north-western boundary of the parish. One is tempted to compare them with a colony of lepers who were kept as far out of sight as possible. All the seven cottages recorded in the census returns and other nineteenth century sources have now gone and a few modern houses have taken their place. The labourers no doubt worked at several of the farms in the vicinity, not just those in Thurlbear, wherever demand arose. Our earliest source of information about them comes from a survey and assessment of the parish of Thurlbear made in 1828 by Mr Ralph Ham, a Taunton surveyor. At the end of the survey we come to a list of encroachments on E. B. Portman's land, namely seven cottages and gardens. The second of the seven entries records Michael Webb's cottage and gardens, covering 32 perches of land, at an annual value of £1.5s.0d. rated at 6¼d. per annum. This information, incidentally, shows that Michael Webb was living here at least four years before his daughter Ann married William Garland of Thornfalcon. Perhaps he had moved here when he married in 1792? The Garlands came into Thurlbear parish to live in a cottage that was already occupied by the Webbs.

The Thurlbear churchwardens' accounts allow us to trace the descent of this property, for regular rate demands were made towards the repair of the parish church. 'Michel Weebb Cotter 6¼' is recorded in 1829 and in a similar manner until 1843. Michael died two years later and in 1846 William Garland's name takes his place. William died in 1852 and in the following year Ann Garland appears in the rate list. She must have died after 1863, when she was last recorded, and before 1865 when Amos Garland became responsible for paying the rates on the cottage. This information enabled me to quickly find her death recorded in the St Catherine's House indexes for March 1864, about the time that Amos and Mary were married. Amos was also recorded in 1867, but unfortunately the accounts then come to an end, so we cannot pinpoint his departure from the parish. His second daughter Jemima was baptised at Thurlbear on 15 November 1868 but on census night in 1871 the family was living at Chardstock, where Elizabeth, their third daughter, had been born a year or more earlier. 1869 seems the likeliest year for their move.

Perhaps the Garlands's cottage was demolished shortly after their departure from Thurlbear. The 1887 6-inch ordnance survey map marks only three cottages alongside the road that passes through Marsh Bay to Taunton. A schedule of cottages on the Portman estate taken in the same year notes that most were built of stone and roofed with thatch. At that time the surviving Marsh Bay cottages shared an 'open well, very shallow, always short of water in summer'. A local mason, James Tarr, lived in 'a very old cottage, roof and floor in a weak state', which was eventually demolished in 1903, and an adjoining cottage, old and disused, was described as a one-up, one-down building with an old timber and thatch linhay, i.e. a shed, open to the front, probably having a lean-to roof.

Nineteenth-century Thurlbear had two carpenters and a black-smith, and extra work was provided from time to time in burning lime for use on the heavy clay soils of the locality. The ruins of a kiln survive in Thurlbear Wood. If Amos Garland found occasional work there, the experience would have stood him in good stead when he moved to Yorkshire to work as a coke-drawer. In 1841 Thurlbear had thirty-six inhabited houses (and two unoccupied), which provided accommodation for 100 men and boys and 94 women and girls; 182 of these parishioners had been born in Somerset. The census returns give the following population figures:

1801: 151	1831: 202	1861: 192	1891: 151
1811: 202	1841: 194	1871: 165	1901: 172
1821: 215	1851: 212	1881: 133	

The Garlands were amongst those who moved out of the parish at the time when it was experiencing its biggest drop in population.

Many of the families that quit the countryside at this time moved to the towns. Somerset did not have any large urban centres, but the county town, Taunton, grew considerably during the course of the nineteenth century, from 5,794 inhabitants in 1801 to 19,525 in 1901. Mary Knight was living in the central parish of St Mary Magdalene at the time of her marriage to Amos Garland in 1864. The town's shops and market must have been a regular attraction for country folk and the magnificent Perpendicular tower of the church must have been a familiar sight. Amos may well have met Mary upon a visit to the town. Others moved on to more distant places; Taunton was connected by rail with London in 1842, and Bristol beckoned those who had decided to try their luck overseas.

The St Mary Magdalene baptism registers record several

Garlands, mostly small tradesmen such as cordwainers, brush-makers, tailors and masons. Lots of Garlands can also be found in Devon; Knight too is a common Devon name, and the Webbs are numerous in Somerset. These branches of my family seem firmly rooted in West Country soil. Sheet 193 of the 1:50,000 ordnance survey map allows the eye to wander over the wooded, undulating countryside south of Taunton, to pick out Otterford and Yarcombe, where the Knights came from, and to find Hemyock, the birthplace of John Knight's bride, Mary Trenchard (another West Country name). A little further west, just inside the Devon border, we come across Garlandhayes. Is this the place that has given rise to my ancestors' surname, or was the hamlet named after a medieval Garland who had already acquired his surname? The question excites and intrigues, all the more so as the latter part of the name is derived from a word meaning 'hedged enclosure', exactly the same as my own surname, Hey.

On turning to J. E. B. Gover, A. Mawer and F. M. Stenton, *The Place-Names of Devon* (1931–2), I found that Garlandhayes was recorded in 1640 and that the first part of the name was derived from the Old English word *gara*, meaning a triangular or wedge-shaped piece of land. As the hamlet lies in a triangular projection of Clayhidon parish, right on the county boundary, the name seems an appropriate one. However, Devon has another Garlandhayes in the parish of Bradninch, where the name was recorded in 1544 and where the position is equally appropriate for such a name. But it turns out that neither of these hamlets is the best candidate for the home of this family name. In the heart of Devon, where the decayed market town and former medieval borough of Chulmleigh occupies a hill above the valley of the Little Dart, the church of St Mary Magdalene serves a large parish that contains several ancient and scattered farms. In the Middle Ages a remote farmstead in the north of the parish bore the name of Garland Farm. It was recorded in 1242 as Gorelaunde and the name was probably derived in a similar manner to Garlandhayes, though Old English *gor* meaning 'dirty land' is a possible alternate source. In his large book on Devon (1954) Professor W. G. Hoskins notes that this farm was the birthplace of John Garland, a remarkable man who became a professor at Toulouse University in 1229 and who wrote treatises on grammar, minerals, counter-point and plain-song. The surname had apparently already been derived from the farm early in the thirteenth century. The present 1:25,000 ordnance survey map shows the boundaries of Chulmleigh, Romansleigh and King's Nympton parishes meeting at Garland Cross. West, Middle and East Garland Farms lie within a triangular-shaped projection of Chulmleigh parish. From the map and on the ground it appears that West Garland Farm may occupy the original site, for it has the most sheltered position and West Garland Moor lies beyond the middle farm, but more detailed research will be necessary before I can come to a firmer conclusion.

On moving from Thurlbear, the place of his birth and his home for thirty years, Amos Garland went first of all to Chardstock on the Dorset-Devon-Somerset border. The parish had once formed part of Dorset but in 1896 it was transferred to Devon. The place-name implies that the settlement had originated as the *stoc* or dependent farm of Chard. Characteristically for this region, the parish contained numerous scattered farms on the hillsides and in the deep coombes, though Chardstock is a decent-sized village, centred on the stone-and-thatch George Inn, the Victorian school and the large church of St Andrew, which was rebuilt in 1864. The tiny river Kit has cut a deep valley to the west of the church, separating the village from the stone farmhouses and cottages that are scattered over the hillside beyond. The lane that winds out of the village in a southerly direction descends this valley and crosses the river by a bridge. In 1871 the Knights and the Garlands lived at the third of the four dwellings in the hamlet of Kitbridge as one approaches from the village. This was just the sort of remote place that they had been used to and one that was very similar in its seclusion to the hamlet where my grandmother was to spend most of her adult life in Yorkshire. As a child she probably attended the church school in the village, a school which had been built in 1839.

Both the Garlands and the Knights had moved on by the time that the next census was taken, or perhaps Mary's parents had died in the meantime. The momentous decision to quit farm labouring and move over 200 miles to the industrial North was taken between 1871 and 1875, when Amos and Mary were in their early or mid thirties with three young children to raise. The crucial question of why they chose south Yorkshire in preference to other industrial areas nearer Somerset cannot now be answered by any surviving member of the family. Did Amos go in search of work and having found employment and accommodation go back to fetch his family? Or did he move in response to an advertisement placed by coal owners in a South-western paper?

The Chard and Ilminster News was established on 7 November 1874, but perhaps the Garlands had gone by then. Amos had no previous family connection with the North, but perhaps friends and relatives had made the move before him? His step-brother, Michael Webb, was a railway labourer in 1861 and he may have passed on some useful information. Whatever the spur to migration, it is clear that the movement of this single labouring family represented a mere trickle in the stream of emigration from the countryside, a stream that swelled again at the time of the Great

---

Plate 4.4 The Village School, Chardstock
The Revd Charles Woodstock, incumbent of Chardstock from 1834 to 1875, was responsible for many changes in his village, including the total rebuilding of the church and the foundation of three schools on the same site. The story is told by the present headmaster, P.J. Wood, in *A History of Education in Chardstock, 1712-1979* (1979).

The schoolhouse shown in the centre of the illustration is still used as the two main classrooms. It was erected in 1839 with a grant from the National Society and altered in 1856 by the addition of a porch and the insertion of new windows. The two wings were used as an Industrial School, founded in 1849 to train poor orphan girls to become proficient domestic servants; the success of the scheme led to similar provision for boys. The vicar wrote that such training was preferable to 'the ruinous and pauperising effect of our present workhouse education, if such it can be called'. Eighteen girls and twelve boys attended the Industrial School in 1871, but the advent of compulsory education brought the scheme to an end.

The illustration can be dated to 1849–58, for in the latter year a large Middle School (later known as St Andrew's College) was erected at the rear. In 1871 it housed forty-three boys aged between eight and eighteen, but three years later the school was transferred to Salisbury and the buildings were eventually demolished. An 1867 Post Office Guide claimed that the children of the Industrial School were 'the hewers of wood and the bearers of water to the upper school'.

As primary education was made compulsory in 1870, my grandmother (who lived at Kit Bridge, Chardstock in 1871) presumably attended the village school. Unfortunately, the admission registers start just too late and she is not mentioned in the school log book which was kept from 1863. Her headmistress would have been Susan Hawkins (appointed in February 1869) and she may have received some reading, writing and singing lessons from the vicar and his sisters. Discipline was firm and the headmistress thought it worthy of comment that one day she 'Conducted the school without once using the cane – only gave one boy a box on the ear'. Children were often absent assisting in the gardens, haymaking, harvesting, apple picking and potato picking, or through illness and bad weather.

Agricultural Depression in the 1870s, the time when the Garlands decided to move.

They moved about the time that F. G. Heath visited some of the villages around Taunton to gather material for his book, *The English Peasantry*. Heath found that in the parishes of Stoke St Gregory, North Curry and Hatch Beauchamp 'a great number of the cottages were very bad, some of them being, in fact, mere mud hovels'; wages in this district were only nine shillings a week and in some parts of the neighbourhood they were as low as eight shillings. He was full of praise for the efforts of Canon Girdlestone, the incumbent of Halberton in north Devon from 1866 to 1872, for the way in which he had directed public attention to the miserable condition of the agricultural labourers, incurring the wrath of local farmers in so doing. Girdlestone poured his energy into organizing a regular system of migration; he had lived in Lancashire where farm labourers were well paid and well housed in comparison and was able to build up a body of contacts who were willing to take on the labourers whom he recommended. During his time at Halberton he was able to send some 400–500 men, two thirds of them with families, to Lancashire, Yorkshire, Durham, Kent, Sussex and elsewhere. Heath was told that almost everything had to be done for the migrant labourers; their luggage addressed, their railway tickets obtained and full and plain directions given. The men who went away, with very few exceptions, prospered and they in turn found situations for their friends and relations. The result was that considerable numbers of families migrated to the North from Devon, Dorset, Somerset and Wiltshire, so much so that eventually the South-western counties experienced a growing shortage of agricultural labour.

Amos Garland's migration therefore fits into a wider pattern of movement. He somehow found employment as a coke drawer in a part of the Yorkshire coalfield where several large pits, for instance the Barrow, Hoyland, Silkstone, Pilley, Rockingham and Tankersley collieries, were being sunk to the Silkstone and Barnsley seams. These pits normally had beehive-shaped coke ovens attached to them for the local seams provided good coking coal. A lot of immigrants, particularly from Staffordshire, had come to this area in search of work. Only a few years before Amos arrived in south Yorkshire the owners of Thorncliffe colliery had imported labour to replace their striking miners and had settled some of them in the secluded Westwood Row down in the valley between High Green and Tankersley. This lonely spot had been the scene of a violent assault on 21 January 1870 when the strikers wreaked havoc with the property of those whom they considered blacklegs. These problems had been resolved by the time that the Garlands arrived but the memories were bitter. Amos worked at the Nancy coke ovens just up the lane from Westwood Row and walked to work across the fields from Hoyland before moving house to the other side of the valley at High Green. He was therefore still doing labouring work in rural surroundings, just as he had done in Somerset. Nancy Pit closed before the First World War and the scene is now entirely pastoral for the site has been outcropped and then restored to farming land. The coke ovens have gone, the old Nancy cottages have been modernized and the pond that once provided water for the pit boiler is now a haven for fishermen.

The row where they lived in 1881 has also been demolished. Hillers Houses had not been built when the survey for the first edition of the 6-inch ordnance survey map was made in 1850–51, and they can be identified only tentatively from the progression of the enumerator of the 1881 census, when plotted on later maps. A number of houses in Mortomley were occupied by people who had the same name as their row, suggesting that they were the owners or builders of small groups of property. Amos would have had about a mile to walk through the woods and across the fields to his place of work.

When Mary Ann Garland married my grandfather in 1900 she was described as the daughter of Amos Garland, coke drawer. This led me to believe that Amos was still alive at the time of her marriage and so I searched twenty-eight years of the indexes at St Catherine's House before I discovered that he had died eight years before the wedding. There was no alternative to this time-consuming task for family memory did not recall when he died or his age at death. When I eventually acquired his certificate I read that he had died on 15 August 1892 at the age of fifty-two, a 'general labourer' who had been suffering from diphtheria for eight months and nephritis for seven months. One of the scourges of the nineteenth century had laid him low. His widow, Mary, died ten years later of a diseased heart and dropsy; her certificate records that her son, Amos Webb Garland, was with her at the time of death and that her late husband had worked as an iron furnaceman.

It has been my good fortune in recent times to make contact with Bill Garland, the youngest of the four children of Amos

Webb Garland, and to find that members of the family still live within a few miles of the old Nancy coke ovens. I learned from him that my grandmother's younger sisters had gone to work in the textile mills a little further north and that they had married men from Hepworth and Denby Dale. We were able to give each other information that surprised us both. An extra dimension to the migration story was obtained when I heard that one of the Knights, Amos's brother-in-law, had also moved up to the same area. Who came first? Or did they come on an adventure together? So there are Knights as well as Garlands in this part of Yorkshire now.

But a much wider dimension was added to the tale when Bill Garland told me that one or two of Amos's elder brothers had emigrated to America and another had gone to South Africa. I have a photograph in my family collection of an unidentified young man in Holyoke, Massachusetts, and Bill recalls a photograph of three shoemakers in a shop at Salt Lake City. This news not only opened up further avenues of personal exploration, but set the Garlands's movement away from the South-west in an even firmer historical context. Together with enormous numbers of other ordinary people from many parts of England, they had left their homes to start life anew thousands of miles away in the hope of a better standard of living.

The story of how the Garlands left the South-west in search of work shows how family history and local history can provide a perspective on our own contemporary world. During the last two or three decades there has been a marked shift of population from the North to the South-east as old manufacturing industries decline and new economic opportunities become much more readily available in southern parts of the country. This is the reverse of the situation a hundred years or so ago. It is also striking that the Yorkshire pits that are now being closed as uneconomic are the very ones that were new and in need of immigrant labour when the Garlands decided to move. Many of the 'traditional' pit villages in fact have been mining villages for no more than three generations or so, a relatively short time in the long span of English history.

THE BATTYS

In the previous chapter we followed the fortunes of some

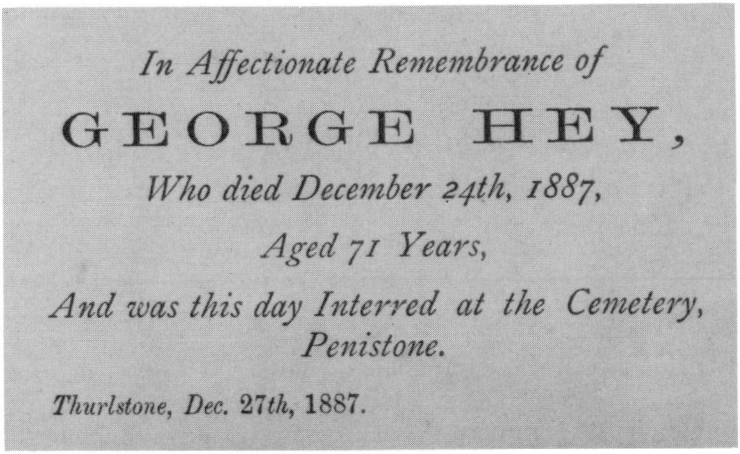

In Affectionate Remembrance of

GEORGE HEY,

Who died December 24th, 1887,

Aged 71 Years,

And was this day Interred at the Cemetery, Penistone.

Thurlstone, Dec. 27th, 1887.

Plate 4.5 A family memento

Most families will have amongst their possessions miscellaneous mementos of their ancestors. This one, edged in black, was printed on the occasion of my great-grandfather's funeral. It gives precise information on his age, date of death and place of burial. Family memorials often provide leads to other sources. Armed with the information on this card, I quickly found George Hey's baptism entry in the local parish register.

members of the Batty family to provide a case study of a representative farming group through the peaks and troughs of agriculture in the Georgian and Victorian eras. Now I wish to consider their activities in more detail in order to demonstrate the range of sources that are available to a family historian who wishes to trace the history of a farming family and to show how by taking all the branches of the North Yorkshire Battys I became aware of broad patterns which were all the more vivid when set against the general trends in British social and economic history. The Battys became interesting not just as my mother's ancestors but as a farming dynasty whose fortunes rose and fell like many another family group during the eighteenth and nineteenth centuries.

From my earliest years my mother regaled me with stories of her ancestors the Batty family, of how they had once been well-to-do farmers in the fertile flat lands north of York, of how my grandfather had not worked until he was thirty-three but had spent his mornings with the local yeomanry and his afternoons dozing upon his couch. Then the day of retribution for such idleness had come with a vengeance and my grandfather had to leave Lund Farm, Easingwold, to seek work as a labourer, returning each night with bleeding hands that were not used to such toil. My mother was born at Topcliffe in north Yorkshire, one of the places they stopped at for a while before the search for work took them into the West Riding, then into Lancashire (where my grandfather was pig-keeper on the Earl of Derby's estate at Peacock Farm, Knowsley, near Liverpool), and a few years later to the Pennine foothills of south-west Yorkshire. As we have seen, my grandfather was eventually able to return to the farm he had left so ignominiously thirty years earlier. I have a photograph of myself taken at the Lund when I was thirteen months old and a postcard written by my mother assuring her mother-in-law that I was happy playing with the pigs and hens. As far as I can remember I only visited Easingwold on two other occasions with my mother during the next thirty years, but my curiosity was kindled by these family stories and kept aflame by their frequent repetition over the years. I became determined to get to the truth behind the family story and to find out all that I could about the places where they had once lived. I was able to confirm its main outlines – stripped of its romantic excesses – and to find a large amount of documentary evidence for the Battys's activities. Moreover, most of the farmhouses which they had once inhabited were still there.

But I was not able to find any Battys. My mother's ancestors had formed merely one of several branches of the Batty family in the northern Vale of York, and some of the others had continued to live in the district after my grandfather had left. Kelly's North Riding directory for 1937 named two men with that surname living in Easingwold, and one of these was still alive in the late 1960s. But now there are no Batty names in the telephone directory for the whole of this part of north Yorkshire. As I showed in the previous chapter, 100 years ago seven different branches of the Batty family had farmed over 1,000 acres of land between them, but since then they had all disappeared. I therefore had no distant relatives to help me pick up the threads of the story. I had to untangle it from records kept at London, York and Northallerton and from visits to the Coxwold–Husthwaite–Easingwold district. Many of the assumptions that I made in the early stages of my enquiry were later proved to be wrong, partly because I did not proceed in a systematic manner (for this was merely a leisure pursuit with frequent bouts of inactivity between spells of feverish enthusiasm), but partly also because of the ambiguity or insufficiency of the records. Many problems remain to be solved, especially the major one of why such a prolific and successful family should have disappeared so completely, but I have now managed to separate the many branches and to locate them in their various homes. In so doing, I have come to understand not only how such a farming dynasty was able to establish a network of connections throughout a neighbourhood, but also to see how subtly different the various communities that existed in that district could be. It did not take me long to realize that Coxwold's history had not run along similar lines to those of its neighbour, Husthwaite, despite their proximity and their similar farming practices.

Coxwold is a neat, stone-built estate village with trim green verges along both sides of the road which descends the hill from St Michael's church into the bottom of the valley. It was the Best Kept Village in the Forest and Vale in 1978, according to an inscription on a public seat, and it is easy to see why it won that award. The village houses and cottages date from the seventeenth to the nineteenth century and they owe much of their present appearance to the influence and authority of the Bellasis family and their successors the Wombwells. Anthony Bellasis, Henry VIII's chaplain, acquired Newburgh Priory in the next township to Coxwold when the house of Augustinian canons there was dissolved at the Reformation. The family subsequently enlarged their property and in time received the title of Earls Fauconberg. Upon the death of the last earl in 1802 their estate passed through the female line to Sir George Orby Wombwell, whose ancestors had lived in the south Yorkshire village of that name. Some of the cottages in the village bear an elaborate inscription with the initials G.O.W. and the dates 1862, 1876 and 1890. Earlier buildings include the old Grammar School, the Fauconberg Arms and, on the opposite side of the street, the Fauconberg Hospital of 1662, a single-storeyed structure with a gabled porch. The influence of the squirearchy on Coxwold is immediately apparent to the visitor. In 1801 the population of the township stood at 289. Thirty years later it had risen to 375, its highest point, and after fluctuating up and down for the rest of the century it fell to 275 in 1901. The good quality of the accommodation provided by the squire had kept the population level reasonably stable at a time when some other agricultural districts were experiencing a fall in numbers as farm labourers moved out.

Plate 4.6   Coxwold and Husthwaite *c.* 1772
Thomas Jefferys's map shows Coxwold village lying close to Newburgh
Priory, the home of the Bellasis family, Earls Fauconberg, who owned
all the land in Coxwold township. Coxwold Park Farm, the eighteenth
century home of the Battys, is marked (without name) to the north of
Angram. To the west of Easingwold stretched a large, low-lying area
of common land, not yet enclosed.

From the earliest times of which we have record Coxwold had
been a centre of local importance. At the time of the great
Domesday survey the manor of Coxwold had six dependent vills
ranging from Thirkleby and Osgodby in the west to Ampleforth
and Yearsley in the east. Over 300 years earlier *Cuha walda* had
been one of the three monasteries referred to in Pope Paul I's letter
of 757 or 758 to Eadberht, King of Northumbria, and his brother
Ecgberht, Archbishop of York. Cuha was an Old English
personal name and *wald* referred to the wooded character of the
area, as did the last element in Easingwold's name. Over the
centuries Cuhawalda was gradually transformed into Coxwold.
The place retained some of its former importance as an early

Christian centre, for well beyond the Middle Ages Coxwold parish covered some 13,000 acres and included several neighbouring townships and the chapelry of Birdforth. The church's dedication to St Michael is one that is often attached to hill-top sites; in medieval art St Michael is commonly portrayed slaying a dragon on a hill. Coxwold was also a neighbourhood centre in another sense, for in 1304 the lord obtained a royal charter empowering him to hold a weekly market and also an annual fair on the eve and day of the Assumption of the Blessed Virgin. The market did not last long, for like hundreds of other village markets throughout England it did not survive the demographic and economic setbacks of the later Middle Ages, but the fair was still being held in the late eighteenth century. By the time of the Wombwells, however, Coxwold had lost all claims to being a local trading centre.

The unusual octagonal tower and the distinctive parapet that crowns the church add to the dignity of St Michael's striking position. The curate of Coxwold from 1760 until his death in 1768 was the Revd Lawrence Sterne, author of *Tristram Shandy* and *A Sentimental Journey*. Sterne lived in the picturesque house known as Shandy Hall which stands a little apart from the village to the west of the church. He must have been a familiar figure to the Battys, who were not only prominent parishioners and, occasionally, churchwardens but near neighbours at Coxwold Park Farm. The farmstead into which Richard Batty moved in the early years of the eighteenth century seems to have acquired its name from a medieval deer park in this part of the parish. In 1257 Thomas Colvill, lord of the manor, obtained a royal grant of free warren, and this general right to hunt on his estate probably led to the creation of the park. No doubt the deer had been removed and the park turned over to farming long before the Battys arrived in the parish. The whole district consisted of good agricultural land and in the Victorian period the fields of Coxwold were said to be 'remarkably fertile'.

As we have seen, at the foot of the western tower of St Michael's church stand seven gravestones that commemorate the lives of ten members of the Batty family. They are of various shapes and sizes and are huddled together close to the churchyard wall, forming a distinctive group. One of the stones was erected in memory of James Batty of Coxwold Park Farm, the elder son of Richard and Frances Batty who were the first members of the family to set up home in the parish. James died on 27 May 1814, aged sixty-four. Buried near to him are some members of the Batty family who had moved to Tollerton and Wallerthwaite, many miles distant, but whose bodies were brought back to be buried in the family's 'home' parish. Tollerton lay about 9 miles from Coxwold and a mile distant from its own parish church at Alne; Wallerthwaite was considerably further away on the western edge of the Vale of York. To the south of St Michael's church three more Batty graves can be found. Two belong to the branch that moved to Thornton Hill, a detached part of the parish 2 miles south of Coxwold. The third is that of John Batty 'of Stillington (but formerly of Whenby)', his wife and their son. Stillington and Whenby both lie several miles away. The family obviously thought of Coxwold as 'their' parish and this sentiment was powerful enough for them to want to be buried there. Tombstones are obviously a major source for the family historian, but we need to be aware that an ancestor may not be buried in the parish where he died.

Another five Batty graves are grouped together in the southwest corner of the churchyard in the neighbouring parish of Husthwaite, where James Batty's younger brother Richard (1755–1833) had established a dynasty. A tombstone that is now sadly broken and propped up against another commemorates Thomas Batty of Woolpots, who died in 1858 at the age of seventy-two, his wife, Elizabeth, and three young children. St Nicholas's churchyard at Husthwaite was as attractive a choice of final resting place for the Battys as was St Michael's churchyard at Coxwold. Here, for example, is the grave of my grandfather's uncle, Thomas Batty of the Lund, Easingwold, who died in 1887 at the age of sixty-one, having been a 'retired farmer' for most of his life, and the graves of Mary (aged three) and John (four), the children of my great-grandparents James and Rosamond Batty, who lived at Mowbray House, Stillington, but who chose Husthwaite as the burial ground for their children, probably because this was the parish church where Rosamond had worshipped before her marriage. The family must have had a certain status in the locality to do such a thing; it is hard to imagine a poor man persuading a minister that family sentiment outweighed all other considerations.

Two other graves contain the mortal remains of members of the Batty family whose bodies had been returned to Husthwaite for burial. Robert Dixon Batty (1823–87) was 'of Easingwold' but 'late of Throstle Nest' a farm to the south of the village. His elder brother, Richard Batty (1820–77), had moved even further, for he had lived at Myton Old Hall on the banks of the river Swale; his widow returned to live in Husthwaite, where she died fourteen years later. The same tombstone records the burial of their son Richard (1850–86), so perhaps this branch of the family came to an end through the lack of male heirs. Here is part of the explanation of why there are no Battys in the district today. Another reason for the disappearance of the Battys from the local scene – one that many family historians will be familiar with – was the unprecedented slaughter of the First World War. A roll of honour inside Husthwaite church names three Battys who were killed between 1914 and 1918; a similar roll at Coxwold includes the name of William Batty of the Highland Light Infantry.

In contrast to Coxwold, Husthwaite was of only minor importance historically. Its name is derived from Old Norse words meaning 'house clearing', for this settlement too was founded when the district was still well-wooded. The parish may have been carved out the territory that was originally served by the monks at Coxwold. It was less than 3,000 acres in extent and included the township of Carlton Husthwaite, which eventually acquired its own small church. When the Dean and Chapter of York Minster became lords of the manor Husthwaite was made into a peculiar ecclesiastical jurisdiction and the church was served by a perpetual curate. The village has an attractive variety of houses of many different shapes and sizes; they range in date from the sixteenth century timber-framed Black Bull Cottage to nineteenth and twentieth century brick and stone structures, which stretch along the three streets that meet at a small green by St Nicholas's church. Their varied and irregular arrangement provides an interesting contrast to the quiet, orderly appearance of the estate village at Coxwold. The church was built in the local brown stone by the Normans, heightened during the Perpendicular phase of English Gothic, and restored by the Victorians, a story that could be paralleled in many other English villages. A good view of the Battys's original home at Coxwold Park Farm, and beyond it the Kilburn White Horse, carved on the hillside, can be gained from the north side of the churchyard. The presence of a Wesleyan chapel nearby reminds us that this was not an estate village dominated by a squire, as at Coxwold. Husthwaite's population rose steadily during the nineteenth century, from 288 in 1801 to 470 in 1871; twenty years later it had dropped to 348, but then it started to pick up again. Meanwhile, the population of the

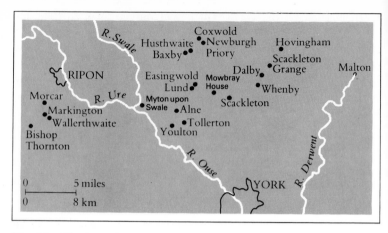

Fig. 4.2 The Battys' Neighbourhood

detached part of Coxwold parish which contained Thornton on the Hill and Baxby township, immediately beyond Husthwaite, fluctuated between 71 in 1801 and 72 100 years later, with a low point of 67 in 1831 and a peak of 97 in 1861.

The second elements in the place-names Coxwold, Easingwold and Husthwaite suggest that in the earliest days of settlement this part of the northern Vale of York was well-wooded. That is decidedly not the case today; modern coniferous plantations cover part of the Howardian Hills in the east and a few old, deciduous springwoods remain near Brafferton and Sessay in the west, but in most parishes the woods have been felled. During the Middle Ages an extensive part of this district lay within the royal Forest of Galtres, whose Scandinavian name meaning 'boars' brush-wood' hints at a hunting connection even before the Norman Conquest. A forest was a royal hunting preserve whose bound-aries were fixed by the Norman kings. The word had a technical meaning and did not imply dense woodland, though tree cover would have been found in many parts of the forest. At its widest extent the Forest of Galtres covered most of the wapentake of Bulmer. It stretched from the Swale and the Ure in the west to the river Derwent in the east, and from the walls of the city of York in the south to the old Roman road from Malton to Aldborough in the north. The line of this abandoned road is preserved by the township boundary between Newburgh and Oulston and part of it is still used as a lane heading west towards

Husthwaite with the significant name Malton Street. *Straet*, the Anglo-Saxon word for a Roman road, is also incorporated in the village names Appleton le Street and Barton le Street much further east near Malton. Coxwold, Newburgh and Yearsley lay beyond the forest boundaries, but Baxby, Husthwaite, Thornton Hill and Oulston formed a small group that were referred to collectively in a 1316 perambulation as the Bailiwick of Easingwold. This northern fringe was not an integral part of the forest in later times; indeed, it may have been reduced to the status of a purlieu when part of Galtres was disafforested in Henry II's reign (1154–89). Certainly, its links with the forest had gone long before Charles I severed the royal connection with the area in 1630 and turned the land to agricultural use.

Part of the district known as The Lund, south-west of Easingwold, was allotted and enclosed in 1630 when Galtres was disafforested. A Lund House was referred to in 1639 and may be identified with the oldest of several Lund Farms; a 1797 rating valuation mentions just one Lund Farm, a holding of 58 acres. Lund is an Old Norse word for a small wood, especially one situated on or near a boundary. This derivation fits the Easingwold Lund perfectly, for just beyond the farms is a stream known as The Kyle, whose leisurely course forms the northern and western boundary of the parish, and close by the oldest farm is a small deciduous wood. Thomas Jefferys's map of Yorkshire (1767–72) marks a large moor to the west of Easingwold and south of Raskelf. Part of this moor was enclosed between 1808 and 1812, together with the remaining open fields, commons and other wastes in Easingwold. The other Lund farms (including my grandfather's) seem to have been created at this time. The style of the buildings and the regularity of the field patterns suggest that this was so, and deeds in my family's possession prove an abstract of title as far back as 1813, the year after the enclosure award. The deeds speak of 30 acres that were 'lately part of certain lands theretofore called the inclosed Moor but the whole of which was lately inclosed . . . divided into seven closes' and of a 'Barn Stable and other Buildings lately erected and built upon the said piece or pracel of Land'. I felt a deep sense of personal loss on a recent visit to find that the old farmhouse, which I had visited as a child, had been almost completely demolished and replaced by a modern bungalow. A small portion of wall remained intact, just enough to show that the house was built of the same local brick as the surviving barn or stable. I knew from a photograph that the farmhouse had once had a pantile roof and Yorkshire- or sliding-sash windows.

Much of the northern Vale of York had been enclosed by the agreement of the freeholders long before the age of parliamentary enclosure began in the mid eighteenth century. Coxwold has no enclosure award for this reason, though ridge and furrow patterns show that part of the township was farmed under an open-field system. Husthwaite does have an enclosure award, ratified in 1845 without the expense of a private act of parliament, but it deals with only 18 acres, 3 roods and 21 perches of waste lands, mainly the broad verges of the village streets and lanes; communal farming in open fields had been abandoned decades if not centuries before, and only a few names such as Long Roods survived as reminders of the old system. Similarly, the neighbouring townships of Crayke, Oulston, Thornton cum Baxby and much of Raskelf and Thormanby had been enclosed by agreement before the end of the seventeenth century. In Husthwaite parish outlying farms with fanciful names like Flower of May and Peep O'Day were probably established when the open fields were enclosed, but their foundation cannot be firmly dated. By the time that the first large-scale maps were made in the middle years of the nineteenth century the settlement patterns of this part of Yorkshire was already ancient.

Where they exist, awards and plans that were made under the terms of the Tithe Commutation Act (1836) are an invaluable source of information for local and family historians. Tithe awards were made on a township or a parish basis and they list all the owners and occupiers of land, they give the names and acreages of the tenements, gardens and fields, and they note whether the fields were used as arable, pasture or meadow. The accompanying plans are often the earliest detailed maps that are available to a local historian and they can sometimes be used to locate the houses of each family in the community. Often they can be correlated with the 1841 or the 1851 census returns. But if tithes had been extinguished prior to the 1836 act, that is at the time of parliamentary enclosure, then no tithe award was made. Thus, fewer than a third of Leicestershire parishes and less than a quarter of Northamptonshire villages have tithe awards, whereas in some other counties the coverage is almost complete. Fortunately, the townships of the northern Vale of York have a reasonably full set of awards, which have been deposited at the Borthwick Institute of Historical Research at York.

The Coxwold and Husthwaite awards (1839) and plans (1840–41) highlight the differences between the estate village and the freeholders' township. All of Coxwold's 1,369 acres, apart from the curate's 2½ acres and another 7½ acres set out as public roads, belonged to George Orby Wombwell, esquire, the future baronet of Newburgh Priory. Even well-to-do men like Richard Harrison, who farmed 175 acres at Coxwold Park, rented their land from the squire. Wombwell also owned all the 1,107 acres of Thornton Hill, though the remaining 333 acres of Thornton cum Baxby township belonged to small freeholders at Baxby, Providence Hill, Woolpots and Throstle Nest. In Husthwaite township, however, Wombwell's interest was minimal, for he owned less than 19 of the 1,621 acres. Most of the land in Husthwaite was farmed by families who were owner-occupiers.

One must always remember that a tithe award might not reveal the full extent of a family's holding, for their farm might have straddled township or parish boundaries. For example, John Dixon owned only 40 acres in his 'home' township of Thornton cum Baxby, but he had another 339 acres across the lane at Acaster Hill in Husthwaite township, where incidentally he was also lord of the manor.

The combination of award and map may enable the historian to locate an ancestor's farmhouse or cottage. Thus, I had no trouble in finding the precise position of the home of James Batty (1782–1866), a Coxwold butcher who was the younger brother of William Batty of Thornton on the Hill. James and his family lived at the top end of the village street, next to St Michael's church, in a house that was rebuilt in 1876 and adorned with George Orby Wombwell's initials. The tithe map marks the house, stables, gardens and the three fields that lay immediately south of the village and which were used as pasture and meadow land; in all the property amounted to 12 acres, 3 roods, 11 perches. The Youlton award and map of 1842 led me to a house that is still standing. Until I saw the map I was not sure which of the three farms in the hamlet was the home of Thomas Batty of Youlton, but it is now clear that it was the interesting old building known as Youlton Hall. In 1842 Thomas was renting 217 acres of land (mostly arable with some grass) that belonged to Edward Swainston Strangeways, esquire. Six of his ten children were born here between 1820 and 1838, and when he moved to Woolpots after his parents had died he was succeeded at Youlton by his eldest son, Richard.

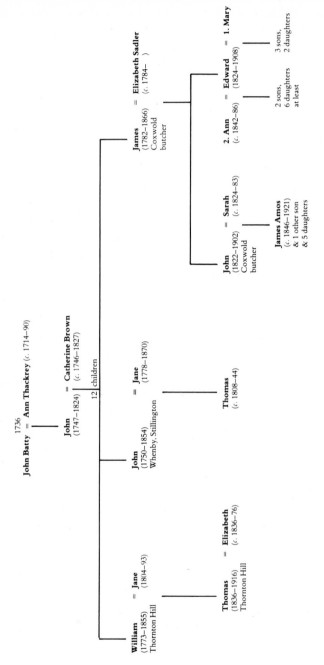

Table 9 The Battys of Thornton on the Hill

Two other tithe awards enabled me to locate holdings occupied by the Batty family. At Dalby on the Howardian Hills, my great-great-grandfather, Thomas Batty, was tenant of 110 acres at the southernmost farm in the township. The Thornton on the Hill tithe award showed that William Batty farmed 103 acres. John and Ann Batty, who married in 1736, were probably the first members of the family to live at this farm. Their son John Batty (1747–1824) was the father of twelve children who were all born at Thornton Hill; three died young, six were daughters and three carried on the family name with branches of their own. John, the second son, moved first to Whenby, then to Stillington; James, the youngest boy, became a Coxwold butcher and the father of eleven children; and William (1773–1855), the eldest, inherited his parents' farm. In time, William was succeeded by his son, Thomas, who lived there until his death at the age of eighty. He was buried at Coxwold in 1916, having outlived his wife, Elizabeth, by forty years. No children were recorded on their tombstone nor in the parish register, so after four generations the Batty family's connections with Thornton Hill came to an end.

The township or civil parish of Thornton on the Hill comprises a mere half dozen scattered farms, a pattern of settlement that has existed for centuries. Near the top of the thorn-hill (which was first recorded in surviving documents in 1167) lie the grassy earth-works of a deserted village. Here can be seen the raised platforms that show where abandoned houses once stood, the depressions which allow the eye to follow the lines of former roads and tracks, and the fishponds that belonged to the lord of the manor. The ordnance survey map marks the position in italic letters as 'Medieval Village (site of)'. Thornton Hill was always a small settlement, the sort that was amongst the first to go when the pestilences of the fourteenth century reduced the national population dramatically. The land was farmed in common fields in 1413, but the township long ago assumed an enclosed appearance, one that has been altered, however, by the destruction of ancient hedges in recent years.

This branch of the Battys were tenants of the Wombwells of Newburgh Priory, as were all the farmers of Thornton on the Hill. For a time I assumed that they had lived at Thornton Hill Farm, where the old farmhouse is now rendered grey and covered with ivy, for they were always described as being of Thornton Hill. However, the tithe award and map make it clear that they lived at an unnamed farm further west. This has now been demolished but the site can be reached along a footpath. The Battys have left no material remains of their long residence in this township.

The commercial and trade directory is another of the local and family historian's most useful sources, and one of the most accessible. Good runs of directories can be readily consulted in public libraries for the Victorian and Edwardian era and some of the larger towns have them for occasional years as far back as the later eighteenth century. William White, a Sheffield man who began to publish directories during the 1830s, claimed that his publications afforded 'one of the best, cheapest, and most permanent mediums for COMMERCIAL ADVERTISEMENTS, as every book is constantly referred to by men of business for a series of years'. Directories became fuller and more reliable as time went on, especially those produced by White, Pigot, Slater and Kelly, who employed full-time agents to collect and classify information. Local publishers and printers also issued directories of their own region from time to time and some of these can be of great use to the historian.

Their chief drawback is that they did not record labourers and servants or other groups of people who worked for an employer; directories were concerned only with the 'principal inhabitants' and with businessmen, farmers and tradesmen. When trying to locate an ancestor one has always to bear in mind that by the time a directory had appeared in print the information which had been collected might have been out of date by up to a year. However, a directory will often provide an address that will be useful when one turns to a contemporary census return; otherwise, much time might be wasted in a misguided search. Directories are also a mine of valuable information about townships, parishes and manors, information that is particularly useful to the historian of those areas that underwent considerable changes in Victorian times. The preamble to each parish entry often contains a potted history of the place, gives the dates of public buildings, comments on the nature of local tenures and states the population figure that was recorded in the previous census.

But like any other historical source directories must be treated with caution. In particular, some of their historical statements should not be taken at face value. I found, for example, that Bulmer's North Riding directory (1890) claimed that at Thornton Hill, 'A farm has been in the occupation of the Batty family for 400 years'. That was manifestly not the case, for the John Batty

who set up home in the first half of the eighteenth century was
the first member of the family to reside at Thornton Hill. For
'400 years' we should read 'a long time', less than 200 years in
fact. We also need to be sceptical about such statements as one
which appeared in White's East and North Riding directory (1840)
and which was repeated in later Kelly's directories. Under the
entry for Youlton in the parish of Alne, White wrote: 'The
farmers are Thos. Wood, Thos. Bell and Thomas Batty. At the
house occupied by the latter, James I halted in his route from
Scotland'. The king must have wandered off his route if he did
stay there. It sounds as if some of my ancestors possessed rather
vivid imaginations.

What are we to make of the following entry relating to a farm
near Husthwaite, where Thomas Batty came to live after his
mother had died? According to the second volume of a directory
of York and the North Riding, published by T. Whellan & Co.
of Beverley in 1859, Woolpots Farm was a neat, plain house that
was erected in 1840 and named after George Potts, 'a dealer in
wool, who resided at it'. This sounds a likely explanation at first,
but a branch of the Batty family were living here earlier than 1840
and the name Woolpots was recorded in the Coxwold parish
register when Frances Batty was baptized in 1795. The farm also
appears to be marked on Thomas Jefferys's map of Yorkshire,
surveyed from 1767 onwards. If George Potts did indeed give his
name to this property, then he must have been there long before
the present house was built.

Whellan's directory says of Husthwaite in general: 'More of the
occupants of the farmhouses here belong to the class of substantial
yeomen, than in most other places in the neighbourhood. The
land is in a high state of cultivation'. On page 671 Whellan
comments:

> In a beautiful sequestered vale is the site of the ancient village of
> Baxby, of which nothing remains but the Manor House, and the
> neighbouring water-mill, though the foundations may be traced to a
> considerable distance.

As one approaches Baxby from Husthwaite village the ridge and
furrow patterns of the former open-fields are also prominent. In
1859 most of Baxby was owned by John Dixon, esquire, who
lived in 'a new well-built house' at Throstle Nest, the next farm
to the south of Woolpots.

Baxby was an old Viking settlement, recorded in Domesday
Book. The second element in the name was the common

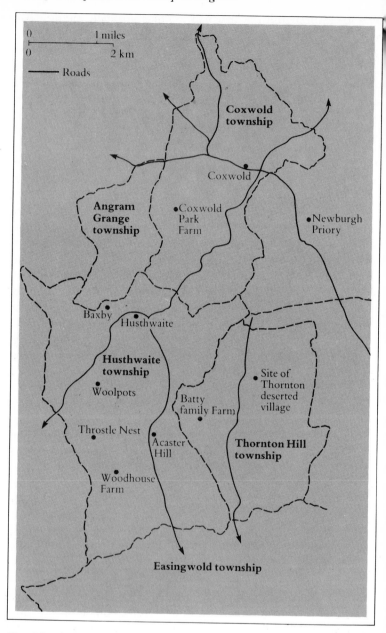

Fig. 4.3 Coxwold, Husthwaite and Thornton Hill townships

Scandinavian term for a farmstead, hamlet or village; the first part was derived from a rare Old Norse personal name. Other Scandinavian place-names in the area include Thormanby, Uppleby and Husthwaite. Although it lay so close to Husthwaite (as close as Uppleby to Easingwold), Baxby was in the parish of Coxwold and once formed a detached part of the township of Thornton on the Hill; in 1839 it covered just over 333 acres. Bulmer's *Directory of the North Riding of Yorkshire* (1890) states that the Baxby estate was taken from Thornton on 25 March 1887 and annexed to Husthwaite for all civil purposes. At that time most of Baxby belonged to the executors of the late Robert Dixon Batty (1823–87), who had lived at Throstle Nest, a mile or so to the south of the deserted village. Earlier census returns had included the Manor House Farm (84 acres). Providence Hill (75 acres), Woolpots (121 acres) and Throstle Nest (40 acres) under the general heading of Baxby. It took me some time to realize that when my ancestors were described as being 'of Baxby' they were in fact living in one of the outlying farms. They never seem to have occupied Baxby Manor but to have lived at Woolpots and Throstle Nest farmhouses in the fields further south. To complicate matters further, although the Baxby estate lay within the parish of Coxwold, most of the Battys who lived in those parts were baptised, married and buried at the nearby church of St Nicholas, Husthwaite.

It was with considerable regret that I finally accepted that although the Battys once owned over half the Baxby estate they did not live in the delightful old Manor House that now offers 'Bed and Breakfast' in a sheltered hollow at the bottom end of Husthwaite village. They preferred instead to live in new brick houses at Woolpots and Throstle Nest. The mellow walls of the Manor House are built of blocks of Jurassic stone, whose weathered appearance blends perfectly with the pantiled roof to make an immediate impression of comfort and hospitality. Sash windows give a superficial impression of the eighteenth century, but their irregular arrangement suggests that they have been inserted into an older structure. Slight clues, such as the ball finial on the gable end and the position of the chimney stacks, reinforce the feeling that this is an older house than appears at first sight. An inspection of the interior confirms that the building is indeed an ancient structure, for the stone walls encase a timber-framed house of unusual design. A curving principal post in the main range is of the type known as a base-cruck, and the roof is supported by a crown post truss which rests on an upper tie-beam. In *Vernacular Houses of North Yorkshire and Cleveland* (1984) Barry Harrison and Barbara Hutton note that Baxby Manor House and Canons' Garth, a few miles away at Helmsley, are so far the only two base-cruck structures that have been found north of the Trent, though ninety-three similar buildings have been discovered further south. The Baxby and Helmsley houses date from about the year 1300. Their roof timbers are heavily sooted, for originally they had no proper chimney but only a vent to allow the smoke to escape.

Until well into the seventeenth century all the farmhouses and cottages in this district were built of oak. A modest but attractive example, which now has a brick lower storey and a pantiled roof, can be found at Husthwaite on the opposite side of the village green from the parish church. Known as the Black Bull Cottage, it is of the lobby-entrance type, whereby the central door opens directly on to the chimney stack, and it is probably mid sixteenth century in date. It consists of a parlour and a living room or kitchen, both of which are heated from the central stack, and a service area in the lean-to at the rear. Judging from the hearth tax returns of the 1660s and 1670s, the northern Vale of York had numerous middling and small houses such as this, but few large ones. The yeomen who could afford to rebuild in warm red brick chose the three-unit, lobby-entrance design of two full storeys just one room deep, which by that time had become fashionable all over England.

A good example of the improved accommodation of the wealthier farmers in the reign of Charles II is provided by the Old Hall at Myton upon Swale, the home of Richard Batty (1820–77), the eldest son of Thomas Batty of Youlton and Woolpots, and my great-grandmother's eldest brother. The house has a 1664 datestone and many of its archictectural features confirm that sort of date. Built of brown brick, now rendered over, it has projecting wings and some mullioned-and-transomed windows in the old style, but also a pediment, pilasters and a hipped roof in vague recognition of newer influences. The builders were moving hesitatingly towards a style that was becoming fashionable further up the social scale but they were not prepared to reject everything that they had learned from the past.

The Georgian farmhouses that were erected between 1750 and 1850 provided much more comfort and a certain elegance. The lobby-entrance plan was abandoned in favour of a new design

Plate 4.7   Myton Old Hall
The old hall at Myton on Swale was built of brick in 1664 with a hipped roof and some classical features that were just becoming fashionable at this social level. The house looks formal and symmetrical and is double-depth in plan. But the builders gave the house projecting wings in the old style, and as sash windows had not yet been invented they used mullions and transoms. (Most of these were eventually replaced by sashes.) Richard Batty (1820–77), the eldest son of my great-great-grand-father, lived here in later life. In 1871 he was farming 500 acres of land and employing four men, three boys and two girl domestic servants.

whereby rooms led off each side of a central hallway. These houses were warm and comfortable, being two rooms deep under a hipped roof, and the external arrangement of windows and chimney stacks gave them a symmetrical appearance. Many of them were roofed with slates rather then pantiles. Bricks were hand-made and of various textures, for it was the common practice to clampburn them locally for each job. Most were mottled pinks and browns and their variety helped to make each house look different. The best examples of this new type of farmhouse are found not in the village streets but out in the countryside surrounded by their fields. In some parts of England they date from immediately after parliamentary enclosure, but in the northern Vale of York, as we have seen, they were often on older sites and reflect the unprecedented level of prosperity that the farmers enjoyed. Today, the traveller through this part of York-shire is struck by the way that, in nearly every case, the eighteenth and nineteenth century farmhouses remain intact but their outbuildings are dwarfed by drab, modern structures and perhaps a silo or two. There is no thought of style nor any feeling for the vernacular tradition in these recent extensions, and the machinery which they house has been used to tear up many of the ancient hedges whose careful maintenance once gave such a pleasing, well-managed look to these farms. But at least most of the Geor-gian farmhouses are still standing.

The Battys lived at a number of fine Georgian farmhouses and were responsible for building some of them. Surviving examples include Coxwold Park Farm, Mowbray House in the township of Stillington, Scackleton Grange, Wallerthwaite, Morcar, Wool-pots and Throstle Nest. All of them stand in isolation, well away from the rest of society. This preference for quiet, rural seclusion was a characteristic that the members of the family seem to have shared throughout the eighteenth and nineteenth centuries; only occasionally did they venture into something as large as a village. There is not the space here to tell the story of all these farms, but let us look at Woolpots, which was one of their major properties for three generations. The farmhouse was built by one of my great-great-grandfathers, Thomas Batty.

Woolpots Farm is reached by a narrow, winding lane that climbs a small hill to the south of Husthwaite and Baxby. Huge new outbuildings, including a silo, indicate at once that this is a prosperous modern concern, but upon approaching the farmhouse a few older buildings come into view. From the outside the farm-house itself looks exactly as it did when the Battys lived here. A high brick wall between the garden and the lane provides some privacy, but the front wall is low so as to allow an uninterrupted view from the downstairs rooms. Woolpots is a perfect example of a Georgian-style farmhouse standing on the highest point of the farm. Built of local bricks and roofed with slate, it is designed to a fashionable double-depth plan, with a range to the rear. The front is composed with pleasing symmetry. A central door opens into the hall, and the two rooms downstairs are lit with bowed windows. In the upper storey three large windows are spread out stylishly and, above, the chimney stacks are balanced at either side of the hipped roof. The bricks and slates are not cut with machine-like regularity and their varied colours, shapes and textures soften the formal appearance of the house. High on the

Plate 4.8 Woolpots Farm
Woolpots Farm was built by my great-great-grandfather, Thomas Batty (1785–1858). His father, Richard Batty (1755–1833), had married the heiress of the estate, Elizabeth Wetherill. Elizabeth died in 1843 and Thomas began to plan his new home. According to an inscription at the rear it was finished on 22 May 1846. Thomas's youngest son, John, inherited the farm, but by the 1890s it was under different ownership as the Great Agricultural Depression drove families into bankruptcy.

upper storey at the rear a rectangular inscription is beginning to peel but can still be made out to read: 'WOOLPOTS, May 22, 1846'. Another inscription on an outbuilding confirms that 1846 was the year of building, not 1840 as stated in Whellan's 1859 directory. The directory date had puzzled me for some time, for the 1841 census return named Elizabeth Batty, aged seventy three, as the head of household. This was not the sort of house that an elderly widow would have built; it made more sense to think that her son had erected it after he had inherited the property in 1843.

I was able to find eighty entries relating to the Batty family in a blanket search of the Coxwold parish registers from 1721 to 1848, thirty-one entries in the Husthwaite registers from 1785 to 1873, and others in nearby parishes such as Alne and Hovingham. From this information I was able to deduce that the first member of the Batty family to set up home at Woolpots was Richard Batty (1755–1833), the younger son of Richard and Frances Batty of Coxwold Park Farm. His elder brother, James, inherited the parental home. Richard may have moved to Woolpots in 1784 upon his marriage to Elizabeth Weatherill. By marrying rich heiresses the Battys moved up from the status of yeomen to become gentlemen-farmers. The Coxwold parish register recorded the baptism of Frances, the daughter of Richard Batty of Woolpots, farmer, on 8 November 1795, so they were certainly here by then.

Another useful source of information was the Husthwaite manorial court book, kept at the North Yorkshire County Record Office, Northallerton. On 22 October 1846 Thomas Batty paid a £21.15s.0d. entry fine and was admitted to some copyhold lands after the court had found that:

> Peter Wetherill formerly of the Woolpots in the Parish of Coxwold in the County of York in or about the year one thousand seven hundred and ninety seven died seized of that Close or parcel of Land called Acres containing by estimation Fifteen Acres more or less The Hough Five Acres more or less and the Red Keld Three Acres more or less situate lying and being in the Township of Husthwaite within and parcel of the said Manor

and that by his last will and testament he had bequeathed this property to his son-in-law Richard Batty and to his daughter, Elizabeth, Richard's wife, for their lives and thereafter to his grandson Thomas Batty and his heirs.

The will of Peter Wetherill of Woolpots, yeoman was proved at York in July 1797 and a copy may be seen at the Borthwick Institute of Historical Research, filed under Bulmer deanery. It provides the additional information that Peter's widow was to receive an annuity of £30 per annum for the rest of her life and that his granddaughters, Elizabeth and Frances (Thomas Batty's younger sisters), were to inherit the freehold estate known as Woodhouse Farm, which lies south-east of Throstle Nest.

On 9 August 1833 Richard Batty of Woolpots, a seventy-eight-year-old farmer, was buried in Husthwaite churchyard. On 16 October 1834 the Husthwaite manorial court found that Richard had died intestate but they admitted Thomas Batty of Youlton, yeoman, as his son and heir, to the tenancy of the fields called Long Roods. Richard had in fact made a will, which was proved at York in June 1834, but this made no mention of his freehold and copyhold estate; by it he merely divided his household furniture between his wife and his daughter Betty, left his wife

Plate 4.9 Youlton Hall
The old hall at Youlton was Thomas Batty's home before he moved to his new house at Woolpots. At Youlton he farmed 217 acres of land as the tenant of Edward Swainston Strangeways, Esq.; the estate at Woolpots was smaller but was freehold.

The curving gable suggests a mid- or late-seventeenth century date for the wing, and the assymetrical arrangement of windows, door and chimney points to a similar date for the main range. If so, the sash windows must have been inserted later.

£150, and shared his personal effects between his three children – Thomas, Betty and Frances Hickes. His farm was not his to bequeath because his father-in-law had already ensured that Thomas would inherit. Here again, it is clear that a will may mislead an historian unless he has access to other documents.

Richard had frequently served as a juror of the Husthwaite manorial court but Thomas did not act in this capacity until 1846, for he probably did not leave Youlton until his new house was ready. At the time of the 1841 census Woolpots was occupied by his widowed mother, Elizabeth, her married daughter Betty and her son-in-law William Dowell, and also nineteen-year-old Eleanor Batty. Eleanor was Betty's illegitimate daughter, born long before her marriage to William Dowell of Coxwold. The tithe awards and plans of the townships of Thornton cum Baxby and Husthwaite show that the family holding comprised about 89 acres around Woolpots and 66 acres in a rectangular block from Woodhouse Farm as far as the parish boundary stream, The Kyle, in the south. They also farmed the 10 acres known as Long Roods which belonged to Thomas.

Elizabeth died at the age of seventy-six and on 26 November 1843 she was buried alongside her husband at Husthwaite. Thomas Batty was now free to build a new house in modern style and to move his family from the old hall at Youlton, where they had lived for more than a quarter of a century. Thomas Batty (1785–1858) undoubtedly improved his fortune further by marrying Elizabeth Dixon, for the Dixons were the wealthiest family in Husthwaite parish. His cousin Richard Batty (1799–1878) married Rosamond, another of the Dixon girls nine years later. Thomas and Elizabeth's first three children – Rose, Frances and Mary – were baptised at Husthwaite between 1813 and 1817 and on each occasion Thomas was described as a Husthwaite farmer. The baptism of Elizabeth, another of the daughters, has not been traced, but seven children were born at Youlton, in the parish of Alne, between 1820 and 1838, the youngest child being my great-grandmother, Rosamond. In 1846 the family moved to Woolpots and there the census enumerator found some of them in 1851. Three of the children had died and four had left home upon their marriages, but Thomas (age 24), John (22) and Rosamond (12) were there, and so was Frances's daughter, Elizabeth Sarah Cass (10).

Thomas Batty made his last appearance at the Husthwaite manor court on 9 April 1858, when he was sworn in as foreman of the jury. He died on 12 December 1858 and probate of his will was granted on 7 May 1859. A copy survives in the family's possession and another was exhibited at the manor court (where his brother-in-law, John Dixon, was lord) on 19 October 1859. The will was made on 1 October 1852 and altered in minor ways by two small codicils in 1852 and 1855. My earlier strictures about the use of wills for family history apply, for the detailed clauses fail to make any provision for Thomas's second son, Robert Dixon Batty (1823–87), who was to inherit his Uncle John Dixon's farm at Throstle Nest. As R. D. Batty did not appear with his family in the various census returns, and because the Batty inter-relationships were so complicated, this absence from the will led me to believe that he belonged to another branch until I found the record of his baptism.

Thomas's eldest son, Richard (1820–77), who had married his second cousin, Frances, and had gone to live at Myton Old Hall, received 'my farm lands and hereditaments and all other my real estate situate in Craike and Easingwold'. The third son, Thomas (1826–87), seems to have been considered unfit to inherit Woolpots; he never married and lived as an 'annuitant' or 'retired farmer' with his youngest sister, Rosamond, for the rest of his life. As we have seen, he was later to use his £1,800 legacy to buy

Lund Farm when James and Rosamond were forced to leave the much larger farm at Mowbray House, halfway between Easingwold and Stillington. Rosamond received a bequest of £600, her married sister Elizabeth Flawith was left £900, and another married sister, Frances Cass, received £300 + £2 per month for the rest of her life. We do not know what financial arrangements had been made to help these children when they had married. Had Thomas's 'dear wife Elizabeth' not died in 1855 at the age of sixty-one, she would have remained at Woolpots with an annuity and 'such part of my household furniture plate linen and china as she shall choose'. The residue of the estate went to the youngest son, John, who was born in 1828.

At this point of the story the web of family connections becomes confusingly intertwined. Three of the children mentioned in Thomas Batty's will married their second cousins. Richard married Frances (1825–91), the elder daughter of Richard and Rosamond Batty; John married Elizabeth, the younger daughter; and Rosamond married James (1830–98), the eldest son of Thomas and Mary Batty. John and Elizabeth Batty lived at Tollerton and then at Thornton Hill before moving into their inheritance at Woolpots Farm in 1858 or 1859. They were recorded in the 1861, 1871 and 1881 census returns as farmers of about 160 acres and in 1873 their annual rental was valued at £277 a year. John Batty was a keen country sportsman who kept the Easingwold Staghounds at Woolpots; a local newspaper reported that he was the starter and judge at a race-meeting in 1855. In the era of Victorian High Farming he lived the life of a gentleman farmer. In 1881 he was employing three farm boys and two female servants and he had two grown sons, Robert Dixon Batty (age 25, and named after his uncle) and John Batty (15) to succeed him. At the time of writing, the 1891 census returns are not available for study, but John Batty does not appear in Kelly's 1893 directory, and the directories for 1897, 1909 and 1913 name Christopher Hird as the farmer of Woolpots. This branch of the Batty family had disappeared from the district, or at least from the types of record in which they had featured so prominently in earlier times. Did they too crash into bankruptcy? There seems no obvious alternate explanation.

The composition of the Batty family and a picture of their farming activities in the northern Vale of York as the Great Agricultural Depression was beginning to bite is provided by the 1881 census returns. James and Rosamond and her brother, Thomas, had already left Mowbray House for a smaller farm at the Lund at the other side of Easingwold. And some Batty properties had passed through female lines upon marriage. At Morcar, seventy-three-year-old Thomas Batty was living in retirement with his daughter Frances and her husband, George Knowles. Myton Old Hall was occupied by Richard Flawith and Youlton Hall was the house of Thomas Flawith; were they the sons of Elizabeth Flawith (née Batty), who was now a widow living as a 'retired farmer's wife' at the Bell Inn, Alne, with her fourteen-year-old domestic servant? If so, in these cases the family continued to farm their holdings though the surname had changed.

The disappearance of the Batty family from Coxwold village is harder to explain, for the brothers John (1822–1902) and Edward (1824–1908) fathered twenty children between them, including seven sons. In 1881 John was still working as a butcher and Edward as a joiner, and John's eldest son, James Amos Batty (c. 1846–1921) had married and had started a butchery business in Husthwaite. John died on 8 December 1902 at Long Street, Easingwold, where he was living in retirement with his son-in-law George Thompson. Were some of the young men who were killed in the First World War from this side of the family? Perhaps some descendants through the female lines are still living in and around Coxwold? Or did some of these Battys join in the migration from the countryside to seek work in the towns?

The five farms in this part of the northern Vale of York that were still occupied by male members of the Batty family in 1881 were as follows:

Farm	Acreage	Head of household	Age
Tollerton	430	Robert Batty	59
Thornton Hill	231	Thomas Batty	44
Woolpots	160	John Batty	52
Throstle Nest	100	Robert Dixon Batty	58
Lund	76	James Batty	50

These were middle-aged men accustomed to the life of well-to-do farmers and perhaps not well suited to adapting to change.

In the absence of later census returns I had to turn instead to the limited information provided by Kelly's directories for 1893, 1897, 1907, 1913, 1921, 1933 and 1937. They confirmed the gradual disappearance of the Batty name from the farms that they still occupied in 1881. I then searched all the indexes of deaths at St Catherine's House for Battys who died in the Easingwold registration district between 1881 and 1950. This laborious task provided a firmer chronological framework for the disappearance of the Battys from that area. Twelve Batty deaths were registered before the end of the nineteenth century, another five before the First World War, and ten more (not including the four killed in the war) between 1914 and 1935. No further deaths were registered between 1935 and the end of 1949.

The story of the Battys has already been told for three of the farms that they occupied in 1881, leaving just Tollerton and Throstle Nest. In 1861 Throstle Nest had been the home of John Dixon (aged 69) and his wife Jane (68). They had built it when they were younger in a similar style to Woolpots, the home of John's sister, Elizabeth Batty. Living with the Dixons was their nephew, Elizabeth's son Robert Dixon Batty (aged 38), who had been promised the inheritance as John and Jane had no children of their own. John Dixon died in the autumn of 1863 and shortly afterwards Robert Dixon Batty married a woman fourteen years his junior. He may not have inherited all the property, however, for whereas the Dixons farmed 220 acres in 1861, ten years later R. D. Batty had only 163 acres; after another decade he, ominously perhaps, farmed only 100 acres. When he died in 1887 his son and namesake (aged 17), succeeded him. This second Robert Dixon Batty died in 1912 at the age of 41, after which the directories cease to record any Battys at Throstle Nest.

In 1881 Tollerton was the largest farm in Batty hands. When Mr Robert Batty died six years later he was succeeded by his son, Richard (*c.* 1857–1931), who was described in Bulmer's 1890 directory as a yeoman and valuer and one of the principal landowners in Tollerton. Three years later he had gone. The 1890 entry for Tollerton also notes his cousin, Dr Dixon Batty (*c.* 1849–1916), the son of Richard Batty of Myton Old Hall, but directories dating from 1893 to 1913 record him as a private resident of Husthwaite, in other words a man who was no longer engaged in farming but who had sufficient income (he seems to have been a bachelor) to live at his ease. Despite their disappearance from the directories, however, the Battys were still at Tollerton at the turn of the century, for one of the group of Coxwold gravestones commemorates the death of the seven-year-old daughter of Robert Marianne Batty of Tollerton in 1901. His unusual middle name was used again when my mother was christened; she knew that her second name was in honour of one of her many cousins.

I do not have any photographs of my Batty ancestors prior to my grandfather, nor do I have many mementos. I have on my shelves a thick, moralizing volume inscribed with a flourish 'Mr Thomas Batty's Book, Youlton, January 1st 1834', but his descendants do not seem to have taken much notice of such sections as 'Indolence, its effects upon men'. The people who flit in and out of the records are illuminated only briefly and inter-mittently. Even the names they are given in these records are too formal, for the many Thomases, Richards, Jameses, Rosamonds, etc. were of course known to their friends and relations as Tom, Dick, Jim and Rosy. I have plenty of tasks to keep me occupied in unravelling their story, for the discovery of information that solves one problem frequently leads to the posing of another. In particular, I want to search the records of the Markington–Bishop Thornton area to see if I can trace them further back, for at the moment my best guess is that this is where they lived in earlier times. A clue is provided by the will of James Batty of Coxwold, yeoman (proved 1814), which refers to his properties in Bishop Thornton, Clint and the Forest of Knaresborough, which he bequeathed to his sons, Richard and Thomas. James's father, 'Richard Batty of Coxwold, Farmer', was one of the adminis-trators of the estate of Thomas Batty of Dale Bank, Bishop Thornton, yeomen, who died in 1757. Perhaps this Thomas was the ancestor of all the Battys who settled in the Coxwold-Husthwaite area? The broad shape of their history is already clear and most of the web of their intricate inter-relationships has been disentangled. Their story is in many ways a typical one. During the Georgian era and the period of Victorian High Farming they prospered and spread, marrying into the richest farming families in the neighbourhood and inheriting other farms by so doing. But later generations, perhaps grown too accustomed to a life of ease, did not have the same driving ambition and resourcefulness of their ancestors and were unable to cope with the effects of the Great Agricultural Depression. Their rise can be chartered more easily than their fall, but fall they did. When my father visited Easingwold in the late 1930s he enquired of a group of men whether any of them knew of the Battys. 'Aye', he was told, 'they're an old broken-down family'.

The late Herbert Finberg once defined local history as the study of the origins, growth and (where appropriate) the decline of local communities. The scope of family history ought to be conceived in similar broad terms. At the moment it is in the same anti-quarian stage of development as local history was (with some outstanding exceptions) a generation or two ago. The antiquary collects facts, the genealogist constructs family trees. Both these tasks provide enjoyment for a lot of people and should not be disparaged, but the rewards in terms of personal satisfaction and contribution to knowledge are so much greater when the family historian tries to see his ancestors as people acting out their lives against a local and national backcloth, people who were caught up, knowingly or unconsciously, in the currents of their time. At its best the study of family history should be concerned with the origin and spread of families, their contrasting fortunes and some-times with their disappearance.

The history of any family can be profitably pursued in this way, though it is natural in the first place to restrict one's enqui-ries to one's own kinsfolk. Sixteen great-great-grandparents are, after all, usually enough to be going on with. I have yet to explore the history of the Websters and the Kells, my East Riding ances-tors on my mother's mother's side with the same thoroughness as I have traced the Heys, Garlands and Battys. I have found most of the basic genealogical information as far back as the fourth generation, but as yet I do not understand their story in the same way that I do with the other branches. They were grooms and farm labourers during the early Victorian period and they are difficult to follow because they moved around quite a lot. They only went short distances at a time but they travelled far enough and often enough to frustrate the person who tries to follow their movements. The Mormom International Genealogical Index has enabled me to trace the marriage of Thomas Kell and Mary Dean at Market Weighton on 29 September 1831; finding it by a pain-staking search of all the local registers would have been a time-consuming task. Microfiche copies of the IGI, as it is known for short, have been placed at the disposal of all enquirers, not just the members of the Church of Jesus Christ of Latter-Day Saints, and this has proved a great benefit for the information is collated from thousands of microfilms of published and manuscript records. This information needs to be checked against the original document, but the IGI microfiche is an invaluable aid which has helped revolutionize the study of family history in recent years.

265

The most difficult period for the family historian is often that which covers the two generations before civil registration began in 1837, that crucial era when the population explosion, parliamentary enclosure, increasing poverty, and the rapid growth of industrial towns and villages created an unprecedented volatile situation for which we have only inadequate records. A fundamental problem that I need to tackle is why the Websters and Kells, the Garlands and Knights, became labourers. Were they younger sons with little or no inheritance? Were they dispossessed through lack of resources, drive and ability? Or had their families always been poor? Our understanding of English social history would be so much deeper if family historians could answer these sort of questions.

When, and if, I can solve such problems, I shall no doubt move on to others. It is in the nature of family history that this should happen. One cannot put aside the writing of a family's story until it is complete because that ideal stage will never be reached. There is a great deal that remains to be discovered about my own ancestors, but I now know enough to be able to appreciate their successes and to understand their trials and tribulations. My ancestors have all been country men and women. None of them lived in a larger place than the little market towns of Pocklington and Easingwold, except one who lived as a child in York. Isolated farmsteads, tiny hamlets and sometimes a village were their preferred abodes. We inherit not just the family face but shared attitudes and assumptions. Like the Revd Francis Kilvert,

> I love to wander on these soft gentle mournful autumn days, alone among the quiet peaceful solitary meadows, tracing out the ancient footpaths and mossy overgrown stiles between farm and hamlet, village and town, musing of the many feet that have trodden these ancient and now well nigh deserted and almost forgotten ways and walking in the footsteps of the generations that have gone before and passed away.

Further reading

Local history and family history each have a vast literature ranging from scholarly volumes to ephemera. In selecting the following list to supplement the works quoted in the text I have limited my choice to books rather than articles and to those which will be of general use to amateur historians from all over the country. Nearly all of them are still in print, and those which are not are available at major libraries. The date of publication is that of the latest edition or reprint.

1. GUIDES TO GENEALOGY AND FAMILY HISTORY

Amongst the best of the books which offer advice on how to trace a family tree are G. Hamilton-Edwards, *In Search of Ancestry* (1983), A. J. Willis and M. Tatchell, *Genealogy for Beginners* (1984), M. Mander, *Tracing Your Ancestors* (1976), C. M. Mathews, *Your Family History* (1982), S. Colwell, *The Family History Book* (1980) and C. D. Rogers, *The Family Tree Detective* (1983).

The beginner who is perplexed by technical and obscure words that he finds in documents should consult T. V. H. Fitzhugh, *The Dictionary of Genealogy* (1985). For broad views of the subject see D. Steel, *Discovering Your Family History* (1980), Sir Anthony Wagner, *English Genealogy* (1983) and N. Currer-Briggs, *Worldwide Family History* (1982). C. R. Humphrey-Smith lists other works in *A Genealogist's Bibliography* (1984).

The Society of Genealogists publishes a quarterly journal, *The Genealogist's Magazine*, and the Federation of Family History Societies keeps us up to date with its *Family History News and Digest*.

2. GUIDES TO LOCAL HISTORY

The best introductions are W. G. Hoskins, *Local History in England* (1984) and W. B. Stephens, *Sources for English Local History* (1981). See also J. Ravensdale, *History on Your Doorstep* (1982), J. Richardson, *The Local Historian's Encyclopaedia* (1982), P. Riden, *Local History: a practical handbook for beginners* (1983) and A. Rogers, *Approaches to Local History* (1977). D. Dymond, *Writing Local History: a practical guide* (1981) should be read before putting pen to paper.

The *Local Historian's* quarterly volumes contain many articles of interest and the magazine *Local History* makes a lively attempt at portraying the current scene. Many useful articles can be found in the annual publications *Northern History, Midland History, Southern History, The Bulletin of Local History: East Midlands Region* and in the transactions of numerous local societies. For general background on the various regions of England see the volumes in the Longman *A Regional History of England* series and the county surveys in the Hodder and Stoughton *The Making of the English Landscape* series.

3. GUIDES TO THE USE OF ARCHIVES

General guidance is provided by J. Shepherd and J. Foster, *British Archives* (1982), A. MacFarlane, *A Guide to English Historical Records* (1983) and F. G. Emmison, *Introduction to Archives* (1978). For rural affairs see W. E. Tate, *The Parish Chest* (1983) and J. West, *Village Records* (1982), and for urban archives J. West, *Town Records* (1984).

Several manuals provide instruction on how to read medieval and early-modern documents, notably L. C. Hector, *The Handwriting of English Documents* (1979), C. T. Martin, *The Record*

Interpreter (1982), F. G. Emmison, *How to Read Local Archives 1500–1700* (1967). H. E. P. Grieve, *Examples of English Handwriting, 1150–1750* (1978) and K. C. Newton, *Medieval Local Records: a reading aid* (1971). Some regional and local record offices have also published guides on how to read the documents in their care.

E. A. Gooder, *Latin for Local History* (1978), is a helpful guide to records that are written in Latin. R. E. Latham (ed.), *Revised Medieval Latin Word List* (1965) and J. L. Fisher, *A Medieval Farming Glossary of Latin and English Words* (1968) translate words that commonly appear in documents.

4. THE MIDDLE AGES

A general view of the social-and-economic history of the early Middle Ages is provided by E. Miller and J. Hatcher, *Medieval England: Rural Society and Economic Change, 1086–1348* (1978). The later medieval period is best represented by a regional work, C. Dyer, *Lords and Peasants in a Changing Society* (1980) and by J. Hatcher, *Plague, Population and the English Economy, 1348–1530* (1977).

For place-names reference should be made to M. Gelling, *Signposts to the Past* (1978). For field names in this and later periods see J. Field, *English Field Names: a dictionary* (1972). Medieval records are covered by N. J. Hone, *The Manor and Manorial Records* (1925). P. D. A. Harvey, *Manorial Records* (1984) and R. F. Hunnisett and J. Post, *Medieval Legal Records* (1978).

5. THE TUDOR AND STUART PERIOD

Recent work on the family is brought together by R. A. Houlbrooke, *The English Family, 1450–1700* (1984), which has a full bibliography. A. Kussmaul, *Servants in Husbandry in Early Modern England* (1984) deals with 'the lower orders of society'. Comprehensive coverage of agrarian history is provided by two volumes of *The Agrarian History of England and Wales*, edited by J. Thirsk; volume IV (1967) covers the period 1500–1640 and volume V (1985) deals with the years 1640–1750. On towns see P. Clark and

P. Slack, *English Towns in Transition, 1500–1700* (1976) and J. Patten, *English Towns, 1500–1700* (1978), and the bibliographies therein.

E. A. Wrigley (ed.), *An Introduction to English Historial Demography* (1966) and A. P. Appleby, *Famine in Tudor and Stuart England* (1978), are good starting points for population history. The serious worker in this field will need to consult E. A. Wrigley and R. S. Schofield, *The Population History of England: a reconstruction* (1981) and articles in the journal *Local Population Studies*. The use of demographic techniques to interpret the social-and-economic history of local communities is best seen in V. Skipp, *Crisis and Development: an ecological case study of the Forest of Arden, 1570–1674* (1978).

R. Millward, *A Glossary of Household and Farming Terms from Sixteenth Century Probate Inventories* (1979) and S. Needham, *A Glossary for East Yorkshire and North Lincolnshire Probate Inventories* (1984) explain the meaning of obscure and archaic words. Collections of inventories with useful introductions include B. Trinder and J. Cox, *Yeomen and Colliers in Telford* (1980), U. Priestley and A. Fenner, *Shops and Shopkeepers in Norwich, 1660–1730* (1985), J. S. Moore (ed.) *The Goods and Chattels of our Forefathers* (1976). F. W. Steer, *Farm and Cottage Inventories of Mid-Essex, 1635–1749* (1969), and L. Munby (ed.), *Life and Death in King's Langley: wills and inventories, 1488–1659* (1981).

Essential genealogical guides not already quoted include D. J. Steel, *General Sources of Births, Marriages and Deaths Before 1837* (1968), J. Cox and T. Padfield, *Tracing Your Ancestors in the Public Record Office* (1981) and C. R. Humphrey-Smith (ed.), *The Phillimore Atlas and Index of Parish Registers* (1984).

6. THE GEORGIAN AND VICTORIAN PERIOD

An outstanding and readable family and local history is M. K. Ashby, *Joseph Ashby of Tysoe, 1859–1919: a study of English village life* (1974). Classic works in addition to those by George Bourne and Flora Thompson include W. H. Hudson, *A. Shepherd's Life* (1957), F. Kitchen, *Brother to the Ox* (1983), R. Jefferies, *Hodge and His Masters* (1979) and H. Rider Haggard, *Rural England* (1902).

Modern works based on oral history as well as on documentary sources are best represented by the books of G. E. Evans, from

Ask the Fellows Who Cut the Hay (1956) to *The Days We Have Seen* (1975) and by the publications of the Ruskin College History Workshop, especially R. Samuel (ed.), *Village Life and Labour* (1975) and R. Samuel (ed.), *Miners, Quarrymen and Saltworkers* (1977). For a comprehensive view of rural society see G. Mingay (ed.), *The Victorian Countryside* (2 vols, 1981), and for urban society J. H. Dyos and M. Wolff (eds). *The Victorian City: images and realities* (2 vols, 1973).

The operation of the poor law is dealt with by D. J. Marshall, *The Old Poor Law, 1795–1834* (1968) and M. E. Rose, *The Relief of Poverty, 1834–1914* (1972). The way that thousands of people emigrated to the New World is vividly illustrated by T. Coleman, *Passage to America* (1972). Guides to enclosure and tithe awards are provided by W. E. Tate (ed. M. E. Turner), *Domesday of English Enclosure Acts and Awards* (1978) and R. J. P. Kain and H. C. Prince, *Tithe Surveys of England and Wales* (1985). Useful guides to other sources include *The Times Handlist of English and Welsh Newspapers, 1620–1920*, (1920). J. E. Norton, *Guide to the National and Provincial Directories of England and Wales, excluding London, published before 1856* (1950) and M. W. Barley, *A Guide to British Topographical Collections* (1974). D. Steel and L. Taylor (eds), *Family History in Focus* (1984) is helpful on the use of old photographs.

Index